MONEY AND ELECTORAL POLITICS

Local parties and funding at general elections

Ron Johnston and Charles Pattie

First published in Great Britain in 2014 by

Policy Press
University of Bristol
6th Floor
Howard House
Queen's Avenue
Clifton
Bristol BS8 1SD
UK
t: +44 (0)117 331 5020
f: +44 (0)117 331 5367
pp-info@bristol.ac.uk
www.policypress.co.uk

North America office:
Policy Press
c/o The University of Chicago Press
1427 East 60th Street
Chicago, IL 60637, USA
t: +1 773 702 7700
f: +1 773 702 9756
sales@press.uchicago.edu
www.press.uchicago.edu

British Library Cataloguing in Publication Data
A catalogue record for this book is available from the British Library

Library of Congress Cataloging-in-Publication Data
A catalog record for this book has been requested

ISBN 978 144730 631 3 paperback
ISBN 978 144730 632 0 hardcover

Cover design by Robin Hawes
Front cover: iStock
Printed and bound in Great Britain by CMP, Poole
Policy Press uses environmentally responsible print partners

Contents

List of tables and figures

Tables

Figures

About the authors

Ron Johnston has been a professor in the School of Geographical Sciences at the University of Bristol since 1995: previously he held posts at Monash University and the Universities of Canterbury, Sheffield and Essex. He has been a recipient of the Royal Geographical Society's Victoria Medal in 1991, a Life-Time Achievement Award from the Association of American Geographers in 2010, and the Political Studies Association's Political Communicator of the Year Award in 2011. He was elected a Fellow of the British Academy in 1989 and awarded an OBE for services to scholarship in 2011.

Charles Pattie is a professor of geography at the University of Sheffield, where he has been based since 1994. Prior to that, he lectured at Nottingham University. In addition to his work with Ron on electoral geography, he has published on citizenship and political participation, on referendums, and on the politics of devolution. He was elected to the Academy of Social Sciences in 2013.

Charles and Ron have worked together on a substantial number of projects in electoral studies for some 25 years – including work on constituency campaigns, spatial variations in voting behaviour at the regional, constituency and neighbourhood scales, biases in the translation of votes into seats, and the redistribution of constituencies in the UK. As well as a large number of academic papers their work has been brought together in a number of books including *A Nation Dividing?* (1988), *The Boundary Commissions* (1999), *From Votes to Seats* (2001) and *Putting Voters in their Place* (2006).

Introduction

In the short three-week campaign leading up to the Eastleigh by-election on 28 February 2013 it was claimed that the Liberal Democrats, who were defending the seat, 'bombarded the electorate with half a million pieces of literature' (an average of seven per elector). Their campaign was contrasted favourably to the Conservatives', whose MPs 'came back to Westminster to complain about the shrivelling of their grass roots' whereas the Liberal Democrats' local organisation was characterised by vigour and 'the enthusiasm with which ... activists swarmed into Hampshire from all over the country'. Labour came only fourth in that contest, barely increasing its share of the votes from that cast at the 2010 General Election (9.6 per cent) despite its substantial lead in the national opinion polls at the time, an outcome that it explained by the lack of an active local organisation.[1]

The Liberal Democrats were not only able to flood the Eastleigh constituency with party activists and supporters promoting their candidate's credentials, but they were also able to raise a substantial sum of money with which to pay for those leaflets, as well as posters and the other costs of an intensive short campaign. The spending limit for candidates contesting a by-election is £100,000; the Liberal Democrats' Mike Thornton reported spending £98,172.26. Two of his opponents also spent close to the maximum allowed: £92,965.74 by the Conservatives' Maria Hutchings and £82,160 by UKIP's Diane James, but the reported expenditure of Labour's John O'Farrell was only about half of that, at £50,194.55.

Because of the context within which it was fought – the resignation after a scandal of a popular local MP and cabinet member who represented the minor party in the Coalition government as well as the growth in support for UKIP, an anti-European Union (EU) and anti-immigration party, in the national opinion polls at the time – its intensity meant that the Eastleigh campaign was not typical of by-elections, let alone general elections in the majority of constituencies. But its general characteristics were nevertheless typical of both of those contests in some constituencies – with relatively large numbers of activists on the streets, doorsteps and telephones contacting potential supporters and encouraging them to turn out and vote, in addition

---

[1] All of the quotes are from http://blogs.lse.ac.uk/politicsandpolicy/archives/30989?utm_source=feedburner&utm_medium=email&utm_campaign=Feed%3A+BritishPoliticsAndPolicyAtLse+%28British+politics+and+policy+at+LSE%29

to large sums of money (within the legally prescribed limits) spent on leaflets, posters, offices and staff. Neither may be sufficient without the other, but much research over the last four decades has shown that in general the more money that parties spend on their local campaigns and the more people who are involved in their delivery, the better their performance, relative to national trends.

Given that situation, the issues of recruiting local party workers and raising substantial funds to spend on campaigning have been central to party strategies, both nationally and in the individual constituencies, especially those marginal seats where a general election is likely to be won or lost. Both have become increasingly problematic, however: party membership has declined very substantially, recruiting and mobilising people to work for a candidate's (re-)election, and raising money to sustain those campaigns, not only in the weeks immediately preceding the contest but, increasingly, in the weeks and months beforehand when the campaigning foundations are laid, has become increasingly difficult. In this book we focus on one of those issues – raising money – as a contribution to both our understanding of the current situation and the ongoing (although frustratingly never coming close to resolution) debates about party funding in the UK.

Over the 20th century's middle decades there was what Johnson (1972, p 53) termed a 'nationalisation' of British politics, a 'process through which local political arenas are increasingly subordinated and integrated into a single national political arena'; 'its preconditions are the improvement of communications and the increasing mobility of the population, its agents are the great national parties, and its results are the gradual ironing out of autonomous local political characteristics, styles and behaviour'. At the same time analysts, as in the classic book by Butler and Stokes (1969, 1974), identified a pattern of what they termed 'uniform swing' across the country: between pairs of adjacent elections the change in the relative support for the two main parties pre-1970 (Conservative and Labour) was virtually the same in all constituencies. This was interpreted by Bogdanor (1983, p 53), for example, as showing that between 1945 and 1970, 'Electoral behaviour came to display a considerable degree of homogeneity since an elector in Cornwall would tend to vote the same way as an elector from a similar class in Glasgow regardless of national or local differences' (see Bogdanor, 1986; Johnston, 1986).

This 'nationalisation' was also associated – at least implicitly – with a growing belief that local campaigns no longer mattered: the country as a whole was swinging from one party to another to the same degree across all constituencies, reflecting the growing importance of national campaigns through the mass media. Kavanagh (1970, pp 10, 87), for example, claimed that 'democratization and modernization of the social and political systems has enervated the local campaign' and 'the political swing during a campaign is negligible [that is, people had made up their minds before it began] and what change does occur is only slightly related to exposure to campaign propaganda'; two decades later Butler and Kavanagh (1992, p 245) argued with regard to the 1992 General Election that it was 'hard to pinpoint any constituencies where the quality of one side's efforts made a decisive difference' (Johnston, 1987, Chapter 2, provides a review of the early literature on spending and its impact). And yet, as early as 1966 Michael Steed wrote in his analyses of the results in the Nuffield *The British general election* … series that substantial regional variations around the national swing were emerging (Steed, 1966; see Johnston, 2012, and also Curtice and Steed, 1982, 1986) – and in any case, Butler and Stokes' (1969, 1974) own analyses were more geographically nuanced than an interpretation suggesting uniform behaviour by members of different classes, whatever their location. Furthermore, statistical analyses not only showed that the conclusions regarding a uniform swing post-1979 were inconsistent with the geography of party support in Great Britain, but also provided strong empirical evidence of very substantial spatial variations in voting behaviour by people of the same social class (Johnston, 1986; Johnston et al, 1988).

A link between that growing spatial variation in voting behaviour, including changes in the geography of party support and local campaigning, was established from the late 1970s on. Initial analyses of a previously little used source – the candidates' campaign expenditure returns for each general election – showed that the more that was spent, the better the performance (Johnston, 1977). Many further analyses sustained this conclusion (see the review in Johnston and Pattie, 2006). Money itself does not buy votes, of course – it facilitates campaigning and canvassing via various forms of advertising as well as the employment of agents and other staff and investment in information technology – but other studies of the intensity of local campaigns using a range of indicators reached similar conclusions (Whiteley and Seyd, 1994; Denver and Hands, 1997), and demonstrated that the amount spent was a good surrogate measure of local campaign intensity.

Nevertheless, questions continue to be asked regarding the efficacy of various forms of political campaigning. According to Schmitt-Beck and Farrell (2002a, p 13), not surprisingly those involved in their delivery believe that 'campaigns matter', including what they term the intentional micro-goals of informing, persuading, mobilising, converting and activating voters. Their book contains nine different case studies of various types of campaign activity and effects, including Denver and Hands' (2002) outline, drawing on Norris' (1997) identification of the development of post-modern campaigns, of how British constituency campaigning has changed in its focus and modes over recent decades. Previously, constituency campaigns had involved identifying the party's supporters and then treating them all the same in the messages delivered; with the use of computers, telephone polling and customised direct mailing it is now possible to prepare and send different messages to different groups. This requires resources – not least financial resources – but where they are deployed they clearly have an impact, as Denver and Hands demonstrated for the 1997 General Election. Reflecting this, and the evidence provided by the other case studies, Schmitt-Beck and Farrell (2002b, p 183) concluded that political campaigns do matter, but how they matter varies in a number of respects and is contingent on circumstances – why otherwise would an increasing proportion of 'calculating' (McAllister, 2002) voters delay their decisions until late in a campaign period, leaving themselves open (probably deliberately) to campaign influence as they receive more information, directly and indirectly, from those seeking their support? Furthermore, Schmitt-Beck and Farrell (2002b, pp 192-3) see these trends continuing:

> ... if it is the case that, as we have seen, campaigns can matter, then it seems reasonable to propose that they will matter even more in the future. Electorates continue to change in ways that make them more responsive to campaign communications. In many democracies, partisan dealignment makes increasing proportions of the electorate susceptible to conversion through campaign communications.... Gone are the days when political parties could rely on the support of particular categories of voters.... The political market has become much more competitive, and the parties, as well as other relevant actors (such as media and interest groups) have had to adapt their modes of operation if only to keep up with the extent of change, and with adaptations by their competitors.

For them, therefore, campaigns are likely to become more intense, and they concluded that 'Campaigns of higher intensity, in turn, are more likely to be effective'.

Those higher-intensity campaigns require resources, both human and financial. Recent decades have seen substantial declines in both parties' membership and the number of activists (not all of them party members) they have been able to mobilise to promote their causes, not only in the few weeks of intensive campaigning immediately prior to an election, but also in the preceding months and years as they seek to establish their visibility and credibility, not least through their activities in local politics and government (Cutts, 2013). How can a party campaign intensively in all of the constituencies where victory is needed if it cannot mobilise sufficient people in sufficient places? One means is by replacing volunteer labour by money – used both to contract out certain functions and to fund others, such as polling by telephone and the printing and despatch of bespoke literature. However, except during (usually brief) periods when they are popular both with large (many of them corporate) donors and individuals prepared to make small contributions (as at the birth of the Social Democratic Party [SDP]: see Crewe and King, 1995, Chapter 13), political parties have found raising sufficient money for intensive campaigns difficult (see Kavanagh and Cowley, 2010; Watt, 2010). Discussion of those difficulties has focused almost entirely on national party organisations, alongside concerns that because they have increasingly relied on large donors, there is considerable potential for the corruption of politics (or at least the perception that they could be corrupted). Little attention has been paid to local party branches, those that enrol the activists who do the door-knocking and leaflet delivery, and that also need money to underpin such activity, not only with leaflets and posters but also with offices, paid staff and computers. How financially sound are they?

The clear implications of research to date have been that either the more financially healthy a local party or the more money that the party centrally directed to local parties, the more intensive their general election campaigns could be, and as a consequence, the better their candidates' performance. Whether either or both of these conclusions was valid could not be fully tested until after 2000, however, when the Political Parties, Elections and Referendums Act required local parties to make returns of their annual accounts to the Electoral Commission if either their annual income or expenditure exceeded £25,000 – material that the Commission published on its website. Initial explorations of these data (Johnston and Pattie, 2008a) found considerable variation across the three main British political parties in the extent to which their local units crossed that £25,000 threshold, and also established that very few of them received substantial financial assistance from party headquarters: money to be spent on local components of general election campaigns had to be raised locally. Furthermore, there was little evidence that the Conservative revival in the opinion polls post-2006 was reflected in more money being raised by local parties with which candidates could fight the next general election (Pattie and Johnston, 2009a), although the party made substantial grants to target seats in marginal constituencies from 2007 on to build the foundations for that contest (Cutts et al, 2012).

This research has established the important role of money in oiling the wheels of constituency campaigning over the last three decades. Although the issue of party funding has been a focus of considerable political and public debate during that period, the local component has attracted little attention, certainly relative to the expressed concerns about large donations to national party organisations. And yet, as that body of research has also demonstrated (much of it through sophisticated statistical analyses), money is important to the election outcomes at constituency level – although few constituency parties have much of it available.

The debates about party funding continue, and form the context for this present book. We review those research findings and present much detailed material in a non-technical format, to inform those involved and interested in the issue – on which legislation is frequently promised but never delivered. Most of the material presented here is based on three main sources, all drawn from the Electoral Commission's published databases. Two are relatively straightforward to access (if not always deploy without considerable 'cleansing' effort) – the candidates' returns of expenditure on their general election campaigns and the returns of all donations above a specified minimum made to political parties and their affiliated accounting units. The third is both less readily deployed and less complete: the constituency party accounts are published by the Electoral Commission (basically by scanning the submitted hard copy documents and placing them on a website), but these do not follow a standard form (despite the Commission's requirements), and there is no collation of the data to provide an overall view of their financial situation.[2] To get that, as with previous analyses of those data, we have had to go through all the published accounts and create our own database, in the course of which a number of decisions about what the data show have had to be made. In general, the totals – of income and expenditure and of assets – are reasonably reliable, but

[2] The Electoral Commission has now made these data available in an online spreadsheet, but covering total income, total expenditure, assets and liabilities only: https://pefonline.electoralcommission.org.uk/Search/SOASearch.aspx.

the greater detail – of sources of income and categories of expenditure – is less so, because of the variations in reporting conventions deployed.

The core of this book, therefore, comprises analyses of those three data sets, to which we have been able to add some collected in the 2010 survey of constituency election agents. We are very grateful to our colleagues Justin Fisher, Ed Fieldhouse and David Cutts for sharing those data with us and allowing us to deploy them here. The goal is not to add another research publication to the substantial number of academic papers and books now available on this subject (we refer to many of them in the text), but rather to make those research findings available to a wider audience, as a contribution to the continuing debates over not just party funding but also the changing roles of parties within British democracy. Although one of the data sets is available for every general election since 1883, when limits on candidate expenditure were first introduced, the other two have only been created since 2000, which largely limits our analyses to the last decade. Within that relatively short period we have confined many of our analyses to the period between the 2005 and 2010 General Elections – in large part because of the changes in constituency boundaries introduced for England and Wales in 2007. The discussion centres, therefore, on preparations for and expenditure on the 2010 General Election. Because of the paucity of data on other parties – including Plaid Cymru and the Scottish National Party (SNP), as well as the several with parliamentary representation from Northern Ireland – our discussion is confined to the three main British political parties only

ONE

Follow the money: cash, party and electioneering in Britain

Money and politics make for an often volatile and controversial mix. Money lubricates politics, enabling parties to carry out activities that are essential for the democratic process, not least informing the voting public of their plans for government. But many fear it also distorts politics in less desirable and even pernicious ways, a sentiment captured dramatically in a scene from *All the President's Men*, the 1976 film of *Washington Post* journalists Bob Woodward and Carl Bernstein's investigation of the Watergate scandal. His investigation stalled, Woodward turns to Deep Throat, his mysterious and well-connected source, in search of new leads. Deep Throat throws out an enigmatic, although ultimately important hint: 'Follow the money'. The cash in question, payments to the Watergate conspirators, is traced back to President Richard Nixon's re-election campaign team (with its oddly appropriate acronym, CREEP, the Campaign to Re-Elect the President). The ensuing scandal not only forced the President's resignation but also caused serious and long-term harm to the American public's trust in their elected politicians. By enabling underhand activity, the Watergate money helped corrupt and undermine the democratic process.

Watergate-style criminal activities aimed at undermining political rivals are, thankfully, almost unheard of in mainstream British politics. But even here there are important questions regarding money's capacity to affect the political process. 'Follow the money' is still an important maxim for those interested in politics. In this book, we take Deep Throat's advice at face value as we trace the story of how British political parties' constituency campaigns are funded and of what effect they have. Just as following the money revealed much about the state of US politics at the time of Watergate, so, we argue, does doing so in early 21st century British elections reveal a great deal about the health of grassroots political activity in the UK. If the central questions for the Watergate investigation were, famously, 'What did the President know, and when did he know it?', our core questions are: 'Where do the funds for modern constituency campaigns come from, what are they spent on, and what effect (if any) do they have on election results?' Before embarking on that task, however, this chapter looks more broadly at the role of parties and of party finance in modern politics.

Politics, parties and campaigning

To understand the changing face of election campaigning, we need to consider the role of political parties in the wider political scene. It is hardly a revelation to say that political parties are not a well-loved part of the contemporary British scene. Most voters have a rather low opinion of them. For instance, before the 2010 General Election the British Election Study (BES) asked people to rate how much they trusted various national institutions on an 11-point scale, running from 0 (no trust) to 10 (a great deal of trust). While trust in some institutions, such as the police, was relatively high (their average score was 6.36), politicians and political parties languished at the bottom of the trust 'league', with average scores of just 3.62 and 3.77 respectively. Even Britain's banks, under much adverse critical scrutiny as a result of their deep involvement in the 2007 financial crisis and the subsequent economic downturn and increase in government debt (a substantial cause of which was the effective nationalisation of several of the largest banks and of their bad debts to avoid a major bank sector collapse), were trusted more, scoring on average 4.27.

Low public ratings for the trustworthiness of the political class were to be expected at the 2010 General Election, following as it did hard on the heels of a 2009 scandal over MPs' expense allowances (vanHeerde-Hudson, 2011; Pattie and Johnston, 2012; Vivyan et al, 2012). And to some extent this is borne out by slightly higher levels of average trust in politicians and parties in responses to similar BES questions at the preceding, 2005, General Election. But the differences are small. In 2005, the average trust rating for politicians was 3.95, while the averages for the Conservatives, Labour and the Liberal Democrats were 4.10, 4.38 and 4.66 respectively – better, granted, than in 2010, but not much better (and lower than trust in any other institution apart from the European Union [EU]).

Nor is it uncommon to hear voters express the view that politicians should put aside their narrow party differences and come together to work in the national interest or, more radically, that the current class of professional politicians should be removed *en masse* and should be replaced by something else. For some, 'ordinary people' should take the place of party politicians, either in elections or through (often internet-based) direct democracy initiatives. For others, parties should be replaced by experts (as with New Labour's decision, in 1997, to cede government control over interest rates to the Bank of England and the Coalition government's 2013 decision to give the Bank of England a greater role in stimulating economic growth). But whatever the preferred replacement, an anti-politics, anti-party mood is evident among a sizeable portion of the British public in the early 21st century.

Unloved though they are by the voters, however, parties remain a cornerstone of the political system (Seyd, 1998). Even in an era of partisan dealignment, for instance, 81 per cent of British adults questioned before the 2010 General Election still said they identified with a particular political party (although only 8 per cent did so very strongly: data from the 2010 BES). With very few exceptions, only candidates standing for political parties – and only those from very few parties at that – have much chance of being elected to Parliament (genuinely independent MPs remain very rare). The government is formed by the party (or parties, in the case of the current Conservative-Liberal Democrat Coalition) that can command a majority of the House of Commons, and the next-largest party in the Commons forms the official opposition. Between them, the government and opposition parties do much to structure the terms of the political debate, and their activities and policy arguments dominate political reporting in the media. And, importantly for the purposes of this book, parties develop (more or less) coherent policy platforms that they then present to the public for their support, and through their campaigning activities they act to focus and mobilise citizens' involvement in the political process. In all these respects, parties are and remain integral to British democracy.

That said, parties have to cope with a constantly changing political and social landscape. In response, parties themselves have changed over time. One major shift has been a substantial decline in party membership since the 1950s (all data from the House of Commons Library, 2012). For much of the 20th century, the Labour and Conservative parties at least could make some claim to being mass membership organisations. In the early 1950s, for instance, the Conservatives claimed almost 3 million members, and Labour around 1 million. Taken at face value, these figures suggest that around 8 per cent of the UK population were party members in the mid-20th century. This is almost certainly an over-estimate of the number of committed party members, as many members of both major parties would not have been active or serious (in some places, for instance, the local Conservative Association served more as a social club than as a political organisation, while Labour's membership figures at the time included individuals who were members of affiliated trade unions and had not personally joined the party themselves). Even so, large numbers of people were involved in some way or other in the parties. But since then, membership has tended to decline (although with some blips along the way). By 2010, both the Conservatives and Labour had shrunk considerably, to just 177,000 and 193,000 members respectively. Liberal Democrat membership then stood at 49,000, down from its peak of just over 100,000 members in the early 1990s (and a quarter of the 190,000 members claimed by the Liberal Party in 1974). Over the same period, the UK's population grew substantially, so that by 2010 only 1 per cent were party members. By any measure, these are no longer mass membership organisations.

Over the same period, parties' internal structures and their external appeals have shifted (Panebianco, 1988; Katz and Mair, 1995, 2009; Mair, 1998). From the late 19th-century extension of the franchise to all adult males until the mid-20th century, the 'mass party' model was perhaps the most successful. Mass parties, obviously enough, had mass memberships. But more than that, they traced their support bases to particular social groups and their political programmes were ideologically distinct from each other (often based in left-right debates around economic redistribution and social reform). In Britain, as in many other countries, this was reflected in strong class cleavages in voting, with working-class voters predominantly supporting parties of the left, such as Labour, and most middle-class voters supporting parties of the right, such as the Conservatives. To a significant extent, mass parties were influenced by their mass memberships (or at least by the most active of those members): party conferences were major decision-making fora in which party leaders regularly faced defeat and censure at the hands of their grassroots activists.

The mass party model 'worked' so long as social group identities remained major sources of voter allegiance and mobilisation. However, from the 1960s onwards it encountered growing problems and challenges. Perhaps the most pressing was the declining electoral importance of social groups such as class. Whereas in 1966 around two-thirds of British electors voted on class lines, by 2010 only around 43 per cent did so (BES data). And social change in the late 20th century, particularly the shift from a predominantly working-class to a mainly middle-class society, created additional problems for parties of the left such as Labour, as their traditional social base was eroding rapidly. For both reasons, parties could no longer assume their 'traditional' support bases would deliver sufficient votes to win elections and they therefore had to widen their appeals to those in other social groups.

At the same time, as discussed above, party memberships were in decline, and the most active among the remaining members were often more extreme in their political views than either their leaders or the public at large (May, 1972; although see Norris, 1995). This could result in party leaders finding themselves committed to policy platforms which they themselves did not fully agree with and which, while likely to please committed party supporters, would be unlikely to appeal to (and could even alienate) those uncommitted voters necessary for victory. Labour found this out to its cost at the 1983 General Election, when its manifesto was lauded by Tony Benn MP, then the leading figure on the left of the party, as 'openly socialist' but condemned by Gerald Kaufman MP, a prominent member of Labour's centre-right, as 'the longest suicide note in history'. Labour lost the election badly.

Parties therefore began to change, moving closer to what Kirchheimer (1966) described as 'catch-all parties'. A mass membership is less critical for such an organisation; its electoral appeal is no longer narrowly based on particular social groups. Rather, it tries to appeal to a wide range of groups and interests (hence 'catch-all'). To achieve this, the party becomes more centralised: power moves towards the leadership and away from the members, and the party professionalises its communications strategy to ensure a clear message is delivered in a competitive media. Its appeal is likely to rest less on the 'positional' politics of ideology and more on the 'valence' politics of policy effectiveness and results. In important ways, the emergence of New Labour in the early 1990s and the intentions of the Conservative party 'modernisers' in the early 2000s reflect the move to a 'catch-all' form of party organisation (Gould, 1998; Evans et al, 1999; Bale, 2010).

For Katz and Mair (1995, 2009), the next step is the emergence of what they call the 'cartel party'. These are dominated by their leaderships, especially those who hold public offices (MPs, government ministers and so on): ordinary members are only weakly involved. They deploy campaign professionals to run their election efforts. Cartel parties depend to a notable extent on state subventions (including preferential access to the state-regulated media such as national broadcasters and substantial amounts of state funding to cover their costs). In effect, they operate as a cartel to protect these interests and to squeeze parties outside the cartel out of the frame. To achieve all this, cartel parties may converge on similar policy positions. All of this reduces the effective choice available to voters; a corollary is that voters will feel increasingly estranged from parties, perceiving the latter to be more willing to act in their own interests than in the interests of the public.

Some aspects of this model fit the British case better than others (Detterbeck, 2005). First-past-the-post elections make it hard for minor parties to break in to Westminster. Election and party television and radio broadcasts are restricted to parties fielding a minimum of 50 candidates in a general election (and only the largest parties are allowed more than one broadcast before any given election). Furthermore, over recent decades Labour and the Conservatives have largely controlled national policy, prior to the formation of the Conservative-Liberal Democrat Coalition in 2010 (a partial exception being the short-lived Lab-Lib pact of 1976-78). But compared to other European nations, state subventions to UK parties are limited (Koß, 2011). And while there has been some policy convergence between Labour and Conservatives, an adversarial model of governing remains the norm in Britain. The current organisation of Britain's major parties is therefore better captured by the catch-all than by the cartel model.

The shift from mass to catch-all parties has implications for how parties campaign, in terms of both whom the campaign tries to reach and who controls its message. So, too, do the major changes in communication technology that have taken place since the mid-20th century. As a result of both developments, parties' election campaign techniques and strategies have evolved and changed considerably over time (Kavanagh, 1995; Lawrence, 2009). Norris (2000, pp 138ff) classifies this evolution into three distinct 'eras': the pre-modern campaign era, running from the mid-19th to the mid-20th centuries; the modern campaign era, from the 1950s to the late 1980s; and, since the 1990s, the post-modern era.

The pre-modern campaign was a highly decentralised affair that changed relatively little from the introduction of the secret ballot in 1872 until the mid-20th century. The ways in which the 1945 General Election campaign was conducted would, in many respects, have been familiar to politicians from the 1880s. Most national political news was carried by newspapers, which were very widely read. Party leaders spent a great deal of their time during an election on the road, travelling from one large set-piece rally to another, giving much the same speech night after night. The bulk of the day-to-day activity of campaigning, however, took place in the constituencies, where local party members worked to get their local candidate elected. Local activists raised the funds needed for the constituency contest, wrote and delivered the leaflets and election material to be delivered to the local electorate, canvassed the voters, organised public meetings in the constituency, drummed out voters (many of them in cars provided gratis by party members) on polling day, and so on. Their constituency campaigns were run almost entirely independently of the national campaign, which was relatively limited and had neither the organisational nor the financial resources to exert much control over the local parties. Opinion polling, focus groups, sophisticated advertising campaigns, news management techniques: none featured in pre-modern elections.

Technological change ushered in the modernist campaign era, as the rapid growth of television ownership in the 1950s transformed the campaign scene. Through televised party election broadcasts and (from the 1959 UK General Election) national television news coverage of elections, parties' campaign messages could be carried direct from the national party organisation into voters' homes, side-stepping the constituency campaign entirely. (The process had begun, in truth, in the 1920s, when the first party broadcasts used then new radio technology, but television accelerated the process.) Attendance at local election meetings declined steeply as voters turned to television for the bulk of their information during election campaigns. This swung the balance of power in election campaigning heavily away from constituency contests and to the parties' national headquarters where senior party members and their staff decided the main campaign themes, organised 'talking heads' for television interviews, arranged the filming and content of party election broadcasts, ran press conferences for journalists from the national news organisations, and so on. There was relatively little place for the constituency campaign in all of this. Indeed, for some, the constituency campaign had become an anachronism, a largely pointless hangover from the pre-modern era that had little or no effect on the election outcome (Kavanagh, 1970). This was always something of an overstatement in practice, and even at the height of the 'modernist' campaign era local campaigns continued and paid some electoral dividends – 25 years later Kavanagh (1995, p 244) accepted that research was indicating that 'the 2 per cent or so of the vote that can be gained by an MP's personality, vigorous campaigning or record of constituency service may therefore make a significant difference overall'. Nevertheless, for many years local activities were a minor feature of the campaign scene and were largely ignored both by the national party headquarters and by the national media.

The marginalisation of constituency campaigns was not permanent, however. They came back into their own with the emergence in the mid-1990s of what Norris refers to as the post-modern campaign. Like modern campaigns, post-modern campaigns are nationally planned and coordinated, with careful attention to news management, to the use of focus groups and opinion polls, and so on. But they differ from the modernist model in several important respects. First, rather than limiting their campaign activities largely to the period before elections, parties have moved onto something nearer to a permanent campaign footing. All major activity, whether in government or opposition, is carried out with at least one eye on how it will 'play' with the voting public.

Second, whereas the modern campaign used broadcast methods, sending the same message via the same media (usually television) to all voters, the post-modern campaign has seen the increasing adoption of narrowcasting techniques. Messages can be targeted to a greater extent to sub-groups of the electorate. For instance, messages aimed at young voters might emphasise different issues than those aimed at pensioners; appeals to confirmed party supporters might contain different exhortations to those aimed at floating voters. Parties' abilities to narrowcast in this way are helped by a variety of developments. Telephone canvassing from national call centres, improved information technology and the use of area socioeconomic classification methods (sending different messages to different groups who are concentrated in particular districts) can help parties build databases of voters in key seats, classifying them by their age profile, their party preferences, their past voting histories and (to some degree) their socioeconomic interests. Desktop publishing software enables the production of bespoke leaflets and materials aimed at different groups, while mail-merge software allows rapid production of mail shots to deliver this material. And, although this remains in its relative infancy in the UK, the internet and new social media provide at least the potential for further targeting of campaign messages to key groups.

To some extent, this reflects expanding possibilities for parties: technological change makes a narrowcasting strategy easier now than in the past. But it also reflects necessity, as changing television consumption patterns make a broadcast strategy less likely to reach most voters. At the height of the 'modern' campaign era in the late 1970s and early 1980s, there were just three television channels in the UK (four after the launch of Channel 4 in 1982). A 'broadcast' strategy targeting these channels therefore reached most households. However, this oligopoly over the nation's televisions was challenged when multi-channel satellite TV entered the UK market in 1989, and had been broken by the mid-2000s (by 2003, around half of all households had access to multichannel TV; by 2011, this had risen to over 90 per cent). Most households now have access to hundreds of TV channels, and more content is now watched online. Viewers are less tied to particular channels than in the past, and can and do 'surf' away from party political broadcasts. 'Broadcast' strategies have become harder and parties have had to adapt to the changing environment. By the time of the 2010 General Election 22 per cent of Conservative, Labour and Liberal Democrat candidates had twitter accounts (for each party separately the percentages were 19, 22 and 26), and on average they sent out 63 tweets each during that campaign (Graham et al, 2013, p 699); around 60 per cent of these tweets were directed at 'the public', mainly giving 'updates from the campaign trail, promoting themselves or party members and critiquing opponents' (p 708). Only about 1 per cent of the electorate received such messages, however, according to the BES post-election survey (Johnston et al, 2012a).

Third, the constituency campaign has become a key element of the national post-modern campaign strategy (Fisher and Denver, 2008; Fisher, 2012). Parties target their constituency efforts at marginal seats, aiming to gain a slight edge there over their rivals by a more effective mobilisation of their support. Decisions on which seats to focus on are taken by the national campaign headquarters, based on judgements of where scarce campaign resources might be best expended. For incumbent governments, this usually means defending those seats that they currently hold by a narrow margin, in an attempt to minimise losses and to retain an overall majority. For opposition parties, meanwhile, the focus is primarily on those government-held marginals where the opposition party could win if a few more votes could be obtained. Party headquarters may refine some of these decisions as more information comes in. If, for instance, it becomes clear that the governing party is almost certain to lose its most marginal seats, then both the government and its opposition rivals might choose to abandon their campaigns there (the former to avoid throwing resources away in a lost cause, and the latter to avoid doing the same on a dead cert) and focus on the next-most marginal layer of constituencies. Information on which voters to contact within these target seats is supplied, in part, by local canvassing returns, but also by telephone canvassing activities from national telephone banks – with an increasing proportion of the electorate difficult to contact via this medium because of the absence of a national database of mobile as against landline telephone numbers. And campaign resources for these constituency campaigns, in the form of material for local leaflets and news stories and, in some cases, financial support (a subject we return to in more detail in later chapters) is also supplied by national party organisations. The local party supplies the labour force which fills envelopes, delivers leaflets, knocks on voters' doors and so on. As party membership dwindles, an increasing proportion is made up not of members but of volunteers and supporters (Fisher et al, 2013a, 2013b).

Pulling together all the different aspects of election campaigns in the early 21st century requires substantial resources, not least of which is hard cash. Campaign staff, media advisers and spokespeople, advertising agencies, polling companies, call centres, video production, web design and many other activities all need to be paid for. No campaign can last for long without money. And comparisons over time of the balance between 'free' campaigning activities (relying purely on volunteer labour) and activities requiring some financial input suggest that '(f)orms of campaigning that incur expenditure are increasing in importance' (Fisher, 2012, p 113). Money is here to stay in modern electioneering.

Party funding and public anxieties: paying the piper, calling the tune?

Following the money trail in British politics starts with identifying the sources of campaign funding – who bankrolls the parties' activities? For many in the media and the electorate, asking this question at all raises worries over whether parties' fundraising needs put them in thrall to a few wealthy individuals or organisations. In large part this reflects the concern that those with the capacity to make major financial contributions to parties will expect some sort of *quid pro quo* for their support. Where parties and candidates are reliant on large donors to fund their campaigns and activities, fears can arise over the extent to which policy might be trimmed to meet the donors' needs. Some idea of the extent of these fears can be gauged from responses to a 2008 survey of the British public's attitudes to party finance (vanHeerde-Hudson and Fisher, 2013). Asked what they thought the motivations for making a donation to a political party might be, 66 per cent of respondents said they thought the goal was to gain a favourable policy outcome. Similar percentages felt that the desire to influence the policy process (64 per cent) or to 'secure personal favours from politicians' (64 per cent) were also prime motivations.

Part of the problem is that the major parties' financial backers have tended to represent particular socioeconomic interests. Traditionally, Labour's main backers were the trade unions, while the Conservatives drew on support from rich donors and private companies, and the Liberals from their party members. The Conservatives were generally seen as the richest, best endowed of the three parties, Labour running a somewhat poorer second, and the Liberals a very much poorer third. For the parties' critics, their paymasters clearly dictated each party's priorities: Labour, went the argument (as it still does in David Cameron's responses at Prime Minister's Questions weekly in the House of Commons), was in thrall to the unions, as were the Conservatives to big business (Pinto-Duschinsky, 1981). The electorate certainly felt as such. The 1987 BES asked respondents how closely they thought each party looked after the interests of various groups in society, including big business and trade unions (see Figure 1.1[a]).[1] Whereas almost everyone (98 per cent) felt the Conservatives looked after the interests of big business closely (and 74 per cent thought they did so very closely), only a minority (40 per cent) thought Labour did so (and only 8 per cent very closely). In contrast, 96 per cent thought Labour looked after the unions' interests closely, compared to just 23 per cent who thought the same of the Conservatives (67 per cent thought Labour paid very close attention to the unions' interests, compared to just 4 per cent who thought the Conservatives did). Not surprisingly, perhaps, respondents tended to see the Liberal/SDP Alliance (the precursor of the modern Liberal Democrats) as somewhere in the middle, less beholden to business than the Conservatives and more than Labour, but more pro-union than the former and less than the latter.

However, structural changes in the economy over the last 30 years or so have meant that neither major party can now rely for its financial health just or even mainly on these 'traditional' funders. Deindustrialisation has hit trade union memberships hard and with that the unions' political funds, from which their donations to Labour are drawn. By the mid-1990s, it was becoming increasingly clear that the party would have to radically diversify its income streams. Similarly for the Conservatives: the decline of the 'maverick' entrepreneurial business leader and the rise of multinational companies and of corporate management, accountable to shareholders for the good stewardship of the company's resources, have made it harder for the party to rely on business donations. The Liberals and their Liberal Democrat successors, meanwhile, did not have the relative luxury of either union or business donations to fall back on when each was an important funding source.

The parties have therefore had to diversify their income sources, and all three now set considerable store on receiving not just many relatively small donations from rank-and-file members and supporters, but also on large one-off donations from the very affluent. This shift has been noted by the public. In 2010, the BES once again asked how

---

[1] Respondents could give one of four possible answers: very closely; closely; not very closely; or not at all closely.

well the parties looked after different groups' interests (Figure 1.1[b]).[2] While the Conservatives were still seen as considerably more pro-business and anti-union than Labour (with the Liberal Democrats once more in the middle), the gap had closed, mainly it must be said

Figure 1.1: Whose interests do voters think the parties look after?

(a) 1987

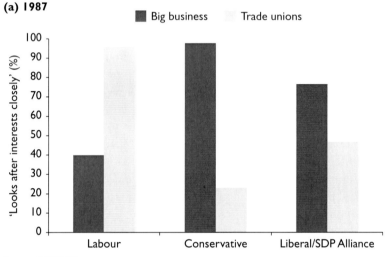

Source: 1987 BES

(b) 2010

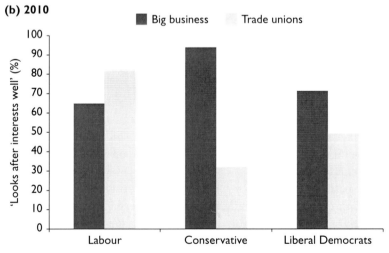

Source: 2010 BES in-person survey

---

[2] This time, they were asked how well, rather than how closely, they thought each party looked after the various groups' interests. The possible answers were: very well; fairly well; not very well; and not at all well.

---

due to changes in voters' perceptions of whose interests Labour served. The proportion thinking the Conservatives looked after the interests of business well was, at 94 per cent, only slightly lower than it had been 23 years before (although the percentage thinking they did this 'very well' dropped more markedly, from 74 to 51 per cent). But the public noticed Labour's shift away from the trade unions and towards business: the percentage thinking the party looked after the former well dropped by 14 percentage points over the quarter century, to 82 per cent in 2010, whereas the percentage thinking it looked after business interests well rose by 25 percentage points, to 65 per cent. Similar shifts occur if we focus just on those who thought the parties looked after business or union interests very well: the percentage thinking Labour looked after 'big business' interests very well almost trebled, to 21 per cent, while the percentage thinking it looked after the unions very well halved, to 31 per cent.

This does not mean that the electorate's concerns about donors' potential influence over parties' programmes have been allayed by the parties' attempts to widen their donor base, however. Even if Labour is no longer as reliant on the unions or the Conservatives on big business for their finances as in the past, they are both increasingly reliant on funding from relatively few very rich individuals. And the public remains deeply sceptical: the main funders may have changed over time, but the fear remains that parties will trim to suit their backers' needs. Some idea of the extent of this public disquiet can be obtained from a YouGov poll conducted in March 2012. Asked how much influence political parties' donors had, 70 per cent of survey respondents said too much; only 10 per cent felt donors had too little influence, and the remainder were not sure either way.

Public concern is not limited only to the potential influence large donors might exert over parties, however. The same YouGov poll also suggests that, by a substantial majority, voters remain uncomfortable with the idea that parties are dependent on a few donors, even if those donors do not influence party policy and action. Survey respondents were asked to choose which of two statements best reflected their views on the appropriate links between parties and donors. Both statements endorsed the view that donors should not receive special favours as a result of their financial support. But their tenor differed. One statement couched things negatively: 'it is wrong for senior MPs and ministers to give special access to people who have given big donations to their party.' The other put the case in a more permissive, positive light: 'as long as they do not receive any special favours, there is nothing wrong with senior MPs and ministers meeting people who give money to their party.' If voters were concerned only about the actual purchasing of influence, then at least as many should have plumped for the second, more permissive, option as plumped for the first, more negative, one. But this is not what actually happened. Given the choice, twice as many people (60 per cent) opted for the more severe-sounding of the two options as did for the less severe one (29 per cent). The implication is that most voters feel politicians should not only be above suspicion when it comes to their dealings with their party's donors, but that, like Caesar's wife, they should be *seen* to be above suspicion.

Nor is the fear that party priorities will be distorted by funders' interests and wishes entirely without foundation, as a few notable examples illustrate. 'Cash for peerages' scandals, involving suggestions that the honours system was being abused by politicians to reward their financial backers (and hence to encourage donations) tainted prominent British prime ministers in the early years of both the 20th and 21st centuries (Lloyd George and Tony Blair respectively). To take another example, in 1997 the newly elected Labour government announced an important public health initiative involving legislation to end tobacco advertising in British sport. But the initiative was swiftly overshadowed by the revelation that one of the leading lights of the Formula 1 car racing world, Bernie Ecclestone, had made a £1 million donation to Labour's 1997 General Election campaign, and had promised more. The problem? Formula 1 had been exempted from the tobacco advertising ban. Not surprisingly, the government insisted that the two events were unconnected, but the suspicion remained in the public mind (a major embarrassment for the new government, as it had campaigned in 1997 partly on a 'clean-up politics' ticket after John Major's Conservative administration had been engulfed by sleaze allegations).

While it is hard to draw direct connections between such events and public attitudes regarding party finance, it is unlikely that there has been no effect. Certainly, many voters fear that fundraising for political parties opens the door to venal and even criminal influence over the political process. Fully 61 per cent of respondents to the 2008 survey discussed earlier disagreed with the statement that 'Despite recent allegations of corruption, on balance UK party finance is clean': only 22 per cent agreed (vanHeerde-Hudson and Fisher, 2013). Whether justified or not, this reflects considerable public distrust of party finance. Given subsequent events, including the 2009 scandal over MPs' expenses, things are unlikely to have improved, and may even have worsened. Even so, it is also worth noting that, public perceptions notwithstanding, political life in Britain is relatively free of corruption

(Triesman, 2000). Money matters, but whether it buys influence to anything like the extent that the public fears is quite another issue.

Furthermore, while British voters are uneasy about private donors' relationships with elected politicians, they are also deeply reluctant to embrace proposals for more extensive state funding of political parties. At present UK political parties do receive some state support (Ewing, 2007, pp 171ff). Candidates at general elections are entitled to a free postal delivery of election material to every voter in their constituency, for instance. Parties fielding more than 50 candidates in an election are entitled to free air time for at least one party broadcast on the main national television and radio channels. And the main opposition parties receive a subvention (the so-called 'Short money') to support their activities in Parliament. But unlike their counterparts in many other democracies, British political parties do not receive substantial grants from the public purse. Nor is it likely that state funding of UK political parties will be extended in the foreseeable future, not least because public opinion is strongly opposed to the possibility. For instance, 75 per cent of those who expressed a view in the March 2012 YouGov poll discussed earlier were opposed to the idea that political parties should be funded by the taxpayer rather than by private donations.[3] The British public may not like the thought of parties seeking money from donors, therefore, but it is not willing to sanction an alternative source of revenue. Questions over who pays the political piper are likely to remain.

An expensive business? How much do elections cost?

Public anxieties over money's place in the political process are not limited to the potential for direct corruption, however. In part, too, there are concerns over the extent to which money in politics distorts a supposedly level playing field for parties and organisations. Money is essential if parties are to campaign effectively. Staff need to be paid; campaigns must be funded. But if some parties are better resourced than others, goes the argument, they are likely to find it easier to gain a hearing than their poorer rivals. When the Conservatives under Mrs Thatcher employed the Saatchi & Saatchi advertising agency as part of their campaign at the 1979 General Election, many commentators felt a Rubicon had been crossed. Had slick advertising stolen the election? (Given the travails of the Callaghan government in

---

[3] Just over one in five respondents (22 per cent) did not know whether they favoured or opposed taxpayer funding: 20 per cent favoured it and 59 per cent were opposed.

the late 1970s, the Conservatives were likely to win in 1979 regardless, but the contrasting images of the Conservatives' well-resourced and professional campaign and Labour's rather more traditional one became part of the folk wisdom surrounding that election.)

In fact, careful media management, astute use of advertising and the deployment of polling data to monitor campaign messages were not new even in 1979 (ironically, given his later reputation as a scourge of image management in elections, Tony Benn built his reputation as a young, rising-star MP in part by running Labour's TV-oriented 1959 General Election campaign). Even so, the 1979 campaign marked something of a watershed in British electioneering. Since then, the major parties have all paid increasing attention to the professionalisation of their campaign activities (Labour's shambolic and amateurish 1983 campaign stands as the main exception and as a baleful warning of what can go wrong). All now routinely strive to ensure, as far as possible, that all those involved in the party's campaign remain resolutely professional and 'on message'. Campaign activities are carefully planned to emphasise the party's chosen campaign themes. Focus groups and opinion polls are used extensively to understand voters' moods, to assess the party's electoral strengths and weaknesses, and to refine which policy proposals and political messages resonate most effectively with voters. Careful attention is paid not just to the words and arguments to be used by campaigners (which are centrally coordinated to minimise the risk of mixed – and even mutually contradictory – messages coming out from different people within the campaign), but also to how the campaign looks, to how it is reported in the media, to who is contacted by the parties and where, to targeting specific messages to particular groups in the electorate, and so on.

All this comes at a financial cost, hence the persistent concern that money can sway results. In their 2008 survey, vanHeerde-Hudson and Fisher (2013) found that almost half (45 per cent) of the British public agreed with the claim that a system of voluntary donations to political parties (in effect, the existing UK system) would mean that some parties would be unfairly advantaged relative to others by their greater capacity to raise funds (only 29 per cent disagreed). There is no reason to expect that there has been much improvement since then in levels of public concern over the potentially distorting effects of variations in party finance on election outcomes. And, as vanHeerde-Hudson and Fisher also discovered, significant numbers of British voters think that the parties spend very large sums indeed on their campaign activities. Asked to estimate each party's expenditure on its national campaign in 2005, 46 per cent of those who thought they had some idea of how much the parties spent overestimated Labour's spending, as did 39 per cent for the Conservatives' and 55 per cent for the Liberal Democrats' expenditure: a sizeable minority, somewhere between one in five and one in three, thought the Labour party alone had spent more then than had actually been spent by all parties together (between 27 and 15 per cent thought the same of the Conservatives). Public estimates of the amounts spent in individual constituency campaigns, meanwhile, were on average three times higher than what is legally permitted.

The reality, however, is often rather less lurid, but no less important for all that. Elections are expensive events, even if not at the levels feared by some voters. At the 2010 General Election, for instance, the combined spending of all political parties on the national campaign amounted to £31.2 million. The vast bulk of this, a total of £29.5 million, was spent by just three parties, the Conservatives (whose national campaign cost £16.7 million), Labour (£8 million) and the Liberal Democrats (£4.8 million). Nor was 2010 an especially expensive election. Just five years before, the 2005 General Election's national campaign cost a total of £42.3 million, £40.2 million of which was spent by the three main parties. If anything, the general climate of austerity gripping the country after the 2007 financial crisis dampened the parties' abilities to raise and therefore spend campaign funds in 2010: the legal limits to the maxima they could spend were unchanged.

Austerity notwithstanding, the amounts spent in 2010 sound large. But how does spending in this election compare with past UK elections, with elections elsewhere, or with other forms of expenditure? Figure 1.2 puts the election into the longer context of spending at British general elections since the 1960s (in this and the subsequent figure, 'Liberal' refers to the Liberal Party between 1964 and 1979, to the Liberal-SDP Alliance in 1983 and 1987, and to the Liberal Democrats from 1992 onwards; data for elections from 1964 to 1997 are derived from Pinto-Duschinsky, 2008).[4]

Two trends stand out. First, the quantities spent by the three largest parties on their election campaigns from the mid-1980s onwards were considerably higher than the amounts spent in the 1960s and 1970s. For instance, at £11.2 million, Conservative spending in 1992 was 10 times higher in cash terms than the party's outlay in the 1964 election (a modest-sounding £1.2 million).

Second, election spending peaked at the 1997 General Election, when the combined amount spent by Labour, the Conservatives and the Liberal Democrats came to £56.4 million (the vast bulk of this was

---

[4] No data are available for the 1966 contest.

Figure 1.2: Spending at UK general elections since 1964

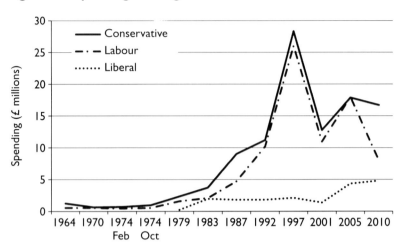

Sources: Data for 1966-97 from Pinto-Duschinksy (2008); data from 2001 onwards from the Electoral Commission

spent by the Conservatives and Labour, who paid out £28.3 million and £26.0 million respectively). Since then, spending levels have come down substantially, running on average at about half the 1997 level. As discussed in more detail in Chapter Two, the factor which contributed most to the downward shift in spending since 1997 was the passage of the Political Parties, Elections and Referendums Act 2000 (PPERA), which for the first time introduced limits on parties' spending on their national campaigns. The legislation has not been the only factor, however. As noted above, both Conservative and especially Labour national campaign spending fell between the 2005 and 2010 elections, beneath those maxima, in large part as a result of the much more difficult economic environment in which the latter election was fought, which made it harder for both parties to raise funds. In the run-up to 2010, Labour suffered the extra difficulty of being a long-lived and increasingly unpopular incumbent government that was widely expected to be about to lose the election. Even in good economic times, potential donors are relatively reluctant to support parties which are not thought to have a chance of winning (why waste money and, for large donors, potential political capital by backing a party liable to be out of office for some time to come); the effect is likely to be more severe in a recession, when money is already scarce. The fall-off in Labour's national spending between 2005 and 2010 was, therefore, much larger than that for the Conservatives.

But, as Figure 1.2 also shows, the 2000 legislation and the post-2007 economic downturn did not affect all parties equally. Labour and the Conservatives, the spending giants of British politics, had to reign in their national expenditure substantially after the passage of PPERA, as their outlays in 1997 far exceeded the new limits, while Labour took by far the biggest 'hit' in 2010. The Liberal Democrats, in contrast, have never been sufficiently well funded to allow them to spend anywhere near the post-2000 limits on their national campaign. Hence, alone of the 'big three' parties, they were able to continue to increase (albeit modestly) their national campaign expenditure between 2001 and 2010.

So far, then, the picture would seem to support a general impression that British general elections have become much more expensive operations over time, albeit with a one-off adjustment due to the introduction of the 2000 Act. An obvious caveat applies, however. Over the near-half century between 1964 and 2010, inflationary pressures have substantially reduced the purchasing power of the pound. To obtain a more accurate impression of the real-terms cost of British general elections, therefore, we need to strip out the effects of inflation. This is done in Figure 1.3, which reproduces data on each party's national campaign spending between 1964 and 2010, but expressed in 2010 prices. In important respects, this provides a major corrective to the impression that British general election spending is growing rapidly. Rather, in around half of the elections over the last half-century, total spending on the national campaigns has been between around £20 and £30 million at 2010 prices, with no long-term tendency

Figure 1.3: UK campaign spending since 1964, at 2010 prices

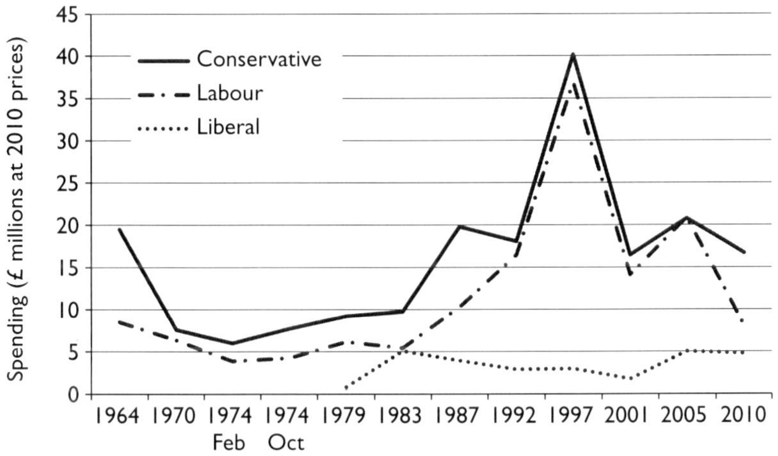

for spending to rise. With the effects of inflation incorporated, for instance, Labour and Conservative spending levels at the 1964 General Election were comparable to the parties' outlays in 2010; seen from the perspective of the real terms cost of their election campaigns, it is as though the intervening 46 years had not happened. On the same basis, election spending in the years from 1970 to 1983 was relatively muted (hitting a low in February 1974, when Labour and the Conservatives combined spent £9.9 million at 2010 prices). The 1997 General Election once again stands out as an unusually expensive contest (with the three parties spending £80 million in total at 2010 prices, over 2.5 times the average total expenditure on the national campaign over the entire period). The cost of British general elections has fluctuated up and down over the years, therefore, but in real terms, and with the exception of the 1997 contest, there are no clear signs of a runaway increase in spending.

The above discussion focuses on money in the national campaign. But (and as discussed in greater detail in subsequent chapters) the local grassroots activity in British elections is focused on the constituency campaigns. At the 2010 General Election, 4,150 candidates stood for election in the UK's 650 constituencies. Many were not serious contenders – some were 'joke' candidates; others were faithfully representing their party in seats where the party had no realistic prospect of winning but where it was important to field a candidate in order to say that the party was competing throughout the country. Few such candidates put much effort or money into their local campaigns. But some candidates in some seats expended much more cash and energy on their local battles. According to the Electoral Commission, a total of £25.2 million was spent by all candidates on constituency campaigning between 1 January 2010 and the election itself on 6 May: £14 million of that was spent in the four weeks after the dissolution of Parliament on 12 April. As with the 2010 national campaign, the 'big three' parties dominated spending on that year's constituency campaigns. The Conservatives spent most (£9.8 million, of which half was spent in the final four weeks). Labour lagged some way behind, spending £6.5 million on its constituency campaigns (£3.6 million after 12 April). And the Liberal Democrats were further behind still: their constituency campaigns cost a total of £5 million, of which £2.7 million was spent in the final month. The combined cost to the main parties of the 2010 General Election can therefore be estimated at around £56.5 million.

How do the costs of a UK general election compare to other sorts of expenditure? It is perhaps no surprise to find that UK elections look positively parsimonious compared to contests in the USA. With a population of around 314 million in 2012, the USA is about five times more populous than the UK (whose 2011 population was 63 million). Even if the *per capita* costs of the two contests were the same, therefore, presidential elections should cost five times more in total than UK general elections. But the actual gap is much wider. According to the US Federal Election Commission, Barack Obama and Mitt Romney spent a combined total of £716 million on the 2012 US presidential election (the Obama campaign's declared expenditure, at £435 million, eclipsed Romney's £281 million).[5] In the same election cycle, a total of £695.7 million was spent on the 435 elections to the US House of Representatives and £473.3 million on the 33 Senate races. The £56.5 million bill for the 2010 UK election pales into insignificance beside this: the ratio of Obama and Romney's 2012 spending to that for the 2010 UK contest is 12.7:1 (the equivalent ratios for the House and Senate contests are 12.3:1 and 8.4:1 respectively). Bizarre though it may sound, there is a case for saying that even the spending behemoth that is a US presidential election represents something of a bargain: if Obama and Romney were to present a bill to every man, woman and child in the USA to recoup their expenses, the average individual would be faced with a payment of just £2.28. But their British counterparts would get off even more lightly: the shared costs of the 2010 General Election campaign amount to just 90p or so per person.

So Britain's elections are cheap compared to contests in the USA, but they are also relatively small budget items when compared to many other forms of expenditure. Most moderately large local authorities spend about the same every fortnight as is spent on a national election. Sheffield City Council, for instance, spent £1,612 million on its services in 2010/11, the equivalent of £62 million every two weeks. Over the course of a four-week election campaign, the council spends £124 million. The city's oldest university, meanwhile, spent £413.5 million in the same year. Even our entertainments often cost more than our elections, as just a few examples attest. In 2010/11, British households spent a total of £3.7 billion on their television licences. A television advertising campaign for beer that ran during the 2007 Rugby World Cup cost £6 million (comparable to Labour's 2010 spend on its national campaign). To take another example, football is an obsession for many Britons, but it is a much more expensive business

---

[5] These figures are based on returns to the Federal Election Commission (FEC) as of 31 December 2012. The sterling estimates are based on the prevailing exchange rate between the pound and the dollar in late 2012.

than the country's politics. During the January 2013 transfer window, for instance, the nation's Premier League clubs spent £120 million on obtaining new players (and this was not a patch on the £225 million they spent on transfers in 2011). Individual transfers, too, rivalled the parties' spending. The two most expensive transfers in the window came close to matching the Conservatives' 2010 national spending, and exceeded Labour's by a factor of more than two: AC Milan spent £19 million to secure the striker Mario Balotelli from Manchester City (eclipsing even the Conservatives' 2010 election expenditure), while Manchester United paid £15 million to bring Wilfried Zaha from Crystal Palace. Set beside these sorts of sums, election spending looks rather less dramatic than the bald figures might originally seem.

Conclusions

A sense of perspective is valuable, therefore. Election campaigns sound expensive and are hardly cheap, but nor are their costs out of control. Furthermore, political parties continue to play a vital role in the democratic process, and it is almost impossible to see how they could fulfil those roles if they did not spend. How else would they be able to communicate with voters? In an increasingly noisy, sophisticated and complex media environment, parties have to work hard to be seen and heard. To do so requires resources. Members and volunteers working for free will help, to some extent. But their reach is limited, their numbers are small and (for members at least) declining, and they can hardly compete with the electronic media for public attention. Even very simple leaflets and constituency newsletters must be paid for. And no major modern party could reasonably do its job without core administrative staff, policy and political advisers, press teams and media advisers, market research activities, and so on. All must be paid for. Money and politics may make a controversy-laden combination, therefore, but the latter could not operate without the former.

That said, much of the discussion around party funding in the UK focuses on parties' national operations. Rather less attention has been paid to funding the parties' grassroots activities in the constituencies, a strong tradition of research on the effectiveness of local constituency campaigns and campaign spending notwithstanding. Yet, as we have seen, the constituency campaign is not only potentially important in its own right but has also been wrapped up into the wider framework of the post-modern election campaign. It can no longer be seen in isolation from parties' national campaigns. The issues of who funds the campaign and with what effect are just as germane at the local as at the national level. In the remainder of this book, therefore, we follow the money down to the grassroots of British electoral politics. That journey begins in the next chapter with a discussion of how much is spent on constituency campaigns and whether it influences the electoral outcome.

TWO

Money matters: local campaigns at British general elections

The nature of British general elections has altered very markedly over the last century, but the law regarding how much candidates can spend on their constituency campaigns has hardly changed at all. In the 19th century, although many candidates stood on a party label there was virtually no party-focused campaigning; each candidate fought his own campaign on a local basis, with some reference to national issues but little call for the voters to ensure that a particular party was able to form a government.

At the beginning of that century, most candidates were seeking election from constituencies with relatively small numbers of registered voters − especially in the so-called 'rotten boroughs'. With neither a secret ballot nor restrictions on the nature of the campaigning, the potential for corruption was large − and frequently realised, particularly through a practice known as 'treating' whereby votes were solicited via, for example, the provision of drink and food by the candidates. As the franchise was extended by the three Reform Acts passed during that century, and the related redistributions of constituencies eliminated most of those with very small electorates, the potential cost of treating increased − giving an advantage to wealthier candidates.

Secret ballots were introduced in the Ballot Act 1872, and regulation of candidates' expenditure by the Corrupt and Illegal Practices Act 1883, whose provisions included limitations on the amount that could be spent on a campaign. (For general introductions to this legislation, see Pinto-Duschinsky, 1981, and Johnston, 1987.) A maximum amount was specified for each of eight types of constituency, as follows:

English, Scottish and Welsh borough seats:
With less than 2,000 electors − £350
With 2,000 or more electors − £380, plus £30 for each additional 1,000 electors.
English, Scottish and Welsh county seats:
With less than 2,000 electors − £650
With 2,000 or more electors − £710, plus £60 for each additional 1,000 electors.

Irish borough seats:
  With less than 500 electors – £200
  With 500–1,000 electors – £250
  With 1,000 or more electors – £275, plus £30 for each additional 1,000 electors.
Irish county seats:
  With less than 2,000 electors – £500
  With 2,000 or more electors – £540, plus £40 for each additional 1,000 electors.

As well as a basic rate for all constituencies, whatever their electorates, these maxima distinguished between urban and rural areas, setting higher spending levels for the latter on the grounds that contacting voters in person was much more difficult there than in the higher density towns and cities. Returns of expenditure – under a number of headings – had to be made within 35 days of an election being held by the candidate's agent, who was legally responsible for all financial matters covered by the law and had to approve all items of expenditure (thus making the appointment of an agent, whether paid or unpaid, obligatory).

As the franchise was extended further – by the 1885 and 1918 Reform Acts (although a full adult franchise was not implemented until 1928) – these regulations were modified by the Representation of the People Act 1918, and its many successors. Over several decades that legislation quite substantially reduced the amount that each candidate could spend during the campaign period. In 1918 it was set at 5 pence per elector (2.08 new pence) in borough and 7 pence (2.92 new pence) in county constituencies; the figure was subsequently reduced, to 6 pence (2.5 new pence) for county constituencies by the Equal Franchise Act 1928 but a comparable reduction of 1 pence for borough seats was blocked by Labour MPs. A further reduction was proposed in 1944 after a Speaker's Conference on aspects of the electoral system – mainly at the behest of Conservative MPs who feared the amounts that Labour candidates were able to raise for their campaigns from the trade unions – but changes were not made until the Representation of the People Act 1949, which introduced a basic formula that has remained at the core of the regulations to the present day:

- in borough constituencies, £450 plus 1.5 (old) pence per registered elector; and
- in county constituencies, £450 plus 2 (old) pence per registered elector.

Those maxima remained unchanged for two decades, so that the real-terms expenditure limits declined substantially. They were then increased – although not necessarily before every election – and 1983 legislation gave the government power to modify them by an Order in Council, avoiding the need for repeated Acts of Parliament. For the 2010 General Election, the maxima were:

- in a county constituency, £7,150 plus 7 pence for every entry in the register of electors in the constituency on the due date;[1] and
- in a borough/burgh constituency, £7,150 plus 5 pence for every entry in the register of electors in the constituency on the due date.

The median constituency electorate then was 70,189: its maximum allowed expenditure for the campaign was £12,063.23 if it was a county constituency and £10,659 if it was a borough (or 'burgh', the Scottish term) constituency.

This was the only legislation to have any impact on campaign expenditure throughout the 20th century. It applied to a short period only – between the date when either the election writ was moved or the individual's candidacy was confirmed (whichever was the later) and election day – almost invariably no more than six weeks and sometimes as short as three. Campaign spending at other times was unregulated until 2001 following passage of the PPERA 2000 (see Chapter Five, this volume), and all campaign expenditure by parties (both nationally and regionally) was separate from that of their candidates.

This status quo for more than a hundred years occurred while the nature of British democracy changed very significantly. Indeed, by the start of the 20th century the UK Parliament was dominated by political parties, and although the campaigns in each constituency were officially between individual candidates, most – and certainly almost all of those with any expectation of victory – were competing under a party's label and committed to its manifesto. Furthermore, those campaigns were increasingly overshadowed – by the end of the century very much so – by national campaigns fought through the mass media, initially the press and then, after some reluctance by their executives to become involved, by radio and television. Party politics were nationalised and increasingly people voted not for the local candidate but for a party, although the candidate's party identification was not

---

[1] This is defined in the Political Parties and Elections Act 2009, Clause 21(4), as 'the register of Parliamentary electors for the constituency in question as it has effect on the last day for publication of notice of the election.'

added to the ballot paper until 1969,[2] and parties were not legally recognised (through registration) until 2000 under the PPERA. In addition, by the mid-20th century large proportions of the electorate identified with a particular party and habitually voted for it, with the main axis of cleavage being social class (see Särlvik and Crewe, 1983); in a much-cited aphorism from that time, Peter Pulzer (1967, p 98) referred to class as the 'basis of British politics: all else is embellishment and detail'. This competition between parties was almost entirely unregulated – certainly the amounts that the parties chose to spend on their national campaigns were subject to no limits – whereas that between their candidates at the local level, increasingly irrelevant to the outcome according to contemporary commentators (see, for example, Butler and Stokes, 1969; Kavanagh, 1970), was subjected to the updated 1883 limits. (The urban–rural distinction was retained: at each redistribution the Boundary Commissions are required to characterise every constituency as borough/burgh or county, for this purpose only.)

In the last decades of the 20th century, however, the 'conventional wisdom' that local campaigns were largely irrelevant to an election outcome came increasingly under question from commentators, reflecting changing political practices. Election campaigns have always had two separate, although linked functions: the first involves socialising voters into support for a party – for its policies, record in government and personnel (especially its leadership); the second involves canvassing electors to identify those who are committed to a party's cause and then, through further contacts, mobilising them to turn out and vote on election day. The former is largely conducted through the national campaign and the mass media: the latter has traditionally involved local party workers assisting candidates to ensure high turnout levels among their supporters, although increasingly the initial canvassing is done by telephone rather than face-to-face contacts, from national and regional call centres rather than from within the constituency. Such contacts are increasingly important as the class cleavage that underpinned voting behaviour for several decades has weakened, and valence politics (the tendency for voters to decide which party to support on the basis of their perceived competence, for example, at managing the economy, rather than for ideological reasons) came to dominate party choice (Clarke et al, 2009).

---

[2] Under the Representation of the People Act 1969, all candidates were allowed up to six words to describe themselves on the ballot paper; most used it to identify the party for which they were standing.

Research over the last three decades has shown that the canvassing and mobilising activities by local party workers are effective: the more intensive candidates' local campaigns the better their performance (and, as a consequence, the less successful their opponents'). Much of that research (especially in the early years) indexed the intensity of the campaigns using the reported amounts spent according to the published returns of candidates' expenditures under the Representation of the People Act provisions (Johnston, 1985, 1987); other work using different measures of intensity, such as the number of campaign workers deployed in a constituency, has produced similar results (see, for example, Whiteley and Seyd, 1994; Denver and Hands, 1997). From the 1980s on, central party organisations recognised the important role of such campaigns, and increasingly coordinated activities across the constituencies to ensure that, as far as possible, the most intensive campaigns were run in the seats where the outcome was least predictable – the marginal constituencies, where victory was uncertain and on which the overall election outcome, and thus which party(ies) would be invited to form a government, depended (Fisher and Denver, 2008, 2009). Target seat campaigns became major elements of each party's national campaigns – some of them very sophisticated, as illustrated by those run by the Conservatives prior to the 2005 and 2010 elections (under the leadership of its former Treasurer and then Deputy Chair, Lord Ashcroft: Ashcroft, 2010; see also Johnston and Pattie, 2007, 2010; Cutts et al, 2012).

Those target seat campaigns have not been limited to the short period between Parliament's prorogation and election day; they have increasingly been initiated months, if not years, before the election was called, with much canvassing of voters to identify supporters followed by contact through a variety of media designed to sustain their support and, in an era of much weakened ideological commitment to individual parties and lower turnout, ensure that votes were cast on election day (or, increasingly, before it by using the more accessible postal voting facility: see Cutts, 2006; Cutts and Shryane, 2006). This was partially recognised in the Political Parties and Elections Act 2009. A retired former senior civil servant, Sir Hayden Phillips, had been asked by the Prime Minister to propose new regulations on party funding, covering both national and local parties and the full inter-election period. He failed to gain all-party agreement (Koß, 2011), however, so the 2009 Act introduced further constraints on candidate expenditure over the last five months of a Parliament only, assuming that it had been sitting for more than 55 months (for more details, see Chapter Five, this volume). The maximum sums that a candidate could spend during those final months before the start of the official ('short') campaign in 2010 were:

- in a county constituency, £25,000 plus 7 pence for every entry in the register of electors in the constituency on the due date; and
- in a borough/burgh constituency, £25,000 plus 5 pence for every entry in the register of electors in the constituency on the due date.

Those maxima only apply if Parliament is dissolved in the 60th month of its five-year term. If it is dissolved earlier, which is very unlikely under the terms of the Fixed-term Parliaments Act 2011, then a percentage of that sum only can be spent (60 per cent if dissolution occurs in the 56th month, 70 per cent in the 57th, 80 per cent in the 58th and 90 per cent in the 59th: see Johnston and Pattie, 2011a).[3]

Those regulations were implemented for the first time at the 2010 General Election. For what became known as the 'long campaign' (the period between January and April 2010), in an average constituency with 70,189 electors the maximum that could be spent in a county constituency was £29,913.23 and in a borough constituency £28,509.45. Combined with the lower limits for the subsequent 'short campaign', this gave maxima that could be spent between the end of 2009 and election day of £41,976.46 in a county constituency and £39,168.45 in a borough seat. Given the range of electorate sizes, the maximum that could be spent varied from £35,199.20 to £55,347.36, although most constituencies fell within the range £39,000-43,000. Many candidates spent well below the maximum, however, as illustrated below.

Most of this money was locally raised, especially that spent on the 'short campaign' in the last weeks before ballots were cast. For both Labour and, to a lesser extent, the Liberal Democrats, the financial situation of their national party organisations has been such in recent decades that they could not afford to allocate funds to constituency branches; indeed, in Labour's case the databases of identified supporters compiled at the national call centres were sold to the constituency parties for use in contacting such voters (Cowley and Kavanagh, 2010). The Conservatives were much better placed financially, and in 2007-09 made substantial grants to local parties to be used in building their candidates' profiles locally and creating local databases of supporters, but few grants were made in 2010. As with the other

---

[3] This means that if an election is suddenly called early within the last five months, candidates could find that they have overspent for that period!

parties, Conservative candidates and their local support groups were responsible for raising funds, through donations and other efforts, to be spent on the constituency campaigns in the last months before the election, although there were considerable stimuli for this to be focused on the marginal seats where the election was going to be won or lost.

The pattern of spending: 1997-2010

If raising money to spend on constituency campaigns was relatively easy and every candidate (at least from the major parties) had at least a plausible chance of winning an election, then all candidates might be expected to raise sufficient funds through their local parties so that they spend close to the local maximum – to ensure that they were not outspent and outvoted by their opponents. But since some forms of fundraising can be costly while others may produce limited returns, and in any case many local parties have few members and hence a limited fundraising capacity, candidates and their supporters are less likely to expend a great deal of effort on them either where they anticipate winning relatively easily or, especially, where they believe they have little chance of victory. On the assumption that the more intensive the local campaign (including the more that is spent on it) the better the likely outcome, the main effort should be reserved for the marginal seats.

The total amounts spent by each party's candidates at each of the four elections between 1997 and 2010, inclusive, in those constituencies where all fielded candidates, are shown in Table 2.1. For the first three elections, data are available for the short campaign only; for the 2010 contest, separate totals are given for both long and short campaigns, as well as the two combined. Four trends stand out from these figures.

- No party spent as much as three-quarters of the maximum possible across the country, and for the Conservatives and Labour the totals declined somewhat over the four contests (Labour spent 71.9 per cent of the maximum in 1997, for example, but only 58.7 per cent in 2005 and just over half – 50.7 per cent – on the 2010 short campaign).
- Over the four elections, the gap between the amount spent by the Conservative and Labour candidates widened – from just 1.6 percentage points in 1997 to 6.7 and 7.2 points in 2001 and 2005 respectively, and then to 18.1 points on the 2010 short campaign, largely because of a substantial decline in Labour spending.

Table 2.1: The total amount spent on the constituency campaigns, by election and party, 1997-2010

	Maximum (£)	Spent (£)	% spent
1997			
Conservative	5,310,890	3,906,076	73.5
Labour	5,310,890	3,821,132	71.9
Liberal Democrat	5,310,890	1,944,498	36.6
2001			
Conservative	5,885,829	4,136,911	70.3
Labour	5,885,829	3,744,047	63.6
Liberal Democrat	5,885,829	1,927,289	32.7
2005			
Conservative	7,133,618	4,692,718	65.8
Labour	7,133,618	4,184,082	58.7
Liberal Democrat	7,133,618	2,479,574	34.8
2010			
Conservative			
Long	16,577,434	4,677,061	28.2
Short	6,486,833	4,466,327	68.9
Combined	23,064,267	9,143,388	39.6
Labour			
Long	16,577,434	2,671,977	16.1
Short	6,486,833	3,287,695	50.7
Combined	23,064,267	5,959,672	25.8
Liberal Democrat			
Long	16,577,434	2,141,762	12.9
Short	6,486,833	2,570,578	39.6
Combined	23,064,267	4,712,340	20.4

- The amounts spent by Liberal Democrat candidates remained relatively constant across the first three contests but then increased on the 2010 short campaign.
- No party spent as much as one-third of the maximum possible on the long campaign in 2010, when the Conservatives substantially outspent their opponents.

The first three of these differences are typical of earlier periods, when the maxima were smaller in relative terms. Thus in 1955, for example, the Conservatives spent 87 of the maximum allowed across all constituencies compared to Labour's 72 per cent. The gap between the two parties closed to only four points when Labour was expected to win in 1964 (92 and 88 per cent respectively), but then widened to an average of some 10 points at most of the subsequent contests (with the Conservatives spending more in each case); in 1979, for example, the gap was 77-67 and in 1992 80-70 with, in general, Labour raising more relative to their main opponent when they were performing relatively well in the opinion polls. The Liberal Democrats spent just 32 per cent of the maximum possible in 1979, 56 per cent in 1983, and 44 per cent in 1992.

Table 2.2 indicates, for the 2010 General Election, how each party's spending in the 566 constituencies for which all three candidates made short campaign returns was distributed across the six separate categories into which those returns were subdivided.[4] At both phases of the campaign the main expenditure was on printed materials, such as leaflets, to be delivered unsolicited to voters; the Labour and Liberal Democrat candidates spent slightly more of their total budgets on this item (73 and 70 per cent respectively during the long campaign and

Table 2.2: The total amount spent on various expenditure categories in the 566 constituencies for which all parties made short campaign returns, 2010 General Election

Party	Conservative	Labour	Liberal Democrat
Long campaign			
Advertising (posters etc)	338,501	132,370	89,821
Unsolicited materials (leaflets etc)	2,902,933	1,947,179	1,508,327
Transport	11,637	7,323	6,706
Public meetings	30,958	16,819	20,761
Agents and paid staff	827,429	199,577	303,587
Accommodation	555,533	354,073	213,227
TOTAL	4,676,710	2,663,961	2,141,762
Short campaign			
Advertising (posters etc)	580,671	359,468	228,163
Unsolicited materials (leaflets etc)	3,062,878	2,378,940	2,017,677
Transport	32,797	31,783	13,645
Public meetings	17,787	8,634	11,221
Agents and paid staff	413,014	84,127	113,919
Accommodation	340,687	369,932	171,898
TOTAL	4,466,327	3,275,270	2,561,922

---

[4] All of the data on spending at the 2010 General Election analysed here were obtained from the Electoral Commission website at www.electoralcommission.org.uk/party-finance/party-finance-analysis/campaign-expenditure/uk-parliamentary-general-election-campaign-expenditure

73 and 79 per cent during the short) compared with the Conservatives (62 and 69 per cent); the latter spent slightly more on posters and similar media. Agents and other paid staff as well as accommodation were also significant expenditure items (especially during the more extended long campaign, although this reflects its greater length – within each party there was little variation between the two campaigns in the amount spent per week on these items), with the Conservatives spending more on these items than their competitors. Little was spent on either transport or public meetings.

The data in Table 2.3 extend the analysis of the volume of spending on the four election campaigns between 1997 and 2010 by looking at the variation across constituencies; in this and most of the subsequent

Table 2.3: Variation in spending across constituencies by election and party, 1997-2010

	Mean	SD	LQ	Med	UQ
1997					
Conservative	72.8	26.3	52.8	84.0	94.3
Labour	72.5	21.7	56.2	72.5	91.7
Liberal Democrat	36.2	31.1	11.3	36.2	57.2
2001					
Conservative	69.4	29.3	42.0	82.9	94.0
Labour	64.3	26.3	41.4	68.0	88.9
Liberal Democrat	32.4	29.5	10.4	19.4	46.1
2005					
Conservative	64.2	28.8	38.8	73.1	88.6
Labour	59.4	28.3	34.0	62.3	85.8
Liberal Democrat	34.6	29.9	11.5	22.5	52.9
2010					
Conservative					
Long	28.2	28.0	4.2	18.7	46.2
Short	68.4	28.2	41.1	78.0	91.0
Combined	39.5	25.8	14.7	35.2	58.4
Labour					
Long	16.3	21.8	0.5	6.3	25.9
Short	51.7	31.0	20.2	55.0	80.6
Combined	26.1	22.0	7.1	20.5	38.8
Liberal Democrat					
Long	12.9	22.9	0.0	10.0	3.2
Short	39.6	33.7	1.2	26.2	9.4
Combined	20.4	24.3	2.6	9.4	28.2

SD – standard deviation; LQ – lower quartile; Med – median; UQ – upper quartile.

analyses, the data analysed are the amounts spent as a percentage of the maximum spending allowed in each constituency, rather than the total amount, to reflect the differences in the maximum allowed. The first two columns indicate the mean and standard deviation in the percentage spent by each party's candidates at the four elections. Relative to the means the standard deviations are large, indicating considerable spatial variation in the amount spent. The other three columns give the median and upper and lower quartile values. These indicate the variation in the central half of the distribution for each set of values: thus, for example, in 1997 in half of the constituencies the Conservative candidates spent between 52.8 per cent and 94.3 per cent, so that in one-quarter of all seats they spent almost to the maximum (that is, those constituencies falling between the upper quartile and 100 per cent). In general at the first three elections the spread of values was approximately the same for the candidates of all three parties, although at a lower average level for the Liberal Democrats than for the other two. In 2010, not only was the inter-quartile range larger (over 60 percentage points for Labour in the short campaign), but in general the lower quartile was small. For Labour's long campaign, for example, it was only 0.5, indicating that in one-quarter of all constituencies it spent virtually nothing then.

One further feature of the variations in spending across parties and constituencies is brought out by the box plots in Figure 2.1: the boxes in these diagrams cover the inter-quartile range, with the median shown by a solid horizontal line, and the stems extend to the maximum and minimum.[5] Thus for the 1997 General Election (Figure 2.1[a]), the diagrams for the Conservative and Labour parties indicate negatively-skewed distributions: spending was clustered towards the upper ends of the distributions, but the longer tails at the lower ends indicate a much wider spread of (low levels of) spending in a minority of the seats. The diagram for the Liberal Democrats, on the other hand, is positively skewed: spending is clustered at the lower end of the vertical axis, with a wider spread of high values encompassed by the upper quartile. The first two parties spent relatively large sums in most constituencies and a small amount in only a few, therefore, but the situation was reversed for the Liberal Democrats. The next two sets of diagrams (Figures 2.1[b-c]) show very similar patterns for the next two elections.

For the 2010 General Election, the graphs for the long campaign (Figure 2.1[d]) show a negatively-skewed distribution for all three parties:

---

[5] Constituencies where the amount spent differed by more than twice the value of the inter-quartile range are separately identified.

Figure 2.1: Box plots of the amounts spent by each party (as a percentage of the maximum allowed) on the constituency campaigns

(a) The 1997 General Election

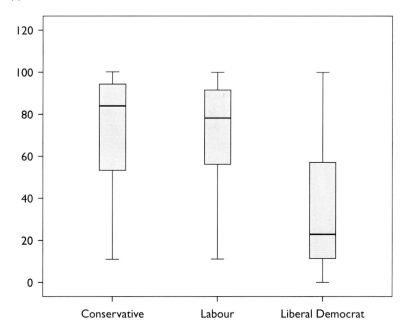

(b) The 2001 General Election

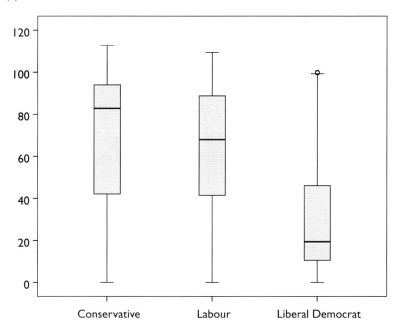

(c) The 2005 General Election

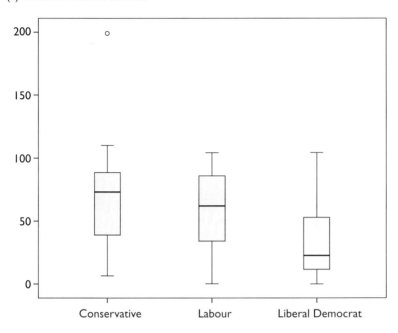

(d) The long campaign before the 2010 General Election

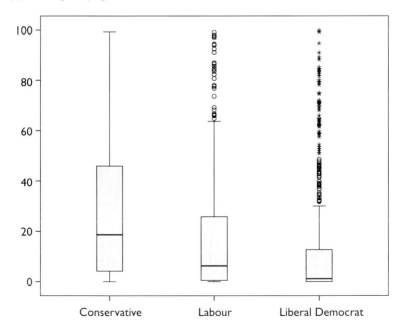

(e) The short campaign before the 2010 General Election

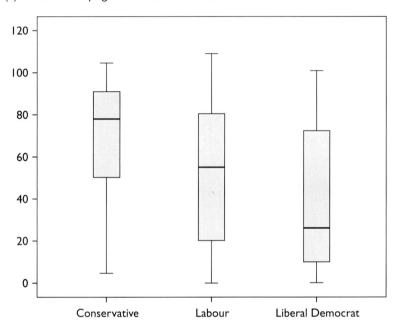

(f) The combined 2010 General Election campaigns

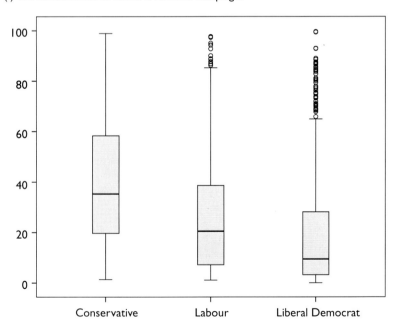

each spent very little in most places, but with a long upper tail indicating substantial spending in only a few (especially for Labour and the Liberal Democrats). For the short campaign (Figure 2.1[e]), the Conservatives have a similarly positively skewed distribution as at the previous three contests. Those for both Labour and the Liberal Democrats show a much wider range of spending within the inter-quartile range, with longer upper than lower tails, indicating high levels of spending in a minority of seats only. The graphs for spending on the combined campaigns (Figure 2.1[f]) show a similar difference between the Conservatives, on the one hand, and the other two parties: each of the latter has a number of outliers where spending was much greater than the average.

Marginality and spending

The variations in spending shown in Tables 2.1-2.3 and Figure 2.1 are considerable, therefore, but are they consistent with the expectation that each party would spend most where it anticipated the greatest returns? Benefit-to-cost analysis suggests that spending money and other resources seeking votes where the party has little chance of success or, to a lesser extent, where victory is virtually assured is of little value; effort should be concentrated on raising and then spending money where it can deliver the greatest benefits – in the marginal constituencies.

The sequence of graphs in Figures 2.2-2.4 inquires whether this was the case over the series of four elections from 1997 to 2010. Each graph shows the pattern of spending for the relevant party across all constituencies for which data are available (which is virtually all of them). The horizontal axes show the marginality of the constituency at the previous general election: a vertical line splits the graph between the seats won at the first contest (to the right of that line) and those lost – the further the constituency is from that line the greater the margin of either victory (the positive figures) or defeat (the negative figures) at the preceding contest. The vertical axes show the party's spending in each constituency at the election being analysed (that is, the subsequent one to that used for calculation of the marginality figures shown on the horizontal axes), as a percentage of the allowed maximum there. A best-fit line is also shown: this indicates the average value on the vertical axis for each value on the horizontal axis.[6]

The general expectation is that all parties spent closest to the maximum around the zero vertical line – that is, in the seats that they

---

[6] Fitting these lines uses the 'lowess' method available in the SPSS graphics package, using the nearest 33 per cent of all values to estimate the average.

either won or lost by a small margin only. This is clearly the case at all four contests for each party, but with important variations across the four elections and the three parties. For Labour, for example, each best-fit line has an inverted-U shape, with its peak close to the zero line. In 1997, however, when Labour was the challenger party (the Conservatives having been in government for the previous 18 years), the peak was to the left of that zero line, indicating that on average Labour candidates spent more in the marginal seats where their party lost in 1992 than in those where it was successful (Figure 2.2[a]).[7] The general expectation in 1997 was that Labour would win the election – after four defeats in a row – and probably win well. The party did not expect to lose many (if any) seats, and its candidates saw little need

Figure 2.2: Scatter plots showing the amount spent on the constituency campaign (as a percentage of the maximum allowed) by Labour in each seat

(a) The 1997 General Election

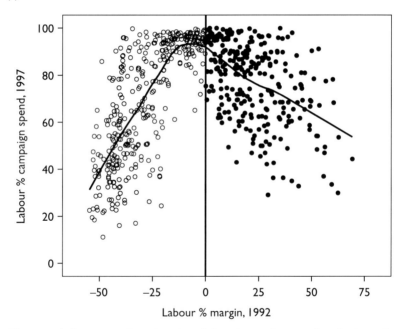

Labour % margin, 1992

The open circles are constituencies where Labour lost at the preceding election and the closed circles are those where it won. The trend lines are the lowess best fits.

[7] The data for the 1992 General Election are estimates, because new constituency boundaries were introduced between that election and 1997. The 'results' for 1992 are estimates of what would have happened if the election then had been held using the new constituencies introduced for 1997 (Rallings and Thrasher, 1995).

(b) The 2001 General Election

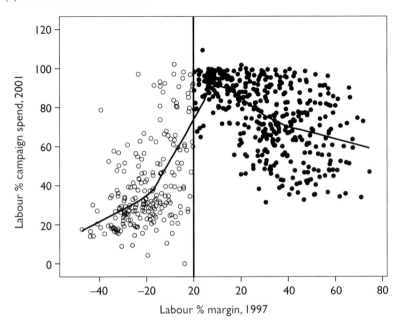

(c) The 2005 General Election

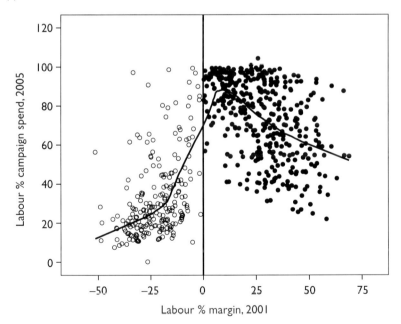

The open circles are constituencies where Labour lost at the preceding election and the closed circles are those where it won. The trend lines are the lowess best fits.

(d) The long campaign before the 2010 General Election

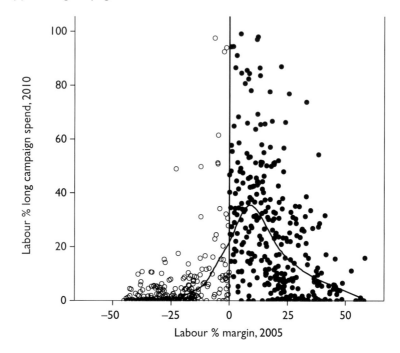

(e) The short campaign before the 2010 General Election

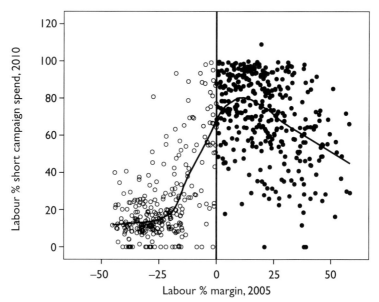

The open circles are constituencies where Labour lost at the preceding election and the closed circles are those where it won. The trend lines are the lowess best fits.

(f) The combined 2010 General Election campaigns

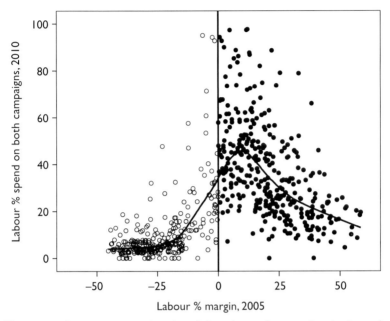

The open circles are constituencies where Labour lost at the preceding election and the closed circles are those where it won. The trend lines are the lowess best fits.

to spend large amounts defending those it already held, even those won by relatively small margins in 1992. Thus there are many more constituencies where close to the maximum was spent to the left of the zero line – that is, in seats won by other parties in 1992 – than in those where Labour was victorious then. Its candidates did not spend relatively large sums in seats where it had little expectation of victory, however. The best-fit line on the left-hand side of the graph is steep, indicating a rapid fall-off in the amount spent as the margin of defeat widened; in seats that were lost by a margin of 25 per cent or more in 1992, for example, it was rare for the local party to spend more than half the maximum. There was a similar, although less steep, fall-off to the right of the zero line: the safer the seat the less spent on its defence, although even in those won by a margin of 25 percentage points, where there was virtually no chance of them being lost, average expenditure was close to 80 per cent of the allowed maximum.

At the next general election, in 2001, Labour was defending the large parliamentary majority won in 1997, and although not expected to lose many seats, nevertheless its strategy was in stark contrast to that deployed four years earlier. Its spending this time was highest in the seats that it won at the preceding contest (see Figure 2.2[b]), with the peak to the right of the zero line and falling away much more gradually than was the case in the seats where it lost in 1997 (shown to the left of that line). Its expectations of displacing the incumbents in the latter seats were low, even in those lost by only a small margin; despite the party's continued popularity, it expected to make few further gains. It spent much less than the maximum on average (less than 80 per cent) in even the most marginal of such constituencies, and in a large number spent very little (less than 40 per cent). Exactly the same pattern is observed at the 2005 General Election (see Figure 2.2[c]), when again Labour was on the defensive and some losses were anticipated; once more its candidates spent relatively little seeking to extend the party's number of seats. But, in line with the data in Table 2.3, it was spending slightly less on average than at the previous contests. In 1997 the peak of the best-fit curve is at over 90 per cent on the vertical axis; in 2001 it had fallen below that level; and in 2005 it was closer to 80 per cent. Over time, Labour was spending less on its local campaigns, even those critical to its continued success – presumably because its local parties were less able to raise funds there since there was no evidence of complacency regarding the overall result, especially in 2005.

These trends are accentuated in the pattern of spending at the 2010 General Election (see Figures 2.2[d-f]), when Labour was very much on the defensive, expecting to lose the election overall and seeking to stem the loss of seats so that the Conservatives could not gain an overall majority. The peak level of spending then was well to the right of the zero line and, apart from a small number of very marginal seats, Labour spent very little in the great majority of seats where it lost in 2005 (less than 20 per cent of the maximum in most of them). The average level of spending was also lower than at previous contests, even in the marginal seats:[8] the range of spending there was greater than in 2005, and the peak of the best-fit curve was only 80 per cent. By the end of its 13 years in office, Labour was spending less overall, with relatively weak campaigns (as indicated by the amount spent on them) in a substantial number of constituencies (including a not-insubstantial number that it won at the previous election). Its spending was concentrated on the defence of seats that it won by margins of 10 percentage points or more then (it being generally assumed that

[8] As for the 1992 General Election, the 'results' for the 2005 contest used in these analyses are estimates because new constituencies were introduced in England and Wales (but not Scotland) in 2007; they are estimates of what the result would have been in 2005 if the election then had been held in the new seats used for the first time in 2010 (Rallings and Thrasher, 2007).

most of those won by smaller margins could not be held), but even in a substantial number of those, its expenditure was substantially less than the maximum it could have spent, were it able to raise the money.

The patterns of spending for the Conservative party are very largely a mirror image of those for Labour: in 1997 the Conservatives were on the defensive and spent most in the seats they won five years earlier (see Figure 2.3[a]), whereas at the following three elections they were seeking to gain additional seats, and their spending was slightly more focused on those where they lost at the previous contest (see Figures 2.3[b-f]). There is, however, one very substantial difference between the patterns of Conservative and Labour spending, especially at the first two contests. In both 1997 and 2001 the best-fit line to the right of the zero line – that is, in seats that the Conservatives were defending – was virtually parallel to the horizontal axis (see Figure 2.3[a-b]): Conservative candidates spent on average as much defending a seat won by a large margin as they did on one where the party only achieved

Figure 2.3: Scatter plots showing the amount spent on the constituency campaign (as a percentage of the maximum allowed) by the Conservatives in each seat

(a) The 1997 General Election

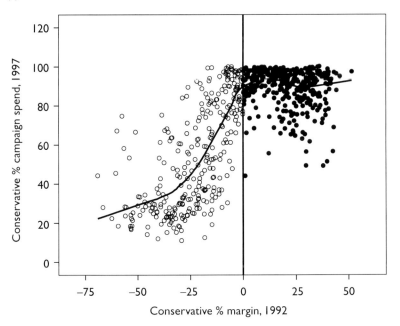

The open circles are constituencies where the Conservatives lost at the preceding election and the closed circles are those where they won. The trend lines are the lowess best fits.

(b) The 2001 General Election

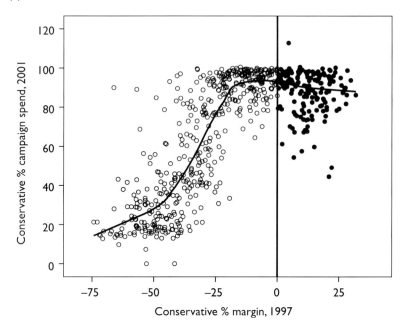

(c) The 2005 General Election

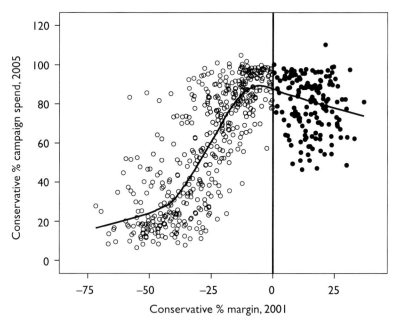

The open circles are constituencies where the Conservatives lost at the preceding election and the closed circles are those where they won. The trend lines are the lowess best fits.

(d) The long campaign before the 2010 General Election

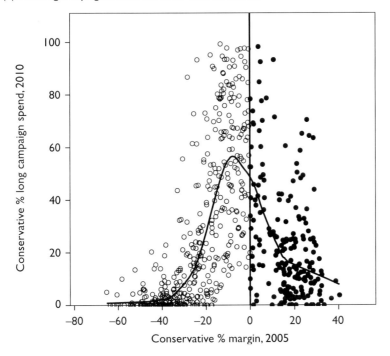

(e) The short campaign before the 2010 General Election

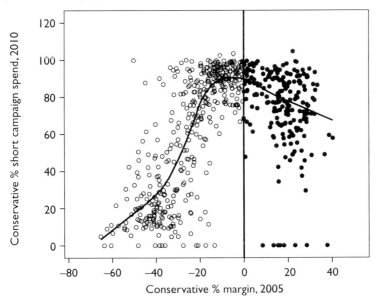

The open circles are constituencies where the Conservatives lost at the preceding election and the closed circles are those where they won. The trend lines are the lowess best fits.

(f) The combined 2010 General Election campaigns

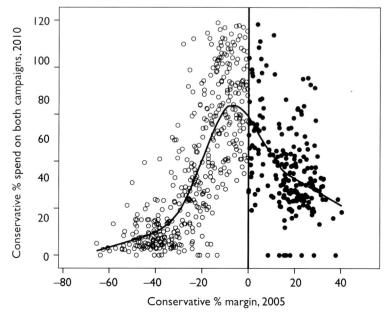

The open circles are constituencies where the Conservatives lost at the preceding election and the closed circles are those where they won. The trend lines are the lowess best fits.

a narrow victory, whereas the safer the seat, the smaller the amount spent on its defence by a Labour incumbent. Furthermore, that line on the Conservative graphs falls at about 90 per cent on the vertical axis, indicating that on average in all of the seats that it was defending the party spent close to the maximum allowed. This tendency was replaced in 2005 (Figure 2.3[c]) and, to a greater extent, 2010, with a fall-away in the amount spent in the party's safest seats (Figure 2.3[d–f]), although the slopes are much less steep than in the Labour graphs. On average, the Conservatives spent more defending their 'heartland' seats than their main opponent did in similar circumstances.

The other major shift in the pattern of Conservative spending is observed to the left of the zero line. In 1997 it did not anticipate many local victories, and although it spent substantial sums in the most marginal seats that it lost in 1992, it spent less than 40 per cent of the maximum in the majority (Figure 2.3[a]), most of which were 'hopeless' to its cause. By 2001, as it sought gains, it spent close to the maximum in a large number of constituencies which it lost in 1997 by as many as 20 percentage points (although spending very little in the 'hopeless cases'), and the same occurred in 2005. Conservative local spending was redirected at those two elections into the seats that had to be won if it was to form a government again, a pattern that was repeated in 2010.

Both of the two largest parties displayed the same general pattern of spending, therefore: when they were the incumbent government they spent on average more defending the seats that they held than in seeking additional gains where they lost at the previous election; and when they were in opposition, their spending was concentrated on the marginal seats that they lost at the previous contest. For the Liberal Democrats too, who were always in opposition, the patterns were consistent across all four elections (Figures 2.4[a-f]). They spent close to the maximum in both the small number of constituencies they were defending (few of which had been won with a substantial majority) as well as in the equally small number of seats where they lost by a small majority last time. In the great majority of cases, however,

Figure 2.4: Scatter plots showing the amount spent on the constituency campaign (as a percentage of the maximum allowed) by the Liberal Democrats in each seat

(a) The 1997 General Election

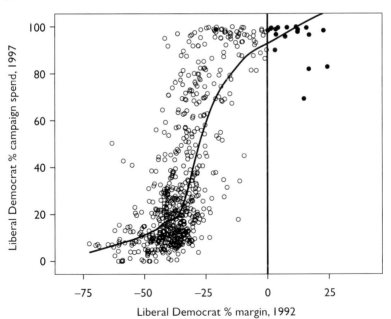

The open circles are constituencies where the Liberal Democrats lost at the preceding election and the closed circles are those where they won. The trend lines are the lowess best fits.

(b) The 2001 General Election

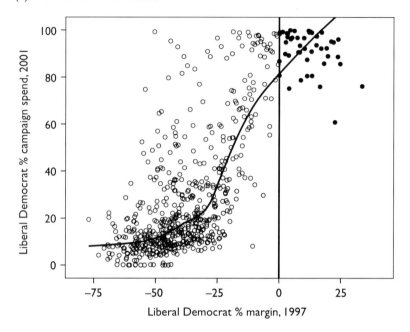

(c) The 2005 General Election

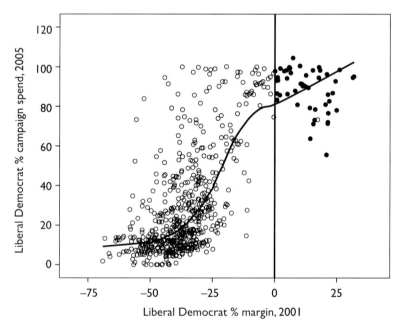

The open circles are constituencies where the Liberal Democrats lost at the preceding election and the closed circles are those where they won. The trend lines are the lowess best fits.

(d) The long campaign before the 2010 General Election

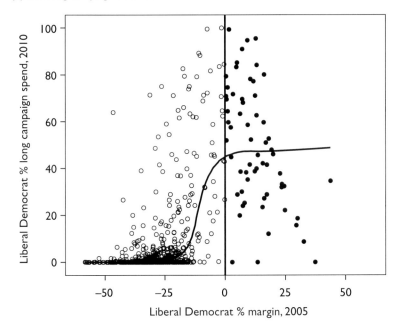

(e) The short campaign before the 2010 General Election

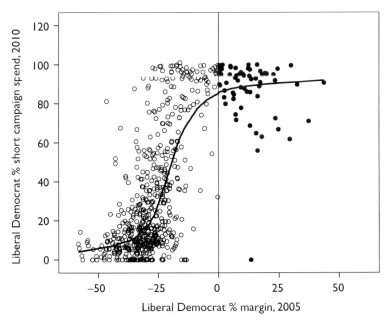

The open circles are constituencies where the Liberal Democrats lost at the preceding election and the closed circles are those where they won. The trend lines are the lowess best fits.

(f) The combined 2010 General Election campaigns

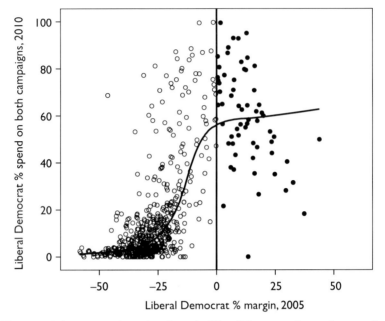

The open circles are constituencies where the Liberal Democrats lost at the preceding election and the closed circles are those where they won. The trend lines are the lowess best fits.

in which they lost by a margin of 25 percentage points or more, they spent very little.

For the 2010 General Election, as noted above, we have data on spending for not only the 'short campaign' (the four weeks between when the election was called and polling day) but also the 'long campaign' (the preceding three months). More could be spent on the latter.[9] In general terms, the patterns of long campaign spending paralleled those on the later short campaign – as the graphs in Figures 2.2[d, e], 2.3[d, e] and 2.4[d, e] show. Labour spent on average more defending seats that it held, the Conservatives more in those it needed to win, and the Liberal Democrats on both types of marginal. But the peaks of the best-fit curves were much lower than for the short campaign spending – averaging only around 55 per cent for the Conservatives, 40 per cent for the Liberal Democrats and 30 per cent

[9] The data analysed here are for all constituencies where the relevant party made a short campaign return. In some cases, there was no long campaign return, which may indicate that they decided to do no campaigning involving expenditure then (although the Electoral Commission suggests that in some there was inaccuracy in the returns).

for Labour – and the range of spending, even in the most marginal seats, was much wider. In the very marginal seats where it lost in 2005, for example, Liberal Democrat spending varied across the full range from 0 to 100 per cent, and there was a similar range in the highly marginal constituencies that both Labour and the Conservatives were defending. During that earlier period, therefore, there was much greater inter-constituency variation in the amounts the parties were able to raise and spend even in the seats where victory mattered most to them.

Those clear differences between the parties in 2010 are brought into stark relief when we combine expenditure on the two campaign periods (Figures 2.2[f], 2.3[f], 2.4[f]). On average, both the Conservatives and the Liberal Democrats were able to raise and spend some 60 per cent of the joint maximum in the seats where their campaigns were most intense, whereas for Labour the average was closer to 40 per cent. At the last election in the four that we have been analysing here, when Labour was under most pressure electorally, therefore, it was least able to raise money to spend on campaigning in the seats where the contest was to be won and lost.

Local competitiveness

The discussion so far, based on patterns of spending that are graphically very clear, has shown that the amount spent by candidates on their local campaigns varied by party, by election, by whether the party was currently in government or opposition, and by the constituency's marginality. By inference, those spending variations are correlated with the intensity of those campaigns more generally: on average, the constituencies where candidates spent more were also those where they were able to mobilise more party workers to canvass on their behalf, for example.

As a check on that assumption, Table 2.4 uses data on a number of campaign intensity indicators obtained from a survey of constituency agents after the 2010 General Election:[10] the number of party members in the constituency (an indicator of the human resources on which the candidate's campaign should be able to draw); the number of locally produced leaflets; the number of active campaign workers across the short campaign; the number of polling stations covered by tellers on polling day; the number of campaigners active on polling day; and a

---

[10] We are grateful to Justin Fisher, Ed Fieldhouse and David Cutts for allowing us access to these data.

---

campaign intensity index which combined those and a range of other indicators. The table shows the mean value for each of those measures according to the percentage of the allowed maximum spent by the party on the 2010 short campaign. The general pattern across all three parties is very clear: the more that was spent, the more intensive other aspects of the campaign – the more people involved, the more leaflets printed and circulated (paid for from the moneys raised) and so on.

These measures and a number of others were combined to provide a composite index of campaign intensity: this has an average value of 0.0

Table 2.4: Mean constituency values on a number of indicators of campaign intensity according to the amount spent there as a percentage of the allowed maximum, 2010 General Election

Amount spent (%)	1-20	21-40	41-60	61-80	81-100
Conservative					
Number of party members	119	123	481	439	500
Number of locally produced leaflets	18,556	16,343	49,671	40,846	74,291
Number of campaign workers	16	12	43	44	43
Number of polling stations covered	14	7	21	24	26
Number of campaigners on polling day	24	18	79	92	122
Campaign intensity index	−0.58	−0.68	0.05	0.44	0.80
Labour					
Number of party members	155	217	338	306	407
Number of locally produced leaflets	10,194	23,983	71,053	56,972	98,827
Number of campaign workers	7	15	24	28	40
Number of polling stations covered	2	3	9	10	13
Number of campaigners on polling day	10	20	45	63	82
Campaign intensity index	−0.90	−0.43	0.48	0.67	0.83
Liberal Democrat					
Number of party members	69	102	121	160	233
Number of locally produced leaflets	19,631	49.693	66,562	143,846	193,372
Number of campaign workers	42	14	17	35	54
Number of polling stations covered	5	8	14	12	17
Number of campaigners on polling day	19	34	37	75	112
Campaign intensity index	−0.88	−0.33	−0.13	0.60	0.97

with positive values indicating the more intensive campaigns. The three graphs showing the relationship between short campaign spending and this index (Figure 2.5) indicate a clear positive link (stronger for the Conservatives and Labour than for the Liberal Democrats) between the two.[11] In general, therefore, the spending data provide a good general index of a local campaign's intensity: where a party spent more it was also more active campaigning and canvassing, as shown by a range of other measures.

A further indicator of the links between how much a party spent on campaigning in 2010 and how much canvassing it undertook there is obtained by using data from the BES. This included a large panel survey in which respondents were interviewed both close to the start of the 'official' campaign (that is, at the end of March–early April 2010) and immediately after the election. In the first of those surveys they were asked if they had been contacted by any of the political parties

Figure 2.5: Scatter plots showing the relationship between short campaign spending and the constituency intensity index at the 2010 General Election

(a) The Conservative party

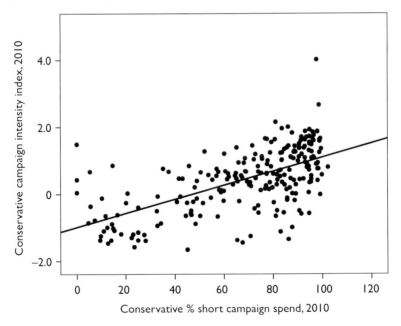

[11] We look at short campaign spending only, since the data collected from the party agents refer almost entirely to that period.

(b) The Labour party

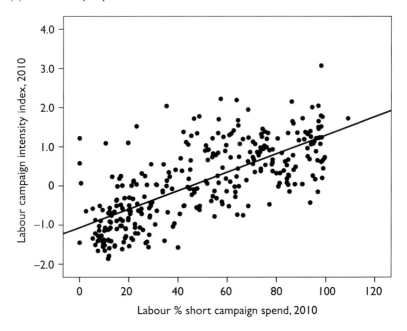

(c) The Liberal Democrat party

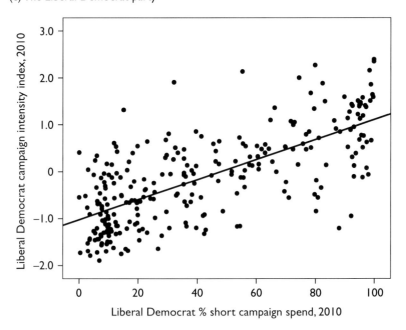

during the preceding six months (that is, covering, but extending back before, the period of the 'long campaign' for spending regulations). In the second they were not only asked whether they had been contacted by a party during the last month (that is, during the 'short campaign' period) but also the nature of that contact – by telephone, leaflet, at home, in the street, by email, by Twitter or other social media, or by text. They were not asked how many times they were contacted through each medium. Such data have their drawbacks, because they rely on recall: the longer the time gap between the contact and the survey, the greater the probability of the respondents having forgotten that contact, especially if it was from parties they didn't support. Even so, the data do provide a broad indication of how voters remembered their encounters with the grassroots campaign. (For further use of these data see Johnston et al, 2012a, 2012b.)

Table 2.5 shows the percentage of the 11,545 survey respondents living in constituencies for which we have both short and long campaign spending data who reported being contacted by each of the three parties in the six months before the short campaign started, according to how much each party spent on the long campaign there. There is a very clear pattern, in the expected direction: the more that a party spent on the long campaign in a constituency, the larger the percentage of residents there who recalled being contacted by that party in the six months before the 'campaign proper' began. Furthermore, in constituencies with intensive campaigns during that period (that is, parties spending more than 75 per cent of the approximate £30,000 maximum allowed), the percentage of respondents reporting a contact was large – well over half by the Conservatives and Liberal Democrats.

Similar patterns are shown in Table 2.6 which indicates the percentages contacted by each of the seven modes, as well as by any of them, by each party, according to its spending on the short campaign in the constituency. Apart from receiving leaflets – the Royal Mail

Table 2.5: Percentage of BES respondents who reported in the pre-campaign survey that they had been contacted by the named party in the months preceding the campaign, according to the amount spent by that party's candidate on the 'long campaign'

% spent	Conservative	Labour	Liberal Democrat
0	9.6	9.5	9.3
1-25	18.8	18.7	18.4
26-50	32.8	35.2	39.5
51-75	44.3	46.0	55.8
76-100	55.7	45.8	63.6

Table 2.6: Percentage of BES respondents who reported in the post-campaign survey that they had been contacted by the named party during the campaign, according to the amount spent by that party's candidate on the 'short campaign'

	T	L	H	S	E	Tw	Te	Any
Conservative								
1-25	0.4	22.7	2.4	1.2	2.3	0.1	0.1	24.2
26-50	0.8	31.5	4.6	1.7	4.7	0.8	0.7	33.6
51-75	2.0	38.1	9.0	2.7	5.3	0.3	0.5	41.7
76-100	4.5	52.2	12.6	3.5	9.1	1.1	1.3	55.3
Labour								
1-25	0.7	25.8	1.4	0.7	1.5	0.3	0.3	26.5
26-50	2.0	35.0	4.1	2.0	3.1	0.5	0.2	36.8
51-75	5.2	45.2	8.4	2.6	3.5	0.9	0.7	47.8
76-100	7.8	53.1	12.6	4.2	5.3	1.1	1.0	56.7
Liberal Democrat								
1-25	0.6	28.5	1.9	0.6	1.7	0.6	0.1	29.6
26-50	0.9	36.0	4.4	1.6	2.2	0.6	0.1	37.5
51-75	2.2	42.9	6.1	1.4	2.9	1.2	0.2	44.6
76-100	7.8	62.3	13.8	4.0	7.6	2.1	0.7	64.6

Type of contact: T – telephone; L – leaflet; H – home; S – street; E – email; Tw – Twitter; Te – Text; A – any.

will deliver one item to each registered elector free-of-charge – only small percentages reported any contact, but in virtually every case more were contacted the more that was spent on the local campaign. Apart from receipt of leaflets, the most common contacts were at the respondents' homes (the traditional locales for canvassing support), by telephone and by email: each party's databases of supporters recorded, where available, both their telephone numbers and email addresses and these were clearly used in those constituencies where campaigning was most intense. Since research has shown that those contacted by a party during an election campaign are more likely to turn out and vote for it, especially those already inclined to support it, the relationships shown in Tables 2.5 and 2.6 give strong support to the argument developed here that parties perform best across the separate constituencies at British elections the more that they spend on their local campaigns there.

On the assumption that spending money on the local campaign is equally efficacious across parties and constituencies (that is, that each pound spent has the same impact on the outcome), then if each party spent the same amount in a constituency, those efforts should cancel each other out. In general, at any election one party's spending does appear to have been more efficacious than another's, especially when comparing the impact of Conservative and Labour spending. Analyses have shown that at the 1983-97 elections, every pound spent by a Conservative candidate had less impact on the party's share of the constituency votes than one spent by Labour, but from 2001 onward this relationship was reversed: Labour candidates' spending was less effective than that of Conservatives' once the former party gained power (Johnston and Pattie, 1997, 2008b; Pattie and Johnston, 2009b). The reason for this appears to be that candidates of the governing party, especially incumbent MPs who won the election for it at the preceding contest, have less need to build up their public profile with the local electorate than their opponents. Incumbents get a great deal of 'free' publicity through their work representing the local community and its interests; their challengers get much less and have to build up their profiles through their activities which attract local media coverage – as well as canvassing support through leaflets and other media on which the bulk of their campaigning funds are spent (see Table 2.2 earlier). Thus in 1997, for example, every extra pound spent by a Labour candidate on average had a greater impact on the election outcome than any additional spending by a Conservative, but in 2005, when Labour had been in power for eight years, the situation was reversed (Pattie and Johnston, 2009b).

Even if each party's candidate's spending was equally as effective as an opponent's, however, if they spent unequal amounts in a constituency, then the bigger spender should gain an advantage. But was this the case, were they competing on equal terms in most constituencies? Take the situation of the two main parties, the Conservatives and Labour. The graphs discussed in the previous section suggest that they were raising and spending money in the same places – in 2010, for example, in the marginal seats Labour was defending against a Conservative challenger. There were substantial differences, however, as shown by the scatter of points on those graphs: on average a Labour candidate spent less than a Conservative, and there was much greater variation in Labour spending. Given those differences, did the Conservatives have a financial advantage in a substantial number of seats?

To explore this issue in more detail, Figure 2.6 looks at the ratio of Conservative to Labour spending at each of the four elections, in those seats where those two parties occupied first and second places at the previous contest. A ratio of 1.0 indicates that both candidates spent the same amount; ratios greater than 1.0 indicate that Conservative candidates outspent their Labour opponents; and ratios of less than

1.0 show seats where Labour candidates spent more. The first four graphs show the relationship for short campaign spending at each of the four elections: the fifth shows spending in 2010 on both campaigns combined. In these graphs, the spending ratios have been converted to natural logarithms to avoid the distortion that can occur with the unconverted values: above 1.0 the range is from 1.0 to ∞; below 1.0 the range is much narrower (0–1.0). Where each party spent the same amount, the logged value of the ratio was 0.0; where the Conservatives outspent Labour the ratio had a positive value, and where Labour outspent the Conservatives it was negative.

Each of the graphs shows the same general pattern, indicative of the Conservatives' greater ability to raise money overall, but the differences became more accentuated over the four contests. Thus on each occasion, spending by the two parties was relatively equal in the more marginal constituencies (that is, those close to the zero vertical line). To the right of that line, where the seats were won by Labour at the previous election, in the great majority Labour's candidate outspent the Conservative candidate, especially in the seats won by large margins (that is, the

Figure 2.6: The ratio of Conservative-to-Labour spending in constituencies where those two parties occupied the first two places at the previous election

(a) The 1997 General Election

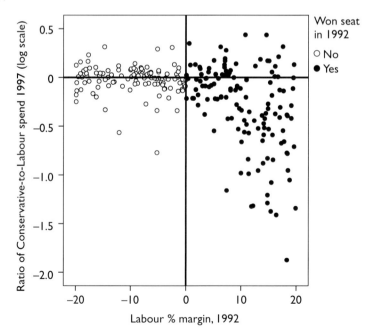

(b) The 2001 General Election

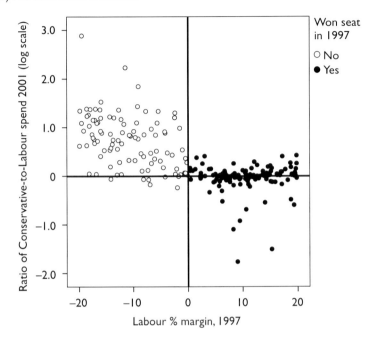

(c) The 2005 General Election

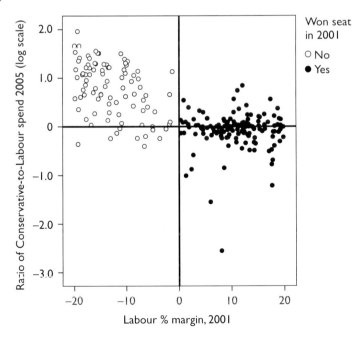

(d) The long campaign before the 2010 General Election

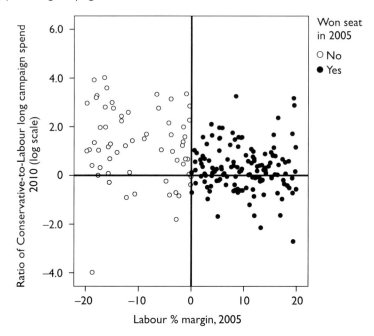

(e) The short campaign before the 2010 General Election

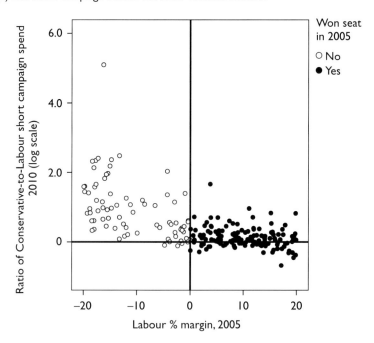

(f) The combined 2010 General Election campaigns

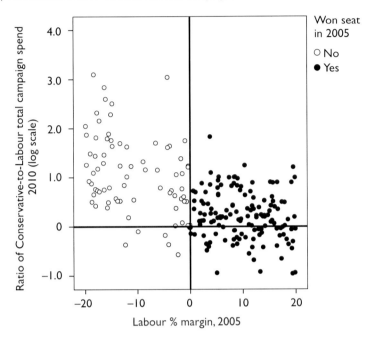

observations that fall below the horizontal line at 0.0 on that axis, which identifies where the two parties spent the same amount). To the left of that line, however, comprising seats won by the Conservatives, their candidate outspent Labour's. Thus each party outspent the other by the largest average ratio in the seats that it was unlikely to lose; where the competition was close, spending was more equal, as expected.

There were major changes in that pattern in spending on the short campaign over the period, however. In 1997, for example, the Conservatives outspent Labour by little more than 2.5:1.0 even in their safest seats, and in many of Labour's safest seats the ratio fell below 0.2 (Figure 2.6[a]). There was also a large number of Conservative-held marginal seats (just to the left of the zero vertical line) where there was virtual parity between the two parties' spending. Four years later (Figure 2.6[b]), there were many fewer constituencies in that latter category, and in the Conservative safe seats the party's candidates outspent their Labour rivals by a greater ratio than previously (in many cases larger than the 2.5 near-maximum in 1997). That difference was even more accentuated at the 2005 election (Figure 2.6[c]) and by 2010 many Conservative candidates were outspending their Labour opponents by more than 6:1 – a difference that is even starker when spending on the two campaigns is combined (Figures 2.6[d–f]).

By combining the pattern of spending by two parties rather than just one (as done in Figures 2.2-2.4 discussed in the previous section), these patterns in Figure 2.6 enable us to evaluate the extent to which the Conservative and Labour parties competed on equal financial terms. Because there was greater equality of spending in the more marginal seats, those graphs suggest that neither party probably gained a substantial advantage from its fundraising. However, if we focus in more detail on those marginal seats, the validity of that conclusion is called into question; for each of the elections, we look just at the marginal seats where change was most likely – for example, at the 1997 General Election, it was in the seats where Labour lost in 1992 and was expecting to make gains; at the subsequent elections, it was in Labour-held seats where the Conservatives hoped to make gains.

For the 1997 General Election, Figure 2.7[a] looks only at those seats lost by Labour in 1992 by a margin of less than 20 percentage points. Although the range of ratio values was relatively small, in around half of those seats Labour was able to outspend its opponent substantially (that is, the constituencies where the logged ratio was less than 0.0). If greater expenditure (and thus a more intensive local campaign) on average brings greater electoral rewards, especially to a party out of government, therefore, Labour should have been able to benefit from its financial superiority in those seats where it outspent its opponent. Four years later, when the Conservatives expected to make some gains at Labour's expense, the two parties spent approximately the same amount in a large proportion of the seats that Labour won by relatively small margins in 1997 (Figure 2.7[b]), with just a few where Labour's expenditure was very substantially greater than the Conservatives'. For the 2005 General Election, Figure 2.7[c] shows that there was again considerable clustering around the 0.0 logged ratio (that is, each party spent approximately the same). Finally, Figures 2.7[d-e] look at the situation in the comparable Labour-held seats in 2010. In the short campaign – Figure 2.7[e] – the Conservatives outspent Labour in a majority of the marginal constituencies, and the reverse situation occurred in only a few where Labour's 2005 margin of victory exceeded 15 percentage points. The same was largely true with spending on the long campaign (Figure 2.7[d]), with the Conservatives outspending their rival in many more seats than those where Labour had the advantage, so that when long and short campaign spending is combined (Figure 2.7[f]) there were many more where the Conservatives had a substantial advantage overall.

Figure 2.7: The ratio of Conservative-to-Labour spending in the marginal constituencies where those two parties occupied the first two places at the previous election

(a) The 1997 General Election

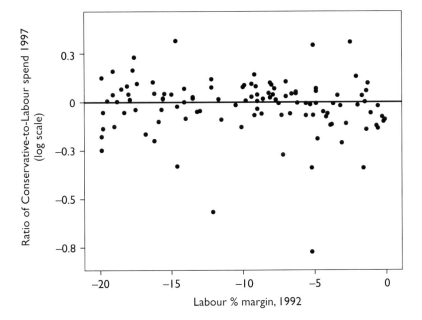

(b) The 2001 General Election

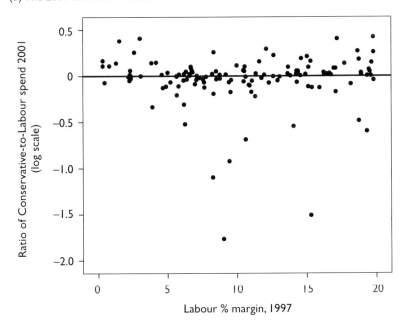

(c) The 2005 General Election

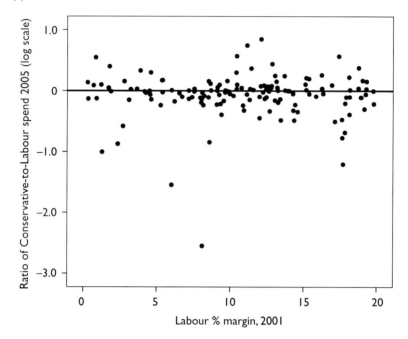

(d) The long campaign before the 2010 General Election

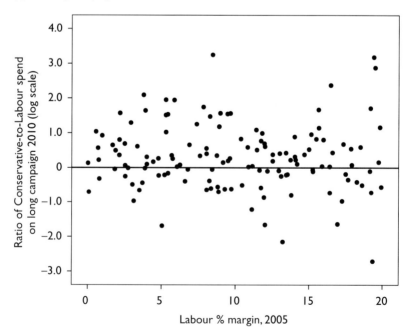

(e) The short campaign before the 2010 General Election

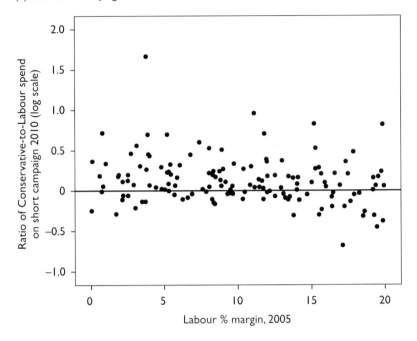

(f) The combined 2010 General Election campaigns

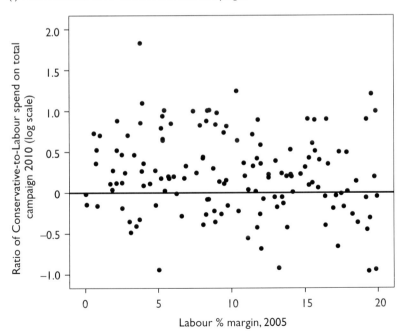

The impact of spending

Parties have varied considerably in how much their candidates spent on their constituency campaigns, even in relatively close contests where the additional effort on a more intensive campaign could well have gained them extra votes and thus increased the probability that they won the seat. But that conclusion depends on the extra effort paying dividends – that the more a party spent on its local campaign, on average, the better its performance there.

Much research in recent decades has indeed shown that this is the case – the more that candidates spent on their local campaign, the better the electoral outcome for them. But how much benefit does such greater effort yield? Tables 2.7-2.8 report the results of analyses that give a general impression of the returns gained from additional spending at each of the four elections, based on statistical analyses.[12] The figures show the average change in the party's performance as a percentage of the votes cast if it spent 25 percentage points more of the maximum allowed in the constituency, with no change in the amounts spent by either of the other two parties. Thus, for example, the first block in Table 2.7 shows that for every additional 25 percentage points of the maximum spent, a Conservative candidate on average gained a further 0.85 per cent share of the votes cast; a 50 percentage point increase thus altered the vote share on average by 1.7 points so that, compared to a Conservative candidate who spent nothing, one who spent the maximum could expect to increase her/his vote share by on average 3.4 percentage points, which in a marginal seat could well be the difference between defeat and victory.

In 1997, both Labour and Liberal Democrat candidates gained substantially in vote shares from greater spending, but the Conservatives, who were in government at the time, substantially less so. For every additional 25 percentage points of the maximum allowed spending, on average a Labour candidate's vote share increased by 2.15 points,

[12] In technical terms they are based on regression analyses in which the dependent variable was the relevant party's share of the votes cast in each constituency at the second election in a pair. The independent variables were its share of the votes at the previous contest there, and the amount spent by each of the three parties. The models are thus estimating the degree of continuity in each party's vote share – whether it polls well in the same places at both elections (and in all cases it does) – and then whether the amount spent on the campaign has a significant (in statistical terms) affect on that outcome. The expectation is that a party's spending will have a positive impact on its voter share – for example, in 1997 it will perform relatively better than it did in 1992 if it spends more there, but less well if its opponents spend more.

Table 2.7: The impact of spending on each party's vote share, by election, if the percentage of the maximum allowed spent by the party increased by 25 percentage points, 1997-2005

	Conservative	Labour	Liberal Democrat
1997			
Conservative spend (%)	0.85	*	*
Labour spend (%)	−0.85	2.15	−1.38
Liberal Democrat spend (%)	*	−1.73	2.35
2001			
Conservative spend (%)	0.33	*	−0.70
Labour spend (%)	−0.55	1.00	−0.45
Liberal Democrat spend (%)	−0.55	−1.23	2.45
2005			
Conservative spend (%)	1.10	−0.90	−1.08
Labour spend (%)	−0.38	*	*
Liberal Democrat spend (%)	−0.45	−0.58	2.95

Note: * an insignificant impact

so that in an average constituency, the difference between a seat where it spent nothing and another where it spent 75 per cent of the total was 6.45 per cent of the votes. For a Liberal Democrat candidate the difference was slightly greater at 7.05 per cent, but for a Conservative it was only 2.56. In addition, the negative figures in the other columns show that the more that the Labour candidate spent, the worse the outcome for each of its opponents: where Labour spent 75 per cent of the maximum, for example, the Conservative vote share was on average 2.55 points lower than in seats where Labour spent nothing, and a similar spending difference generated an average difference of 4.13 points in the Liberal Democrat's performance. The amount that the Liberal Democrat candidates spent also had a negative impact on the Labour performance, but although Conservative spending had a positive impact on the party's own performance it did not also significantly eat into its opponents' vote shares. After 18 years in government, Conservative candidates who ran intensive local campaigns were able to sustain their vote shares slightly but not enough to hold back their opponents' advance where they spent the same amount.

At the 2001 General Election when the expectation was a further clear Labour victory, although all three parties performed better, relative to 1997, the more that their candidates spent on the local

Table 2.8: The impact of spending on each party's vote share, by election, if the percentage of the maximum allowed spent by the party increased by 25 percentage points, 2010 General Election

	Conservative	Labour	Liberal Democrat
Long campaign			
Conservative spend (%)	0.65	−0.75	−0.30
Labour spend (%)	*	1.73	−0.98
Liberal Democrat (%)	−0.53	*	2.75
Short campaign			
Conservative spend (%)	0.83	−2.38	*
Labour spend (%)	*	3.05	−1.03
Liberal Democrat (%)	−0.28	−0.38	2.08
Combined campaigns			
Conservative spend (%)	0.83	−1.65	*
Labour spend (%)	*	2.93	−1.43
Liberal Democrat (%)	−0.58	*	3.33

Note: * an insignificant impact

campaigns, the Liberal Democrats were by far the major beneficiaries of additional spending – on average their vote share was 2.45 percentage points higher where they spent 25 per cent of the allowed maximum compared to those constituencies where they spent nothing. The Conservatives gained relatively little from more intensive campaigns – only 0.33 percentage points in the vote share for an increase in spending of 25 points. With one exception, the more that each party spent the worse the outcome for its opponents, but Labour spending had no significant impact on Conservative vote-winning: again, defenders reaped fewer benefits from their spending.

To a large extent, the analyses of the 2005 General Election repeat the findings for the previous contest: the Liberal Democrat candidates benefited most from their spending, and their Conservative opponents got a greater return than previously. The main difference, in line with earlier findings, was that Labour candidates' spending had no significant impact on their own performance then. At all three of the elections, candidates of the incumbent government got a smaller yield from intensive local campaigns than their opponents, but only in 2005 did the (Labour) incumbents get no benefit at all. They were able to raise less money for that contest than the previous two, and on average it brought them little positive return (although the negative values in the other blocks indicate that greater spending by Labour did reduce the impact of their opponents' campaigns).

For 2010 we have data on both long and short campaign spending, and its impact has been analysed both separately and in combination (see Table 2.8). For long campaign spending, all three parties' candidates got a positive return from their expenditure, Liberal Democrat and Labour candidates substantially more than the Conservatives. On average, of course, the former two parties spent little in most constituencies relative to the Conservatives: in the small number where they did spend a large percentage of the allowed maximum, however, it yielded considerable returns. For short campaign spending, again those two parties gained greater benefits from increased spending than the Conservatives where they were able to raise substantial funding – as with the long campaign, Conservative candidates were the largest spenders both overall and in the marginal constituencies. The Conservative campaigns did substantially cut into Labour's ability to win votes, however: spending 25 per cent of the allowed total brought Labour candidates on average a 3.05 percentage points' increase in their vote share, but if their Conservative rivals matched that spending, the gain was reduced by 2.38 points. Labour had to match Conservative spending to gain a net benefit from the campaign – but, as our previous analyses have shown, this was rarely the case.

Finally, the data on the combined 2010 campaigns at the foot of Table 2.8 replicate the two sets of results for the separate components. The parties that spent less overall gained most from that expenditure where it was made.

What difference does it make?

The results of the analyses just discussed show that, in general, the more that a party's candidates spent on their constituency campaigns, the greater their share of the votes and the smaller their opponents'. But did those changes in vote shares, some of which were quite substantial, have an impact on the most important aspect of the election outcome – the number of seats won by each party? To address that question, the statistical analyses underpinning the data reported in Tables 2.7-2.8 have been used to predict the number of seats that each party would have won with different patterns of spending. Six out of a very large number of possible outcomes have been simulated:

- All three parties spent the amount reported in the official returns (that is, the actual pattern, although not the actual outcome[13]).

---

[13] These differ because the models look at the average impact of a party's campaigning

- All three parties' candidates spent nothing on their constituency campaigns.
- All three parties' candidates spent 50 per cent of the maximum allowed on their constituency campaigns.
- The Conservative candidates spent 75 per cent of the maximum allowed on their constituency campaigns, the Liberal Democrats spent 50 per cent, and:
  - the Labour candidate spent 60 per cent of the maximum allowed;
  - the Labour candidate spent 75 per cent of the maximum allowed; and
  - the Labour candidate spent 90 per cent of the maximum allowed.

These allow an evaluation of the impact of differences in each party's spending, particularly Labour.

In 1997, spending benefited the other two parties more than it did the Conservatives. If all candidates in every constituency spent nothing, then the Conservatives would have won 229 seats, for example, whereas if all spent half of the allowed maximum everywhere, they would have won 14 fewer seats, while Labour would have gained 12 more and the Liberal Democrats 2 (see Table 2.9). Holding the amount of Conservative and Liberal Democrat spending constant across all constituencies (at 75 and 50 per cent respectively), as Labour candidates' spending increased, so did their party's share of the seats: if they spent 60 per cent of the maximum everywhere, the party won 402 seats; if they spent 75 per cent it gained another 11 (413); and with 90 per cent its total increased to 428 – with the number of Conservative MPs declining accordingly. As the average maximum expenditure per constituency at that election was about £8,500, this means that increasing its expenditure per seat from about £5,100 (60 per cent of the maximum) to about £7,650 (90 per cent) – a total of approximately £1.6 million across all constituencies – would have brought Labour an additional 26 seats.

In 2001 and 2005, when the returns to Labour of additional expenditure were on average smaller (as shown in Table 2.7), the difference in the number of seats Labour would have won at different average spending levels was considerably smaller (just 8 and 3 seats respectively at the two elections). But the returns on Liberal Democrat spending at those two contests were quite considerable: the party would have gained 7 extra seats (from a baseline of 30) from spending 50 per cent of the maximum everywhere (when each of its opponents

---

across all seats where it spent a particular amount.

did also) compared to the situation when all spent nothing; in 2005 its gain from such a difference would have been 14 seats. Finally, the last block of Table 2.9 shows the simulated outcomes in 2010 according to expenditure on the short campaign. Labour's financial situation then

Table 2.9: The number of seats that would have been won by each party using the simulations described in the text, 1997-2010

	Seats won by		
	Conservative	Labour	Liberal Democrat
1997			
Actual spend	193	415	33
All spent zero	229	388	24
All spent 50%	215	400	26
Conservative spent 75%, Liberal Democrat spent 50% and			
Labour spent 60%	214	402	25
Labour spent 75%	205	413	23
Labour spent 90%	190	428	23
2001			
Actual spend	176	414	47
All spent zero	200	409	30
All spent 50%	193	409	37
Conservative spent 75%, Liberal Democrat spent 50% and			
Labour spent 60%	195	409	35
Labour spent 75%	189	414	36
Labour spent 90%	186	417	36
2005			
Actual spend	200	366	60
All spent zero	185	404	39
All spent 50%	191	384	53
Conservative spent 75%, Liberal Democrat spent 50% and			
Labour spent 60%	206	377	45
Labour spent 75%	202	379	47
Labour spent 90%	201	380	47
2010 short campaign			
Actual spend	303	262	54
All spent zero	288	296	46
All spent 50%	300	277	53
Conservative spent 75%, Liberal Democrat spent 50% and			
Labour spent 60%	320	258	52
Labour spent 75%	308	276	46
Labour spent 90%	290	299	41

was such that it spent much less overall than at the previous contests (especially 1997), but the estimates show that if it had been able to raise substantial funds, these could have brought it a substantial return; indeed, the last three rows show that, with Conservative and Liberal Democrat spending held constant at 75 and 50 per cent respectively in every constituency, increasing Labour spending from 60 to 90 per cent everywhere would have brought it 41 additional seats, and made it the largest party in the House of Commons (and able to form a viable coalition government with the Liberal Democrats).

These simulations are, of course, artificial in that they take no account of other factors that might influence a party's share of the votes cast (such as whether a seat was being defended by an incumbent MP, which generally brought the party a better return than if it was being contested by a first-time candidate); they also assume that each party's spending is equally efficacious everywhere. The real world is not like that. Nevertheless, by looking at what would happen if one party's spending varied while the others' did not, those simulations give a clear indication of the relative impact of intensive constituency campaigns. Not only is it the case that the more a candidate spends the better the electoral outcome, but also the more that a party's candidates spend, relative to their opponents, the more seats the party can expect to win (Johnston et al, 2013).

Conclusions

In this chapter we have reviewed the role of money in candidates' campaigns at each of the last four general elections in Great Britain. On the assumptions that the amount spent on a candidate's campaign is a good indicator of its overall intensity and that the more spent – and thus the more intensive the campaign – the better the campaign's performance, several hypotheses followed.

The first hypothesis was that spending would be concentrated on those constituencies where the outcome was most in doubt – the marginal seats where a relatively small shift in voter preferences could produce a change in the successful party. The data presented here sustained that argument very clearly: in each of the three parties, candidates in marginal seats spent more than those either defending safe seats or, even more so, those contesting constituencies where their chances of victory were slim. There were significant differences across the four elections, however, particularly for the Labour and Conservative parties. In 1997, when Labour was expecting to unseat the incumbent Conservative government, its candidates spent most in the marginal seats where Labour was defeated in 1992, whereas its opponent's candidates spent most defending those seats. At the subsequent three elections, when Labour was defending parliamentary majorities, its candidates spent most in the marginal constituencies where they won at the previous election – with the Conservatives spending most in those same places. The governing party's candidates spent most defending the marginal seats that they won last time, and the main opposition's candidates spent most seeking victory there.

Although the patterns in the data clearly support that first hypothesis, nevertheless there was variation in the amounts spent. Over the period of the four elections, the amounts spent by Labour candidates in comparable seats declined, suggesting increased problems in raising sufficient money to enable spending at the maximum; in very marginal seats, for example, Labour candidates were spending on average about 90 per cent of the maximum at the first of the four contests, but only around 80 per cent at the last (in 2010). There was no comparable decline in Conservative spending, however, so that in many of the more marginal contests where the election was to be won or lost, whereas in 1997 the two main parties' candidates competed with local campaigns of similar intensity, by 2010 in many places the Conservatives substantially outspent their Labour opponents. For the Liberal Democrats, most of their spending – and, by implication, their intensive local campaigns – were focused on the seats that they won at the previous election as well as the small number where they came a close second and where they sought further victories.

These changes had important consequences regarding the second hypothesis – that the more candidates spent on their campaigns, the better their performance. Again, this argument is clearly sustained by the analyses: the more intensive a candidate's local campaign, the better her/his performance. Thus, the better financed a party's campaigns across the constituencies, the more seats it gained – intensive campaigns won seats. But because Labour candidates in general spent less than their Conservative opponents at the later contests, they were unable to win some seats that more money – and more intensive campaigns – might have yielded. As Labour's financial situation apparently declined, its competitive edge in many of the key marginal constituencies was eroded – which leads into the next chapter and its discussion of the financial health of the local parties from which candidates obtain most of their campaign resources.

THREE

The financial health of local parties: the key to electoral success?

The discussion in the previous chapter has shown that the amount of money spent by each political party's candidates on their local campaigns (mainly on materials advertising themselves and their policies) is a good indicator of the intensity of those campaigns. Further, and importantly, the amount spent is linked to the election outcome – greater spending is associated with better election results, although the extent of this influence varies according to the local context. This does not, of course, imply that money buys elections in Great Britain, but it does show that intensive local campaigning effort – of which money is a crucial component – brings electoral returns.

Given this conclusion, which has been consistently identified over the sequence of elections held since 1950 (Johnston, 1987), one might anticipate that parties would respond by allocating money from their central coffers to the constituencies where they anticipate that the seat might be won or lost. Spending money there could either gain a victory or prevent a defeat, which would affect the overall election outcome – and, for two of the parties at least, influence whether they formed the next government. A rational party would put its money where the votes that matter might be won or lost.

To a very considerable extent this does not happen at British elections. In recent decades, however, although central party organisations, realising the efficacy of well-run local campaigns, have increasingly coordinated them, substantial allocation of central party funds to local parties for their conduct during the year in which an election is held has not been the norm. Other resources have been provided, such as the organisation of constituency visits by leading party members, the secondment of staff to coordinate local campaigns (often for groups of, rather than single, constituencies),[1] polling voters

---

[1] In 2012 the Conservatives announced that they were putting a central party officer to prepare for the 2015 General Election in each of 40 marginal constituencies they needed to win then if they were to obtain an overall majority of seats in the House of Commons, and also in 40 of the most vulnerable of their own seats. In early 2013, Labour announced its 106 target seats.

from national and regional call centres to provide databases that local party organisations can use in mobilising support,[2] cheap printing of standard leaflets, and suggesting which constituencies activists might campaign in – but on few occasions has this involved the transfer of funds from the centre to the constituencies. The years preceding the 2010 General Election saw some change from this situation for two of the parties, however, as detailed below.

Given the general absence of central financial support, constituency parties and their candidates are largely dependent on their own resources and fundraising abilities. Little is known in detail about the sources on which they rely, and whether there are significant inter-constituency differences. Although each candidate's agent is required to make a return of not only expenditure during the campaign period (two periods – the long and short campaigns – from 2010 onwards) but also sources of income, in 2010 the latter returns were aggregated by the Electoral Commission prior to publication, and only the totals received were revealed; the full details remain available for inspection at local returning officers' offices only (and are destroyed one year after the election date). After the 1997 General Election, a research project obtained copies of those returns from the returning officers (covering some 1,524 candidates), but they revealed very little about the sources tapped (Johnston et al, 1999). In just over half of the cases only a single source was named – either the candidate's constituency party or a fighting fund it had established, which together accounted for 83 per cent of all income returned. (Fighting funds were much more common as sources for the Conservative and Liberal Democrat candidates, accounting for 25-30 per cent of all income. For Labour, on average only 1.8 per cent of the income was so designated; the second largest source for its candidates, 8 per cent on average, was one or more trade unions.)

As Rawlings (1988) observed, if money is given for the specific purpose of funding the campaign, it has to be recorded as such and spent accordingly. If it is donated to the party then, until recent legislation (see below), the source remained opaque and the party could use the money as it saw best; the system of transfers from a local party to a candidate's campaign via a fighting fund meant that the latter's income sources need not be revealed, especially if the fighting funds were established separate from the local party's accounts. The Berwickshire, Roxburgh and Selkirk local Conservative party

---

[2] At the 2010 General Election, Labour charged its local parties for access to that database!

reported in 2010, for example, that it operated a separate fighting fund that had an income of £39,840 in that year and spent £49,407. Its own accounts included an income of only £35,086 for 2010 and of similar sums in each of the three previous years. In 2008 it transferred £11,025 to the fighting fund, which at the start of 2010 had reserves of £55,502. In 2009, the Kettering Conservative constituency party reported having a separate fighting fund of £41,436. Not all local parties acted in that way, however: in 2010 the North Warwickshire local Conservative party reported £11,765 income from, rather than to, its fighting fund.

This lacuna in the information base regarding the funding of local campaigns was partly filled after implementation of the PPERA 2000, which for the first time introduced regulation of party finances. For local parties no limits on their financial activities were introduced, but to achieve greater transparency all accounting units (the official term in the legislation) affiliated with a registered party must make an annual return of their audited accounts to the Electoral Commission if their 'gross income or total expenditure in a financial year exceeds £25,000' (Schedule 5, 6[1]). (Such units included both regional and local parties, with some of the latter covering more than one constituency.) Those audited accounts must comply with 'such requirements as to ... [their] form and contents as may be prescribed by regulations made by the Commission' (Clause 42[2]); the Commission requires a standard reporting period (the calendar year) with income and expenditure statements deploying suggested categories (although there is a great deal of variation in the degree to which these are used, despite the publication of a best practice guide), comparable data for the preceding year, a statement of assets held and a review of activities during the reporting year (including a statement of membership, which a considerable number fail to provide).

Although this source contains information on the financial health of local parties that could be linked to data on their candidates' campaign spending (the Commission publishes the returns on its website; they are redacted only to remove information that would divulge the addresses of those making the returns), it was clear that the limit of £25,000 below which returns were not required meant that the coverage would be far from complete. When implementation of the requirements began in 2003, Pinto-Duschinsky (2008) obtained the published accounts not only for all those local parties that had a gross income or expenditure exceeding £25,000, but in addition the results of a survey conducted by the Commission in that year of all accounting units that fell below the threshold. Table 3.1 shows the results, in which

Table 3.1: The financial situation of local party accounting units in 2003: results of an Electoral Commission survey

	Conservative	Labour	Liberal Democrat
Number of parties	492	547	74
Expenditure (£)			
Minimum	121	6	35
Lower quartile	8,459	3,059	1,770
Median	27,934	6,112	7,990
Upper quartile	52,398	11,274	31,437
Maximum	343,059	165,235	63,695

returns were obtained from many more Labour and Conservative local parties than Liberal Democrats. (In London, for example, most of the Liberal Democrat accounting units relate to the separate boroughs rather than individual constituencies.) For both Labour and Liberal Democrats the amounts spent by the great majority of their local parties in 2003 (a non-general election year) were relatively small and well below the £25,000 threshold for annual reporting to the Electoral Commission; over half of the Conservative local parties from which data were obtained spent more than £25,000 during the year, however. The stark differences are emphasised in Figure 3.1, which shows the distributions of gross expenditure for each of the three parties. The £25,000 threshold is incorporated in these histograms to illustrate those differences: whereas over half of the local Conservative parties for which data were available had expenditure of over £25,000 (259 of 492), that was the case for only 24 of the 547 local Labour parties. For the Liberal Democrats only 74 returns were obtained, of which just over one-third had above-threshold expenditures, and it can reasonably be inferred that, as with Labour for which many more returns were obtained, the great majority of local Liberal Democrat parties had a very small turnover.

The clear implication to be drawn from this 2003 snapshot of local party finances is that in general the Conservatives were much healthier financially at the local level than either of their opponents. This was confirmed in a study using the returns for the two years 2004-05, which included the 2005 General Election (Johnston and Pattie, 2008b). Whereas 248 and 252 returns were made by Conservative parties for 2004 and 2005 respectively, the comparable figures for Labour were 22 and 42, and for the Liberal Democrats 61 and 63. (The number of local Labour parties crossing the threshold virtually doubled in the election year, but still covered only 6 per cent of all constituencies.)

Figure 3.1: Histograms showing the annual expenditure of local accounting units in 2003 according to the Electoral Commission survey then

(a) Conservatives

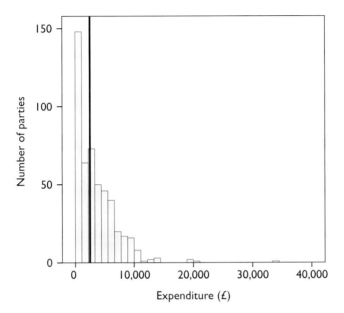

(b) Labour

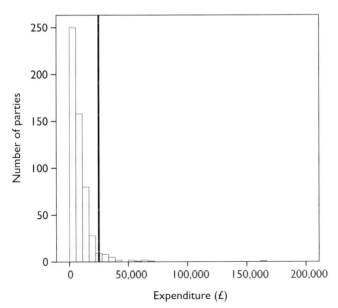

(c) Liberal Democrats

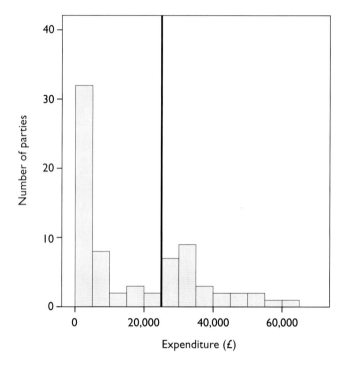

Party finances, 2007-10

In the remainder of this chapter we focus on the financial situation in local parties from 2007 on; the new constituencies to be deployed for the next general election were approved then and any necessary local restructuring of party organisations had been undertaken so that the constituency parties served the new territorial structure. The four years 2007-10 for which data are analysed here thus represent the period during which local parties prepared for and fought the 2010 General Election.

The number of such separate local parties – excluding those operating at a regional level – with either an annual income or expenditure exceeding £25,000 in each year is shown in Table 3.2 (in a few cases returns were made by parties which fell below the threshold). Three general features stand out. The first, and by far the clearest, is that many more local Conservative parties made returns in each year than either Labour or the Liberal Democrats. Second, the number of local parties returning their accounts increased over the four years, in part probably reflecting inflation (which was not taken into account in any uprating of the reporting threshold) but more so the preparations for the 2010

Table 3.2: The number of local party accounting units which made returns of their accounts to the Electoral Commission, 2007-10

	Conservative	Labour	Liberal Democrat
2007			
Single-constituency	328	43	54
Multi-constituency	25	5	31
2008			
Single-constituency	321	43	67
Multi-constituency	25	10	34
2009			
Single-constituency	365	68	87
Multi-constituency	32	11	34
2010			
Single-constituency	359	80	80
Multi-constituency	23	12	36

General Election. This increase was largest for Labour – which made the fewest returns overall – and smallest (certainly in relative terms) for the Conservatives. Finally, the Liberal Democrats were much more likely to have multi- than single-constituency branches; in many areas they were organised at a larger local scale than the Conservatives.

The straightforward implication to be drawn from those initial figures is that local Conservative parties were much healthier than their counterparts in the other two parties. This conclusion is sustained by the summary statistics in Tables 3.3–3.5, for which, because of the incompleteness of many of the returns (especially but not only with regard to membership numbers), it was not possible to draw up data that are fully comparable; as the goal is to provide a general picture of patterns and differences, this has had to be accepted, and while the exact numbers (for example, the means) would undoubtedly differ if such an ideal data set could be collated, it is very unlikely that the overall patterns would differ significantly from those presented here. The summary figures presented include five to show the range of values – minimum, lower quartile, median, upper quartile and maximum – as well as the mean; comparison of the latter with the median indicates whether the distribution of values is skewed. (If the mean is much larger than the median, this indicates that there is a small number of very large values; this turns out to be the case with virtually all of the distributions portrayed.) Five indicators of overall health are given – the number of members, annual income, expenditure, reserves and fixed assets.

The data for Conservative single-constituency branches (Table 3.3) indicate that around half of all constituencies had a local party that made a separate return (there were 650 in the UK during those four years but only 631, that is, excluding the Northern Ireland constituencies as well as Buckingham, being defended by the Speaker

Table 3.3: The financial situation of Conservative single-constituency local party accounting units 2007-10: summary statistics

	Members	Income	Expenditure	Reserves	Fixed assets
2007					
Minimum	35	9,837	5,282	−29,558	0
Lower quartile	326	38,234	32,419	20,578	0
Median	490	53,961	52,880	50,265	2,759
Upper quartile	769	81,772	78,528	118,307	51,011
Maximum	2,255	330,400	314,991	1,520,660	1,400,709
Mean	584	65,080	62,680	87,394	45,384
Number	306	328	327	307	313
2008					
Minimum	65	11,240	8,529	−21,925	0
Lower quartile	318	35,548	34,269	17,034	0
Median	453	52,450	51,208	53,978	3,028
Upper quartile	722	77,842	76,826	128,256	56,692
Maximum	211,341	615,910	371,097	1,540,575	1,400,571
Mean	1,299	65,005	60,953	96,252	47,911
Number	286	321	321	316	304
2009					
Minimum	33	265	1,497	−29,767	0
Lower quartile	259	32,468	33,241	20,887	0
Median	399	50,567	50,727	45,182	2,469
Upper quartile	643	75,907	76,923	112,897	50,027
Maximum	2,076	289,965	301,488	1,514,551	1,401,633
Mean	483	60,908	61,724	86,540	45,618
Number	325	362	365	357	350
2010					
Minimum	41	1,253	19,055	−23,724	0
Lower quartile	247	36,320	40,727	16,980	0
Median	391	50,906	55,561	45,398	1,654
Upper quartile	607	77,795	78,282	109,679	48,278
Maximum	37,363	240,655	243,898	1,502,361	1,400,185
Mean	578	61,808	64,610	83,818	46,111
Number	302	358	359	352	346

who, by tradition, was not challenged by the major parties, where Conservative candidates contested the 2010 General Election). The median income varied little over the four-year period – indeed it was smaller in 2009 and 2010 than in the previous two years. In part this may reflect that the local parties which crossed the threshold during the period (30 more made returns in 2010 than 2007) reduced that average somewhat, but the mean also declined, suggesting that, although it was much larger than the median in each year, indicating a small number of parties with very much larger incomes than normal, overall local parties found it relatively hard to increase their income substantially, even during the run-up to a crucial general election which the Conservatives expected to win, although they were uncertain about the size of their victory. Indeed, if we just look at the data for the 287 single-constituency parties that made returns in each of the four years, the mean income increased only slightly over the period – from £64,939 in 2007 through £62,890 and £65,093 in 2008 and 2009 respectively, to £67,802 in 2010. (Given the rate of inflation over those years, this means that in real terms incomes were at best stable.)

There was very little difference between the level of income and expenditure at any point on the distribution – at either the median, for example, or the lower quartile. Most local Conservative parties spent virtually all of their income each year; indeed, the median annual excess of income over expenditure was only £941 in 2007 and £1,169 in 2008 – and in 2009 and 2010 the median party made a loss of £144 and £2,745 respectively. Few local parties were apparently able to build up substantial reserves to spend in an election year, therefore (apart from those which transferred money into fighting funds), and perhaps as a consequence, most had an excess of expenditure over income in 2010, presumably reflecting greater expenditure than usual because it was a general election year (the local parties are also involved in local government elections as well as elections to the devolved bodies in Scotland and Wales). This situation is also illustrated by the data on reserves: some local parties had substantial reserves (one in excess of £1.5 million), but the median figures show that the average party had no more than £50,000, less than the average annual level of expenditure. A considerable number had much less in reserve, with a few in debt. Fixed assets were even more unevenly distributed. Many had small sums – usually representing the value of computer and other equipment plus furniture – and at least a quarter had none. Around a quarter had fixed assets valued at more than £50,000, with a small number having much more extensive financial foundations. In almost all cases, those extensive holdings involved buildings owned by the local party, which in most cases they occupied and which also, for some, provided substantial income streams from their tenants – which in some cases included local MPs and MEPs. Those with the largest fixed assets tended to have the largest reserves, and in turn those with the largest reserves tended to have the largest annual incomes. Similarly, as Figure 3.2 shows for 2010, in all three cases those local parties with most members on average also had the largest incomes.

Turning to the small number of single-constituency local Labour parties filing a report, Table 3.4 paints a very different picture from that for their Conservative opponents. Not only did few Labour parties cross the income/expenditure threshold, but those that did were on average in a much weaker situation than their Conservative counterparts. The median income for a reporting Labour constituency in 2007 was £35,755, for example, compared to £53,961 for the Conservatives; the gap closed slightly over the four years, but even so the median Labour constituency party returning a report raised only £36,601 compared to the Conservative median of £50,906 in

Figure 3.2: The relationship for each party between local accounting unit income in 2010 and the number of registered members then

(a) Conservatives

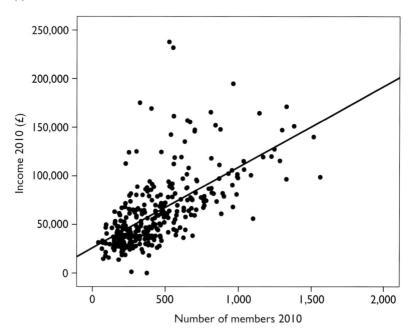

(b) Labour

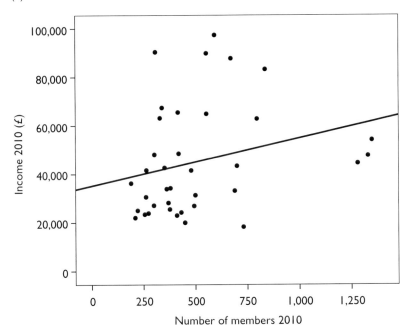

(c) Liberal Democrats

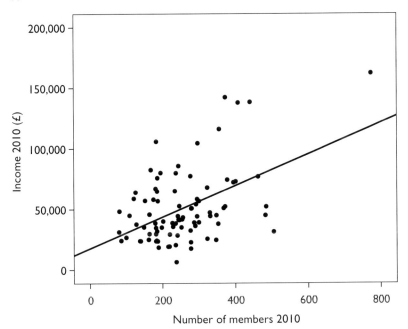

each year. The difference was even greater at the upper ends of the distribution: the maximum Labour income in any year was at best only half of that for a local Conservative party. Expenditure in many cases equalled if not exceeded income – the median Labour constituency party returned a deficit of almost £4,500 in 2010 (election year), and

Table 3.4: The financial situation of Labour single-constituency local party accounting units 2007-10: summary statistics

	Members	Income	Expenditure	Reserves	Fixed assets
2007					
Minimum	229	10,468	9,795	−17,833	0
Lower quartile	230	27,605	23,345	3,019	0
Median	300	35,755	30,943	50,063	506
Upper quartile	565	57,342	46,874	258,282	208,268
Maximum	931	103,216	93,240	954,460	1,053,758
Mean	405	43,181	38,312	169,388	130,505
Number	6	24	24	24	24
2008					
Minimum	211	7,412	5,815	−9,720	0
Lower quartile	285	25,697	23,420	11,433	0
Median	392	34,544	32,594	45,407	0
Upper quartile	396	46,680	51,109	144,943	53,259
Maximum	1,986	99,553	189,981	759,149	750,000
Mean	233	39,034	40,060	115,111	65,426
Number	21	43	43	43	43
2009					
Minimum	132	2,936	4,034	0	0
Lower quartile	218	15,407	16,831	12,355	0
Median	294	30,132	26,333	29,910	0
Upper quartile	401	42,800	44,606	163,085	130,314
Maximum	900	114,597	99,422	749,890	755,813
Mean	344	32,914	31,953	106,420	64,553
Number	24	68	67	61	50
2010					
Minimum	190	13,423	4,886	−18,506	0
Lower quartile	303	25,630	32,638	7,244	0
Median	411	36,601	38,513	22,017	0
Upper quartile	672	53,874	54,562	107,431	33,064
Maximum	1,348	123,836	128,909	776,144	821,139
Mean	507	42,104	46,584	88,576	60,748
Number	35	80	80	72	72

few had substantial reserves on which to call (the difference between the median and the mean indicates a very skewed distribution); over half reported no fixed assets and almost all of the few that were well-endowed owned property. In 2010, for example, 34 local Labour parties reported receiving rental income, totalling £510,409; 81 Conservative local parties declared a total of £1,245,849 in rental income; and 22 local Liberal Democrat parties together received a much lower total of only £169,178. Aylesbury Conservative party alone received rental income of £237,653 in 2008, from a building that has made it one of the most prosperous local parties for several decades; until the late 1990s local Conservative parties were largely independent of the national body, but were invited to make contributions to the national party against a quota determined by each local party's size (number of members), wealth and electoral strength. Not all made contributions and others did not meet their quota, despite the amounts remitted being reported in the party's annual *Conference handbook* and various levels of awards recognising the volume of those contributions being made at the annual conference immediately prior to the leaders' speech (see Pattie and Johnston, 1996). A few gave more than requested, and Aylesbury local party was almost invariably in that group: in 1993-94, for example, it remitted £61,672, which was 663 per cent of its quota.

Most local parties earned much less than the Aylesbury Conservatives from rents, however: Cheadle Liberal Democrats received £11,922 and £10,733 in 2007 and 2008 respectively from leasing out office space. Others obtained one-off income from their properties: Orpington Liberal Democrats, for example, received £90,000 from Tesco as compensation for allowing access to a car park.[3] But properties generate expenditure as well as income: in 2010, for example, the Bath and Battersea Labour parties reported spending £41,309 and £29,797 respectively on their buildings, from which they received rents of £64,664 and £33,463; the Braintree Labour party received rents of £99,893 but spent £78,230 on the building, and the comparable figures for the Brentwood and Isleworth party were £34,388 and £40,729. (Both had similar levels of income and expenditure in 2009, when the Braintree party also reported receiving £66,000 for car parking.) Bath Labour party also had a substantial property portfolio: it owned flats valued at £558,679 in 2009, when it reported that most of its income (£67,003) and expenditure (£45,916) that year related to its property.

---

[3] There were other windfalls: Hastings and Rye Labour party received a legacy of £45,000 in 2008.

As with the other parties, there was a substantial increase in the number of single-constituency Liberal Democrat branches that made financial returns between 2007 and 2010. Those local parties on average had less income than their Conservative contemporaries, but slightly more than Labour (see Table 3.5). Over the four years

Table 3.5:The financial situation of Liberal Democrat single-constituency local party accounting units 2007-10: summary statistics

	Members	Income	Expenditure	Reserves	Fixed assets
2007					
Minimum	110	17,762	14,599	−6,776	0
Lower quartile	193	30,878	33,316	4,035	0
Median	270	47,944	48,079	8,458	713
Upper quartile	357	53,717	55,931	25,327	6,249
Maximum	478	198,135	158,596	496,330	484,000
Mean	279	47,944	48,079	31,285	28,939
Number	37	54	54	54	52
2008					
Minimum	101	9,824	5,521	−1,851	0
Lower quartile	194	27,457	25,079	5,948	0
Median	256	39,556	37,702	12,095	333
Upper quartile	335	49,826	49,431	34,786	4,714
Maximum	477	124,920	111,377	486,073	470,900
Mean	269	42,907	39,697	35,930	23,792
Number	49	67	67	67	67
2009					
Minimum	77	5,619	7,978	−4,058	0
Lower quartile	183	25,255	25,748	6,784	0
Median	235	40,175	38,443	15,428	0
Upper quartile	305	55,390	51,099	28,355	2,923
Maximum	480	141,022	136,516	471,749	200,000
Mean	247	43,902	43,961	33,109	14,199
Number	71	87	87	84	83
2010					
Minimum	80	6,461	14,656	−28,061	0
Lower quartile	182	26,628	32,284	3,925	0
Median	241	40,740	41,346	10,893	0
Upper quartile	295	53,743	55,307	28,647	2,085
Maximum	485	116,036	119,292	586,828	200,000
Mean	245	44,238	47,268	782,915	16,328
Number	67	80	80	78	76

there was relatively little change in several of the key indicators – the median, upper quartile and mean – and apart from the small number with incomes above the upper quartile, in general expenditure exceeded income. Reserves were not built up over the period in most constituencies, therefore; furthermore, by 2010 less than half of the 76 units had any fixed assets, and in most cases these were of low value only. Additionally, like the Conservatives, local Liberal Democrat parties were only able to raise a small amount of extra income in election year relative to the previous three; for the 50 single-constituency units that made returns in all four years, the mean income was £46,179 in 2007, £46,110 in 2008, £53,242 in 2009 and then £52,675 in 2010.

The geography of party strength

The analyses reported in the previous chapter showed that money matters in British general election campaigns – the more money spent by a party/candidate in a constituency, the better the performance there. But although the expenditure of additional money may be related to how well a candidate performs, it may have no impact on the number of seats each party wins. If, for example, it is spent either in seats that the candidates are going to lose or in those that they are going to win, then changing their vote share somewhat may have no substantial impact on whether the seat is more winnable. Money matters most in those constituencies where the situation is marginal, and a candidate who wins a few hundred extra votes may be able to turn what would otherwise be a small defeat into a marginal victory. Thus the geography of money – of where a party can raise income – matters; the parties need their financially healthy local accounting units to be in constituencies where intensive campaigns matter most.

Where are the financially healthy local parties? Table 3.6 looks at their regional distribution, using the nine standard regions of England as well as Scotland and Wales; the number of parties in each region who returned their accounts in each year is shown, alongside the number who made such a return in all of the four years under consideration. For the Conservatives, there is a very clear geography: it had a 'healthy' local party in most of the constituencies in the East of England, the South East and the South West as well as a substantial minority (more than one-third but less than one-half) in London and the two Midlands regions, but in very few of the seats in England's three northern regions, as well as Scotland and Wales. As might be expected, these local strengths were concentrated in their electoral heartlands so that most of the Conservatives' multi-constituency local parties

Table 3.6: The regional distribution of local party accounting units which made returns of their accounts to the Electoral Commission, 2007-10

Region	NC	2007	2008	2009	2010	AF
Conservative						
East of England	46	46	45	50	49	40
East Midlands	58	25	24	27	27	21
Greater London	73	33	33	36	34	24
North East	29	3	2	4	3	2
North West	75	21	23	23	27	13
South East	84	71	68	66	73	60
South West	55	44	45	47	48	42
West Midlands	59	25	24	23	30	20
Yorkshire and the Humber	54	16	18	19	20	12
Scotland	59	18	14	16	16	13
Wales	40	8	8	10	12	7
Labour						
East of England	58	2	3	3	6	2
East Midlands	46	1	1	1	1	0
Greater London	73	12	19	18	24	9
North East	29	0	0	0	1	0
North West	75	0	1	0	8	0
South East	84	3	5	5	8	3
South West	55	2	3	4	6	1
West Midlands	59	0	0	0	1	0
Yorkshire and the Humber	54	0	1	3	5	0
Scotland	59	0	0	0	2	0
Wales	40	1	2	4	3	1
Liberal Democrat						
East of England	58	5	6	7	5	4
East Midlands	46	1	1	1	1	1
Greater London	73	2	2	4	3	2
North East	29	0	1	0	2	0
North West	75	6	6	7	6	5
South East	84	9	11	12	13	9
South West	55	12	12	17	17	10
West Midlands	59	3	2	3	3	2
Yorkshire and the Humber.	54	5	6	6	6	5
Scotland	59	5	6	7	8	3
Wales	40	2	2	2	1	9

NC – number of constituencies; AF – made returns in all four years.

were in those regions where the party was relatively weak, not only at recent parliamentary elections but also in the local governments there – there were combined accounting units for the cities of Bradford, Bury, Doncaster, Liverpool, Nottingham, Sunderland and Sheffield, for example. Over the four years, as the next general election approached, coverage increased slightly in some of those regions, but overall there was little change to that geography.

Turning to Labour, by far the dominant feature in the table is the concentration of its small number of local parties who met the £25,000 threshold each year in Greater London – fully 12 of the 21 in 2007. As the 2010 General Election approached, the number in other regions increased somewhat, but that in London doubled, and by election year it was still the case that 24 of the 65 local parties for which we have returns were in the capital. Several of its multi-constituency units were in the same northern areas as the Conservatives (Liverpool, Sheffield and York, for example, as well as Manchester); there were comparable units in some southern cities (Milton Keynes, Norwich, Portsmouth and Southampton) as well as four in London boroughs (Croydon, Lambeth, Newham and Tower Hamlets).

The regional distribution of Liberal Democrat single-constituency local parties with incomes exceeding £25,000 also shows strong geographical concentration – in the South East and South West of England (the latter having been the party's main heartland for much of the preceding decades). Like the Conservatives, the Liberal Democrats were, on this measure, particularly weak in terms of local organisational structure in the North East of England, and many of their multi-constituency units were also in their southern heartlands (especially the London boroughs of Brent, Camden, Haringey, Islington, Kingston, Lewisham, Sutton, Twickenham and Richmond, and Tower Hamlets, for example).

Table 3.6 portrays a clear geography to each party's local organisational strength, therefore, with the main concentrations for the Conservatives and the Liberal Democrats being in the southern regions; Labour is a partial exception to this because although it has traditional areas of electoral strength in London that are expressed in these data, unlike the other two parties it was apparently weak on this particular index in its main electoral heartlands of northern England, Scotland and Wales. But where each party was strong within those regions, was that strength in its relatively safe seats?

Table 3.7 addresses this question for each of the parties, with constituencies classed into whether they were won or lost at the 2005 General Election and by what margin (with the latter expressed in six categories, from the very safe/hopeless – margins of 20 percentage points or more – to the marginal – margins of less than 10 points).[4] The Conservatives had a 'financially healthy' local organisation throughout the period in most of the constituencies that they won in 2005, and by 2010 had such a situation in virtually all of them. They also had a

Table 3.7: The electoral situation in constituencies where local party accounting units made returns of their accounts to the Electoral Commission, 2007-10

Margin	NC	2007	2008	2009	2010	AF
Conservative						
Seats won						
20%<	10	10	10	10	9	9
10-20%	115	106	101	101	106	92
0-10%	86	76	73	72	75	65
Seats lost						
0-10%	160	91	96	105	112	71
10-20%	158	25	22	29	33	15
20%<	103	3	2	4	4	2
Labour						
Seats won						
20%<	172	2	5	7	13	1
10-20%	91	5	10	12	20	4
0-10%	87	8	11	12	18	6
Seats lost						
0-10%	45	3	5	3	8	2
10-20%	63	1	1	2	2	1
20%<	281	2	3	2	2	2
Liberal Democrat						
Seats won						
20%<	10	3	5	3	5	1
10-20%	24	16	16	16	16	13
0-10%	28	15	15	18	18	14
Seats lost						
0-10%	31	10	10	16	16	8
10-20%	81	4	7	9	8	4
20%<	457	2	2	4	2	1

NC – number of constituencies; AF – made returns in all four years.

[4] Recall (as discussed in the previous chapter) that the 2005 'election results' used are calculations based on the best expectations of the outcome then if the election had been fought in the new constituencies introduced in 2007 for the 2010 contest.

similar organisational strength in a substantial minority of the seats that they lost in 2005 by less than 10 percentage points; many of them they would have anticipated winning in 2010 given the shift in national preferences towards the party (and in some cases these will be the successor organisations in seats that they last won in 1992). Labour, on the other hand, was organisationally weak whatever the local electoral situation – even in those where they won by a substantial margin in 2005.

The Liberal Democrats were estimated to have won 62 seats if the 2005 General Election had been held in the new constituencies introduced in 2007, and by 2010 they had a local organisation turning over £25,000 or more in a majority of them (39; a number of the seats that they won in 2005 were included in the multi-constituency units). Unlike the Conservatives, however, they had very few, long-running, similarly strong local organisations in those seats that they lost in 2005 by small majorities and which they would have targeted in 2010, although the number of such organisations did increase over the four-year period.

Income sources and expenditure streams

What sources of income did the local units rely on, and how did they spend their money? Creating comparable data sets – within each party let alone across all three – is not straightforward, in part because of the varying formats in which the annual returns are made (disregarding the Commission's 'best practice' suggestions) and also because of variations in local situations; in 2007, for example, the Conservative MP for Bosworth contributed £23,375 in 'overhead costs' and quite a few MPs rented space for their constituency offices from the local party (in 2008, for example, the Liberal Democrat MP for Dunfermline and West Fife, along with an MEP, paid £21,750). In addition, the parties vary in the degree to which they raise income through subscriptions. For example, 302 Conservative units – some of which indicated that £25 was the minimum expected from a local member – reported both their number of members and the subscription income raised in 2010. The latter totalled £3,916,704 (20 per cent of their total income) and averaged £22.40 per member; by contrast, of the 35 Labour units for which we have comparable data, subscription income totalled £100,603 (6 per cent of the total income) and averaged just £5.66 per member. For the Liberal Democrats, many local units gave membership totals but no subscription income; of the 33 that gave both, the total subscription income of £53,693 was 3.5 per cent of total income and averaged £6.55 per member. Some units in all three parties also obtained substantial income from local (often ward) branches, which in some cases may have included subscription income, and the Conservatives raised considerable amounts in some constituencies from subscriptions to separate clubs: Basingstoke's 'Portcullis Club' provided £13,747 in 2007, for example. Others reported income from 'patrons' (£18,259 in 2010 in the Berwick-on-Tweed constituency, for example); the Oxford West and Abingdon party reported an income of £10,544 from its patrons in 2010, but also noted that this involved an expenditure (presumably on dinners and other such events) of £6,422; and in 2008 the Witney constituency reported an income of £30,400 from its 'Principal Patrons'.[5] Brentwood and Ongar's Conservatives Portcullis Club raised £10,500 from a dinner with David Cameron in the same year that it received £5,622 from its Patrons Club.

Income

Given these difficulties, Table 3.8 reports income totals for each year under a small number of main headings only, which are sufficient to identify general patterns. There were very substantial inter-party differences in their reliance on donations, although in all three the relative importance of this source increased over the four-year period leading to the 2010 General Election. For the Liberal Democrats, donations comprised over 45 per cent of their income in each year, and over half in 2010, whereas for the Conservatives the percentage in the early years was only 10, increasing to 16 by 2010. Labour fell between the two, getting about one-fifth of its income from donations in 2007-08 and over two-fifths in 2010. A further major difference across the three parties is in the relative as well as absolute amounts they could raise through appeals and contributions to fighting funds; in 2010, the Conservatives raised almost as much through appeals as through donations (a more than six-fold increase over the 2007 total, indicating their ability to attract funds as an election approached), but the other two parties raised only small amounts via this route.

Whereas donations and appeals involve the parties asking for money (although some donations may be unsolicited), the other main source

---

[5] A report in the *Daily Mirror* (20 December 2007) about the Principal Patrons Club in David Cameron's Witney constituency said that its members paid 'up to £200 to have lunch or dinner in the Commons'; a party spokesperson responded that members paid an annual subscription of £480, which was below the £1,000 limit for reporting donations.

Table 3.8: The main sources of income (in £) for local party accounting units, 2007-10

	2007	2008	2009	2010
Conservative				
Donations	2,285,316	2,087,658	2,914,478	3,736,991
Appeals	536,522	633,503	1,191,727	3,493,634
Fundraising	6,001,999	5,126,288	5,688,069	3,910,975
Central grants	597,233	677,086	974,464	164,421
TOTAL INCOME	23,043,572	22,506,386	23,633,587	23,539,677
Labour				
Donations	232,546	400,643	786,916	1,719,349
Appeals	11,811	26	8,858	71,729
Fundraising	155,391	248,458	377,649	449,950
Central grants	1,176	19,679	13,020	20,339
TOTAL INCOME	1,207,208	2,013,448	2,727,108	4,035,344
Liberal Democrat				
Donations	1,733,842	1,905,432	2,460,874	2,696,757
Appeals	22,289	36,097	59,815	113,369
Fundraising	440,184	540,607	650,257	521,954
Central grants	407,958	656,384	833,901	635,333
TOTAL INCOME	3,578,051	4,241,643	5,421,661	5,282,639

reflecting their own efforts is through fundraising activities, which take a variety of forms (annual dinners and other events, regular lotteries, and so on). Here again, the Conservatives were able to raise much more than their opponents, throughout the electoral cycle (with a lower total for 2010 than the other three years, suggesting that they were building funds up for the election; not all of the income was a net gain, however, as many of those events had considerable costs – reporting whether the income was gross or net was not clear in some cases, however, and the presentation here assumes it was gross[6]). Their income from fundraising events comprised 17 per cent of the total in 2010 and 24 per cent in the previous year; Labour raised only 11 per cent by that route in 2010 and the Liberal Democrats 10 per cent.[7]

[6] In 2010, for example, of those Conservative units that reported fundraising income, the total received was £3,791,027, whereas the reported cost of fundraising events in the expenditure columns was £1,519,294 – a 150 per cent return on the investment.

[7] In a 2006 survey of local parties, Unlock Democracy (Graham, 2006) reported that whereas local Labour parties on average held two to three social and fundraising events per annum, this contrasted with an average of 12 by the Conservatives in the seats that they held and at least four in all other constituencies. (The average Liberal Democrat local party also held on average four such events annually.)

Central grants to local parties

One final difference across the three parties is in the amounts of money received from the national party organisation – registered in Table 3.8 as 'central grants'. In 2007, the Conservative party initiated a target seat campaign directed and partly funded by Lord Ashcroft, a Deputy Chair and former Treasurer. He had pioneered such activities at the 2005 General Election, making grants to local parties who presented him with business cases showing how investment in their campaigning activities could help the party to win marginal seats. Between 2001 and 2005 his company Bearwood Services Limited made 120 separate donations to 68 different constituency parties, totalling £828,798, more than twice the amount given by the next largest donor, the Midlands Industrial Council (38 donations, totalling £367,690 to 30 separate constituencies), which was following a similar strategy. These donations enabled the local parties to spend more on the 2005 short campaign than might otherwise have been the case, and they benefited accordingly, with several of the targeted seats yielding Conservative victories (Johnston and Pattie, 2007).

For the 2010 General Election, Lord Ashcroft's strategy was extended and integrated within the central party organisation – part of the target seats programme that he established and oversaw involved extensive telephone polling and leafleting from party headquarters; another part, as in 2005, involved making grants to local parties in target constituencies (almost all of them marginal seats). Not all parties received grants, however, only those that submitted convincing business plans, and these covered six-month periods. If polling suggested that further investment was not needed because the seat looked to be either increasingly 'safe' or 'hopeless' for the Conservatives, then it did not qualify for further grants (Johnston and Pattie, 2010; Cutts et al, 2012). As Table 3.8 shows, for single-constituency units alone these grants totalled around £600,000 in both 2007 and 2008 and almost £1 million in 2009; as the programme was intended to lay the foundations for the final months of campaigning in 2010, there were few grants then, and local parties were left to their own fundraising efforts to cover the costs of the long and short campaigns – for which in most seats the legislation allowed a total expenditure of some £40,000.

More detail on these grants is given in Table 3.9; this is not necessarily a complete list, since no details have been published about the strategy by either Lord Ashcroft or the party, so the table only reports on grants that are separately identified in the local accounting units' annual financial returns.[8] Some may have been made to smaller local parties (that is, with a turnover of less than £25,000) and are therefore omitted from the table, as might others that were reported elsewhere in the accounts and not separately identified in the supporting annual report. (Interestingly, virtually none of the annual reports made any reference to receipt of these grants, although they were separately identified in the income statement.) Almost all of the grants were made to single-constituency accounting units; most were for less than £10,000, but there was considerable variation around the mean and median values. Most grants were made in 2009, when nearly £1 million was reported as being received. Few were allocated in 2010, and these were in general much smaller than those in previous years. The intention of the target seats programme was clear, therefore: to fund the mobilisation of support well before the 'official' campaigns of 2010. The money was to be spent when it was received, not retained to be spent on the 'long' and 'short' campaigns that followed. The programme was a foundation to later spending on those campaigns, which had to be funded by the local parties and the candidates themselves.

Table 3.9: Grants allocated by the Conservative central party organisation to local accounting units, 2007-10: summary statistics

	2007	2008	2009	2010
Single-constituency units				
Number of grants	56	67	94	28
Minimum grant (£)	1,629	1,346	489	483
Median grant (£)	8,262	8,587	9,641	3,809
Maximum grant (£)	37,277	42,497	31,326	18,176
Mean grant (£)	10,665	9,968	10,203	5,571
Standard deviation (£)	8,614	7,241	6,734	4,571
TOTAL (£)	597,233	667,834	959,114	155,988
Multiple-constituency units				
Number of grants	0	1	2	1
Minimum grant (£)	–	–	5,400	–
Median grant (£)	–	9,252	7,675	8,433
Maximum grant (£)	–	–	9,950	–
Mean grant (£)	–	–	7,675	–
Standard deviation (£)	–	–	–	–
TOTAL (£)	–	9,252	15,350	8,433

---

[8] Some grants went indirectly to the constituency units; in 2009 the Halesowen and Rowley Regis constituency party reported that its target seat grant came through the West Midlands regional accounting unit.

That this strategy was carefully targeted on places where pre-2010 campaigning could enhance the party's prospects for the general election is shown by the geography of grants made (see Table 3.10). Very few, in any of the four years, went to local parties in ultra-safe seats where the Conservatives lost by more than 20 percentage points in 2005, and similarly there was only a very small number to local parties where they won by a similar margin then. The focus was on the marginal seats – won by less than 10 percentage points at the previous contest – especially those where the Conservatives lost and victory was necessary if they were to form the next government. In the first years of the programme, several grants were made to local parties in seats that the Conservatives won marginally in 2005 (several of them where the incumbent was not planning to stand again), to protect their hold on the seat, but as the general election approached and a Conservative victory seemed more likely, the grants to such local parties became smaller in value, and there were only three in 2010, when the focus was very much on the seats the party needed to win. There is clear evidence that the canvassing undertaken using those grants received in 2007-09 improved the Conservatives' electoral performance at the general election; Cutts et al (2012) have shown that the party was far more likely to win in a Labour-held constituency if its local party received grants in both 2007 and 2008.

Liberal Democrat headquarters made grants to local party units, as did the Association of Liberal Democrat Councillors; the latter were for local election campaigning, but as the two types of campaign are substantially integrated by most local parties, data on them have been combined here. The amounts allocated were smaller than the Conservatives', but comprised over 10 per cent of the local parties' total income in each year. Given the relative importance of multi-constituency local accounting units in the party's organisation, not

Table 3.10: The number and total value of grants from the Conservative central party organisation to single-constituency local accounting units, 2007-10, by constituency marginality

	2007		2008		2009		2010	
	N	£	N	£	N	£	N	£
Ultra-safe lost	0	0	2	8,682	4	32,956	2	10,517
Safe lost	13	47,434	16	126,301	31	351,695	13	75,550
Marginal lost	29	374,892	37	454,725	46	512,520	11	62,995
Marginal won	11	141,109	9	76,971	13	71,872	3	15,359
Safe won	1	8,201	2	5,548	0	0	0	0
Ultra-safe won	2	25,687	2	4,859	2	5,421	0	0

surprisingly they received around one-third of all the grants in number each year, and a larger proportion of the total value in the last two (Table 3.11), reflecting the presence of marginal seats within those units (as, for example, with the Brent, Haringey and Sutton London Borough accounting units). One difference between the Liberal Democrats and the Conservatives is that in two of the years the former made a much larger maximum grant to a local party – £98,042 and £116,946 in 2008 and 2009 respectively. Both were to the same local party – Streatham – which was not a very marginal constituency (Labour's lead over the second-placed Liberal Democrats in the estimated 2005 General Election was 17 percentage points).[9] A further grant in 2010 was for £24,152, when the local party also attracted £51,310 in donations; there was also a grant of £31,977 in 2007 so that over the four years the local party received £290,540.[10] (And the impact of all this investment there was only small: the Liberal Democrats came second again in 2010, 7 percentage points behind Labour.)

As with the Conservatives, most of the Liberal Democrat grants to local parties were to those in marginal constituencies – although this can only be assessed for those made to single-constituency units.[11] Thus in each year the majority of grants were to local units where the Liberal Democrats either won or lost in 2005 by less than 10 percentage points (see Table 3.12), although the large grants made to

---

[9] The Liberal Democrats won 10 of the 24 seats on Lambeth Council at the 2010 local elections in the eight wards that form the Streatham parliamentary constituency.

[10] The Liberal Democrat candidate, Chris Nicholson, was a wealthy businessman, who was accused in the local newspaper in 2010 of trying to buy the seat (www.streathamguardian.co.uk/news/5051752.Election_candidate_accused_of__attempting_to_buy_a_parliamentary_seat_/), having personally donated over £283,000 to the party in the previous three years. According to the Electoral Commission's register of donations, discussed in detail in Chapter Four, Mr Nicholson gave £439,109.26 to the Liberal Democrats during the period 2003-11 (most of it in 2008-09). A total of £85,104.26 went to his Streatham constituency party, and there were smaller donations to the Kingston Borough accounting unit, the London region unit and the Leeds North West constituency party; the bulk of the money, £333,600, went to the national party organisation.

[11] In the multi-constituency units, it was almost certainly the case that most of the expenditure took place in their more marginal seats: in the London Borough of Brent, for example, most was probably spent in the marginal seat of Brent Central – won by Sarah Teather by just 1,345 votes – rather than Brent North, where the Liberal Democrats came third in a safe Labour seat.

Table 3.11: Grants allocated by the Liberal Democrat central party organisation to local accounting units, 2007-10: summary statistics

	2007	2008	2009	2010
Single-constituency units				
Number of grants	22	27	39	32
Minimum grant (£)	492	1,100	500	862
Median grant (£)	10,326	5,684	7,105	9,422
Maximum grant (£)	31,977	98,042	116,946	36,364
Mean grant (£)	10,795	12,414	13,737	11,414
Standard deviation (£)	7,881	18,883	19,216	8,894
TOTAL (£)	237,487	335,186	535,753	365,254
Multiple-constituency units				
Number of grants	13	19	16	19
Minimum grant (£)	3,496	1,450	378	412
Median grant (£)	11,032	15,000	19,508	14,553
Maximum grant (£)	30,195	43,302	43,155	57,677
Mean grant (£)	13,113	16,910	18,634	14,214
Standard deviation (£)	8,649	11,498	12,409	13,471
TOTAL (£)	170,471	321,298	298,148	270,079

Table 3.12: The number and total value of grants from the Liberal Democrat central party organisation to single-constituency local accounting units, 2007-10, by constituency marginality

	2007		2008		2009		2010	
	N	£	N	£	N	£	N	£
Ultra-safe lost	1	18,990	2	5,785	3	9,998	3	31,742
Safe lost	4	60,385	5	159,259	6	175,034	4	80,960
Marginal lost	6	65,367	7	63,595	11	134,671	10	109,411
Marginal won	6	66,872	8	78,414	15	153,686	12	123,514
Safe won	4	25,223	5	28,133	4	62,364	3	19,627
Ultra-safe won	1	650	0	0	1	18,122	0	0

the Streatham party meant that a substantial proportion of the money went outside that band of marginal constituencies.

Expenditure

Turning to expenditure, Table 3.13 reports this under three headings only: salaries, print/post (which in most cases also includes the costs of stationery), and electioneering. Expenditure on the first two includes

Table 3.13: The main items of expenditure (in £) for local party accounting units, 2007-10

	2007	2008	2009	2010
Conservative				
Salaries	6,818,028	6,740,523	6,994,620	6,274,310
Print/post	2,876,932	2,483,853	3,117,827	3,127,654
Elections	2,753,503	2,753,050	3,282,649	5,521,030
TOTAL	22,178,622	21,270,255	24,232,023	24,850,507
Labour				
Salaries	238,174	305,224	418,071	446,049
Print/post	80,495	274,583	426,458	1,090,676
Elections	104,634	229,876	265,325	1,139,634
TOTAL	1,075,168	2,118,063	2,588,139	4,538,697
Liberal Democrat				
Salaries	804,725	898,417	1,096,895	872,223
Print/post	795,106	819,175	1,451,972	1,589,161
Elections	834,310	685,591	1,123,082	1,809,668
TOTAL	3,514,718	3,792,698	5,395,115	5,675,993

activities other than electioneering – money is spent on printing and postage to maintain contact with members in all years, for example, but the increase in the amount spent over the four years by Labour and the Liberal Democrats as the 2010 General Election approached strongly suggests that much of it was associated with campaigning. Expenditure on electioneering also increased substantially from 2007 to 2010, both absolutely and relatively; some of that spent before 2010 was on local government and European Parliament elections (some units separated out this expenditure) and elections to the Scottish Parliament and the National Assembly of Wales, but much – especially by local Conservative and Liberal Democrat parties – was spent on promoting their candidate for the forthcoming general election. By contrast, spending on salaries and associated costs varied much less, although for all three parties it declined in relative terms towards the end of the period as more was spent on electioneering.

A considerable number of the local parties' annual reports provide insights into the nature of their electioneering expenditure (which one, the Arundel and South Downs Conservative party, called spending on 'political promotion'). In some cases, there were contributions to the efforts in neighbouring seats: the Bedfordshire North East party reported campaigning in Bedford in 2010, for example, because its own Conservative incumbent MP had a large majority to defend (24.6 per cent compared to the Conservatives being 8.1 per cent behind Labour in Bedford), and the Buckingham party – having no contest locally since their constituency was represented by the Speaker – undertook campaigning in Milton Keynes (where the Conservatives won both seats from Labour). Similarly, the Wiltshire South West party (Wiltshire South West is a safe Conservative seat) reported that 50 of its members went to campaign in Chippenham, where the Liberal Democrats were defending a notional majority of 2,183, and reported distributing 377,000 printed items to constituents in 2010. Newbury's Conservatives provided campaigning support in Reading, and the New Forest West party transferred £5,000 to their neighbours in the marginal seat of Romsey and Southampton North; Richmond (Yorkshire) Conservatives reported donations of £2,000 each to the Calder Valley and Halifax constituency parties in 2010; and in 2009, Beverley and Holderness Conservatives reported that they were twinned with the nearby 'battleground seat' of Cleethorpes and also provided assistance in Dewsbury (where the candidate was chair of the Beverley and Holderness party).

A substantial number of local Conservative parties shared administrative services with their neighbours; in Wiltshire, for example, Chippenham, Devizes, Wiltshire North and Wiltshire South West (none of which reported any expenditure on salaries) transferred £33,372, £76,867, £55,619, and £42,385 respectively to the 'North Wilts Group', and three in East Devon jointly employed an agent. Most of those joint Conservative organisations are not registered as accounting units affiliated to the party. For example, in 2010 five of the six constituency parties in Gloucestershire together transferred £441,061 to 'Gloucestershire Conservatives' with The Cotswolds party alone contributing £128,758.[12] Each of the local parties had a quota to meet, and over the four years 2007-10 they transferred over £1.2 million to that organisation.[13]

In some cases, the annual reports give details on the nature of the electioneering activities. In 2009, for example, the Conservative party in Dover reported that its parliamentary candidate engaged in doorstep canvassing every weekend (he won the seat in 2010, overturning a notional Labour majority of 5,005; the party did not receive a grant from the target seats campaign in any of the four years, however). In Renfrewshire East there was a 'high profile doorstep and leaflet

---

[12] No return was available for the sixth constituency party in 2010 (Cheltenham); in 2009 it contributed £45,000 to 'Gloucestershire Conservatives'.

[13] It has a website (www.gloucestershireconservatives.org) which carries news and announcements of events, most of which involve the individual constituency parties.

campaign' (Labour had a 6,000 vote lead over the Conservatives in 2005, and 10,000 in 2010); in Edmonton, the candidate (facing a Labour lead of 10,000 votes) conducted a high profile campaign in 2009 using his own money (he failed to unseat the incumbent, whose 2010 majority was over 9,500). In Ipswich during that year half of the electorate was surveyed (a Labour 2005 majority of over 5,000 became a Conservative victory by 2,000 in 2010); and in Croydon Central £43,362 was spent in 2008 on 'professional printing' (Labour won there in 2005 by 328 votes). Maidstone and the Weald constituency party adopted a new candidate in 2008, and spent £31,413 on a campaign to promote her to the electorate (the retiring Conservative MP, Anne Widdicombe's, notional majority in 2005 was over 12,000; her replacement won in 2010 by less than 6,000). The Pudsey local party received a large donation in 2008, which it placed in a fighting fund, from which £12,788 was spent on postage and stationery.

Some local Conservative parties gave details of how they used the target seat grants. In 2009, for example, the Somerton and Frome Conservative constituency party conducted a survey of the whole electorate as well as contributing £46,300 to a joint working group with the neighbouring Wells party. (Somerton and Frome was held by the Liberal Democrats with a notional 2005 majority of 595; Wells was a Conservative-held seat, with a notional 2005 majority of 3,040. The Liberal Democrats held Somerton and Frome in 2010 and won Wells.) The Brigg and Goole party received a grant of £22,001 in 2008, which was spent 'raising the profile' of their candidate (he faced a Labour majority of 3,227, and won in 2010 by 5,147). In 2008, the local party in Carmarthen West and Pembrokeshire South reported meeting with the central party unit established by Lord Ashcroft, which had suggested that they set up a fighting fund called the 'Donations for Westminster Campaign'; the party received a grant in 2009. In 2010 they won the seat by 3,243 votes, overturning a notional Labour majority in 2005 of 2,043. Harlow constituency party spent part of its central grants in 2008 and 2009 on contacting voters through Facebook and Twitter; Birmingham, Edgbaston received a target grant of £20,000 in 2007, some of which was spent on a reply-paid questionnaire to all households in three of the constituency's four wards;[14] the local party

---

[14] The Conservatives failed to win that seat. The Labour MP's notional majority there was only 1,555 (1.01 per cent), but she held it by 1,274 votes. It was one of the constituencies where, according to Peter Hain (2012, p 439; original emphasis) Labour 'won against the tide because – through years of patient work in the community – they mobilised hundreds of *supporters*, and not just members, to campaign for Labour.'

also received grants in 2008 and 2009, but was unable to unseat the Labour incumbent MP whose majority was only 1,555 in 2005 (4 per cent: she won by 1,274 in 2010). The Calder Valley constituency party received a grant of £25,300 in 2007: £945 was spent on newspaper advertisements, £6,591 on leaflets and £16,449 on a survey; Reading West received only a small grant in 2007 (£3,089) but in the months after the May local elections delivered more than 100,000 pieces of literature in the constituency. Some constituency parties were not in need of grants and so themselves contributed to the target seats campaign: Tatton Conservatives, for example (where the Portcullis Club provided £50,930 in 2008), donated £7,000 each year to the North West region target seats campaign.

The annual reports of Liberal Democrat and Labour accounting units provide similar insights to their activities, although of course in fewer constituencies than for the Conservatives. In election year 2010, for example, donations of £44,268 to the Liberal Democrats in Bath – one of their safer seats with a notional majority of 5,624 in 2005 and 11,973 in 2010 (and hence no grants from the party's central office) – were used to fund not only leaflet printing but also £9,430 on opinion polling. The Eastleigh party (a marginal seat but with no grant income) not only raised £66,529 in donations in 2010 but also £30,299 for doing printing for other parties, allowing it to spend £56,504 on the election.

Few local Labour parties gave much detail on their campaigning activities, although in 2010 the Burton party reported that it spent £14,862 on the long campaign and £8,969 on the short, figures that tally with the Electoral Commissions' returns. (Labour won Burton in 2005 with a notional majority of 2,132 but lost it in 2010 by 6,304 votes.) Barking constituency Labour party reported in 2009 that it had received numerous donations (its total then was £22,372) to help in the campaigning effort against the British National Party (for which Barking was their prime target – their candidate was the party's leader, who came third in 2010 with 6,620 votes compared to the Labour candidate's 24,628); the party received £36,716 in donations the following year (more than the median income for all Labour single-constituency accounting units then). Barking was one of the three constituencies identified by Hain (2012, p 439) as places where Labour was able to mobilise a large number of non-member supporters to campaign for its candidate and stem the tide of support flowing away from the party. Fisher et al (2013) have analysed data on the number of such supporters recruited by each party, showing that, for those constituencies for which they obtained data, 75 per cent of

Conservative and Labour parties recruited supporters to assist members in their campaigns, as did 86 per cent of local Liberal Democrat parties; the average number of recruits was 20. Most of their work involved delivering leaflets, alongside party members who were much more likely to be involved in canvassing; the more supporters who were active in a party's local campaign, the better its performance there.

The intensity with which the Conservative and Liberal Democrat parties invested in campaigns during the years preceding the 2010 General Election is illustrated by one of the few three-way marginal constituencies being fought then – Watford. The notional outcome there in 2005 saw Labour with 33.6 per cent of the votes cast, the Liberal Democrats 31.2 per cent, and the Conservatives 29.6 per cent. Table 3.14 shows that over the four years 2007-10 each of the local Conservative and Liberal Democrat parties raised approximately £250,000 from either target grants or donations and appeals, with the Liberal Democrats' central party organisations providing twice as much as the Conservatives' (most of whose money was provided in a single year, 2009). Much of this money was spent preparing the

Table 3.14:Target grants and other major income sources for the Watford constituency parties, 2007-10

	Conservative	Liberal Democrat
2007		
Target grant	2,400	21,300
Donations and appeals	5,142	13,177
TOTAL	7,542	34,477
2008		
Target grant	42,497	22,392
Donations and appeals	6,757	10,124
TOTAL	49,254	32,516
2009		
Target grant	2,400	24,192
Donations and appeals	122,507	6,694
TOTAL	124,907	30,886
2010		
Target grant	0	14,347
Donations and appeals	78,128	133,430
TOTAL	78,128	147,777
Totals		
Target grants	47,297	82,231
Donations and appeals	212,984	163,425
TOTAL	260,281	245,656

ground for the general election, when the Conservatives and Liberal Democrats spent £37,552 and £35,158 respectively on the long and short campaigns combined. Labour, whose local party made no return of its annual accounts in any of the four years 2007–10, spent only £13,391. The Conservative candidate won the seat with 34.9 per cent of the votes, with the Liberal Democrat and Labour candidates getting 32.4 and 26.7 per cent respectively.

Where local Conservative parties received grants from their central party organisation between 2007–09, did this lead to more intensive campaigns in 2010, indexed by the amount of money spent, than in those that were reliant on their own fundraising? (Unfortunately similar analyses cannot be undertaken for the Liberal Democrats because of their relatively small number of single-constituency accounting units, with most of those in marginal constituencies in receipt of grants.) This was certainly the case in 2008 and 2009. Looking first at those constituencies where the Conservatives lost by less than 10 percentage points in 2005, to ensure some comparability of the 'demand' for expenditure, in 2007 there was virtually no difference between those parties that received grants and those that did not: the average spending on elections in the former was £7,092 and in the latter £7,074. In 2008 and 2009 the gap was much wider, however: the parties in receipt of grants spent on average £11,266 and £13,586 respectively in the two years whereas those without grants spent only £5,048 and £2,144 on average. The gap then closed in election year: the small number of parties in receipt of grants spent £13,945 on average whereas in the remainder mean expenditure was £13,507. Turning to the marginal seats where the Conservatives won in 2005, the amounts spent electioneering were generally much smaller, but with substantial differences in each year between the small number of constituency parties that received grants and the larger number that did not. Thus in 2007, average expenditure in the former seats was £8,198 compared to only £591 in the latter; in 2008 and 2009 respectively the means were £7,932 and £6,613 for the first year and £7,981 and £5,584 in the second; and finally, in 2010, when only three parties received grants, £23,540 was spent, compared to £13,733 in the much larger number that did not. The three constituencies in receipt of grants were: Guildford, where the Conservatives were estimated to have won by only 89 votes over the Liberal Democrats in 2005 and the latter strongly targeted the seat – they spent £12,142 there on the short campaign in 2010 (96.9 per cent of the maximum allowed), and £8,092 on the long campaign – but the Conservatives held the seat by a majority of 7,782; Solihull, where the estimated Conservative lead was 124 but which the Liberal Democrats won in 2010 by 175;[15] and Wirral West, which the Conservatives were estimated to have won by 569 votes over Labour in 2005, and which was only slightly changed in by redistricting in 2007 – the Conservatives' 2010 majority was 2,436.

Local finances and election spending

A key assumption underpinning the arguments being developed here is that the financially healthier local parties will be those best able to raise substantial sums to spend on general election campaigns. This is not to imply that those with a turnover of less than £25,000 per annum, even in an election year, may not be able to raise substantial sums even though their income is below that threshold; they may spend little on other activities, employ no staff (or only a small, probably part-time, element) and yet be able to obtain money for campaigning activities through donations and other sources. Furthermore, the maximum amount that can be spent on the short campaign is less than half of the annual income necessary for annual accounts to be returned to the Electoral Commission, so it would be quite feasible for a local party for which we have no accounts to fund a full-blown short campaign. The amount that can be spent on the long campaign is on average more than twice that for the short, however, and in total the cost of the two campaigns combined if the maximum were spent would be more than £40,000 – a substantial sum to be raised by a local party that normally turns over less than half that amount, and (as the data in Table 2.4 show) probably has very few members to undertake the effort necessary to raise such funds.

To explore the veracity of the assumption, therefore, Tables 3.15–3.17 cross-classify, for each party, each local unit's annual income in 2010 against its expenditure on the long campaign, the short campaign and the two campaigns combined; the number of parties spending the varying sums shown in the column headings are expressed as percentages of the total number of constituencies in that row (thus, for example, 75 per cent of Conservative parties whose incomes were less than £25,000 in 2010 spent less than £5,000 on the long campaign; see Table 3.15). In general terms, the expectations are realised.

For long campaign expenditure, Table 3.15 shows that local Conservative parties which made no return to the Electoral Commission in General Election year were much less likely to spend

[15] The Liberal Democrats won the former seat of Solihull in 2005 by 279 votes; the seat was only slightly changed in the 2007 redistribution.

Table 3.15: The amount spent in constituencies on the 2010 long campaign according to the local party's reported income in that year*

Income 2010	Long campaign spend (£k)							N
	0	0-5	5-10	10-15	15-20	20-25	25<	
Conservative								
<25,000	21	54	13	4	3	3	2	294
25-50,000	5	28	19	19	15	10	5	156
50-75,000	4	28	23	18	7	15	6	83
75-100,000	2	33	27	15	7	9	7	55
100,000<	7	23	9	16	16	11	8	44
Labour								
<25,000	21	57	12	7	2	1	1	565
25-50,000	2	11	22	33	18	7	5	44
50-75,000	0	0	29	7	14	29	21	14
75-100,000	(0)	(2)	(1)	(0)	(1)	(0)	(2)	6
100,000<	(0)	(1)	(0)	(0)	(0)	(0)	(0)	1
Liberal Democrat								
<25,000	37	51	6	3	2	1	1	565
25-50,000	0	10	25	15	20	25	5	40
50-75,000	0	0	13	25	25	25	13	16
75-100,000	(0)	(0)	(0)	(1)	(0)	(4)	(1)	6
100,000<	(0)	(0)	(0)	(0)	(1)	(1)	(1)	3

*The figures are percentages of the total number of constituencies in each row except where the number of constituencies is less than 10 where the absolute number is shown in brackets.

N – number of constituencies

£5,000 or more on that part of the campaign than those with a larger turnover; only 25 per cent of them spent more than that amount, most of them between £5-10,000. There was little difference across the local parties with more substantial incomes in the percentage that spent small amounts only on that campaign. This was even more the case with Labour and the Liberal Democrats, most of whose local units had an annual income then below the £25,000 threshold. Relatively heavy spending on the long campaign was much more likely among the small number with an annual turnover exceeding £50,000.

Turning to the short campaign – for which the maxima were substantially smaller – the differences are, if anything, even starker (see Table 3.16). Across all three parties, spending less than £5,000 during that four-week period was almost entirely confined to local units with an annual income of less than £25,000. Of those whose

Table 3.16: The amount spent in constituencies on the 2010 short campaign according to the local party's reported income in that year*

Income 2010	Short campaign spend (£k)						N
	0	0-2.5	2-5-5	5-7.5	7.5-10	10<	
Conservative							
<25,000	3	29	21	15	24	8	294
25-50,000	0	1	1	9	44	46	156
50-75,000	0	0	1	12	37	49	83
75-100,000	0	0	0	9	31	60	55
100,000<	0	0	5	7	25	64	44
Labour							
<25,000	3	28	18	21	22	9	565
25-50,000	2	0	7	9	36	45	44
50-75,000	0	0	0	21	43	36	14
75-100,000	(0)	(1)	(0)	(1)	(2)	(2)	6
100,000<	(0)	(0)	(1)	(0)	(0)	(0)	1
Liberal Democrat							
<25,000	7	50	18	11	8	8	565
25-50,000	0	0	0	5	25	70	40
50-75,000	0	0	0	0	19	81	16
75-100,000	(0)	(0)	(0)	(0)	(2)	(4)	6
100,000<	(0)	(0)	(0)	(0)	(2)	(1)	3

* The figures are percentages of the total number of constituencies in each row except where the number of constituencies is less than 10 where the absolute number is shown in brackets.

N – number of constituencies

incomes exceeded that threshold, the great majority spent more than £7,500 (about two-thirds of the average maximum allowed), although in general at any income level local Labour parties spent less on the campaign than their two opponents.

Combining the two sets of spending confirms these patterns (Table 3.17). In general, the greater a local party's annual income, the more it spent on campaigning there between January and May 2010. This relationship held for each of the three parties. Because there were many more local Conservative than Labour and Liberal Democrat local units with not only annual incomes above the £25,000 threshold but also with incomes well above that level, however, this means that the Conservatives had a very considerable advantage when it came to preparing for and conducting the campaigns.

Table 3.17: The amount spent in constituencies on the 2010 long and short campaigns combined according to the local party's reported income in that year*

Income 2010	Total campaign spend (£k)							N
	0	0-5	5-10	10-15	15-20	20-25	25<	
Conservative								
<25,000	2	41	23	14	9	3	8	294
25-50,000	0	0	11	23	19	19	29	156
50-75,000	0	0	15	18	23	17	28	83
75-100,000	0	0	6	29	22	16	27	55
100,000<	0	0	9	21	9	14	48	44
Labour								
<25,000	1	40	25	15	11	4	3	565
25-50,000	0	0	5	18	20	27	30	44
50-75,000	0	0	0	21	7	7	64	14
75-100,000	(0)	(1)	(1)	(0)	(1)	(0)	(3)	6
100,000<	(0)	(0)	(1)	(0)	(0)	(0)	(0)	1
Liberal Democrat								
<25,000	4	63	18	4	3	3	4	565
25-50,000	0	0	3	13	10	20	55	40
50-75,000	0	0	0	0	0	38	62	16
75-100,000	(0)	(0)	(0)	(0)	(0)	(1)	(5)	6
100,000<	(0)	(0)	(0)	(0)	(0)	(0)	(3)	3

*The figures are percentages of the total number of constituencies in each row except where the number of constituencies is less than 10 where the absolute number is shown in brackets.

N – number of constituencies

Conclusions

Money is not necessarily the key to success in local election campaigns, as some recent analyses of their nature and impact have shown; party activists and supporters canvassing voters in their homes and on the streets are important too, although in general local parties with more money (both income and assets) tend also to be those with more members, so the two key ingredients are to a very considerable extent complementary. Where parties are strong locally, they are better able to mount intensive campaigns, and benefit accordingly.

In general, the analyses reported here of the, incomplete and far from uniform in their quality, annual accounts of local political parties show that in the years leading up to the 2010 General Election the majority of local parties were far from strong locally – if we take the £25,000 annual income or expenditure threshold as an arbitrary but (in part because nothing else is available) useful dividing line between relatively weak and relatively strong local parties. There was considerable variation across the three political parties, however: the Conservatives had many more relatively strong local parties than Labour and the Liberal Democrats combined and, in addition, the Conservative and Liberal Democrat central party organisations were able to provide grants to local parties to aid their campaigning activities, which Labour was unable to do. In all three cases, most of the money to fund the long and short campaigns immediately preceding the 2010 General Election had to be raised by the candidates and their local party organisations themselves, however, and the stronger local parties were better able to raise sufficient to approach the maximum amount they could spend on their campaigns. The foundations for intensive campaigns varied considerably, therefore, both across parties and (geographically) within each.

FOUR

Raising the money: donations to local parties

Chapter Three has shown that donations are a substantial source of income to local constituency parties, and thus indirectly to their candidates' campaigns. In 2009, for example, over £6 million was donated to those units that made returns of their income and expenditure to the Electoral Commission, and in 2010 that sum exceeded £8 million (see Table 3.8). Given that only a minority of local parties reported on their income and expenditure to the Commission – albeit in general those which spent most on their general election campaigns in the latter year – this is undoubtedly an understatement of the total amount donated to the three parties' local accounting units; the total amount donated in 2010 almost certainly exceeded £10 million. What sources were being tapped and which local parties were the recipients of the largest amounts? In this chapter, we explore two separate sources of information that can be used to address that question.

Reported campaign donations in 2010

The data published by the Electoral Commission for spending on the long and short campaigns – discussed in Chapter Two – include not only the total amounts spent by each candidate in each constituency, but also the amount that the candidates received in donations, divided into those which were under and those which exceeded £50. (This threshold is applied because for donations below £50 candidates do not have to check whether they comply with the legal requirements.) No information is provided on the number of donations, however, which limits the utility of these data. Nevertheless, they provide some insights into how local campaigns were funded.

In a large number of cases – and especially for spending on the short campaign (that is, in the period between the writs being served and polling day) – the amount received in donations exactly equals the reported amount spent. This is in line with earlier research on the funding of local campaigns: analysis of the detailed returns made by each candidate for the 1997 General Election – and therefore for the short campaign only – showed that the great majority obtained the financial resources from a single source only, the local political party (Johnston et al, 1999). That this was the case again in 2010 is made very clear in Figure 4.1, which shows for each of the parties the amount spent on the short campaign and the amount received in donations then exceeding £50. The great majority of constituencies fall on the main diagonal of that relationship, where the amount spent exactly equals the amount received. Whether the latter was delivered as a single sum cannot be determined, nor can we know whether the amount spent was the total amount made available by the local party (or, as discussed in Chapter Three, its fighting fund), or the amount donated was the amount spent and requested, although from the data on the financial situation of most local parties the former is the more likely. In other words, in the majority of cases either the local party (or a fighting fund that it had established) provided the candidate with a sum of money and that was the amount spent, or the candidate claimed a sum from the local party equal to the reported amount that was expended on the campaign after the event.

Figure 4.1: The relationship between the total amount received in donations and the amount spent on the 2010 short campaign

(a) Conservative party candidates

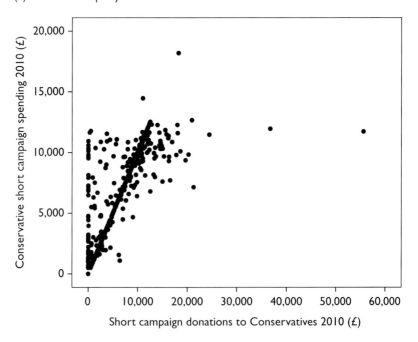

(b) Labour party candidates

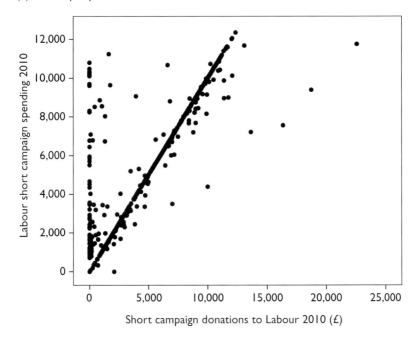

(c) Liberal Democrat party candidates

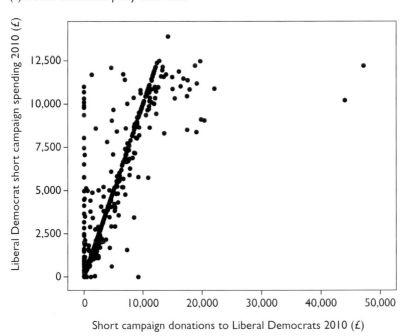

Despite the limitations of the data, some important findings do emerge. For example, few candidates received much money as small donations (less than £50) for the long campaigns. Only 84 Labour candidates (out of 631) received any money at all through such donations; the mean total received was only £622 (and the median just £63, indicating that most of them were very small: the largest received by any candidate was £13,921); the total donated to all candidates was only £52,244. Almost twice as many (160) Liberal Democrat candidates received money through small donations, but the total amount was not much larger than Labour's (£62,838); the maximum received by any candidate was £3,933 and the mean £394. Finally, 118 of the Conservative candidates received small donation moneys for the long campaign; the total amount received was much larger than for the other two parties, however (£176,524), as was the mean per candidate (£1,496).

Although Figure 4.1 shows that in most cases all of the money received by the candidates equalled that spent on their campaigns, nevertheless in a few cases more was spent than received, and in others, less. Thus 112 Conservative candidates 'over-spent' on their long campaigns (Figure 4.2[a]) by slightly more on average than candidates

Figure 4.2: The relationship between the total amount received in donations and the amount spent on the 2010 long campaign

(a) Conservative party candidates

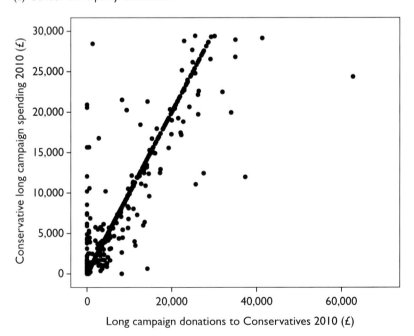

(b) Labour party candidates

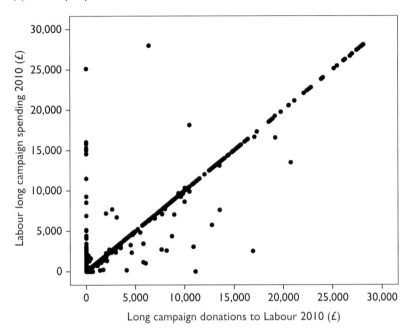

(c) Liberal Democrat party candidates

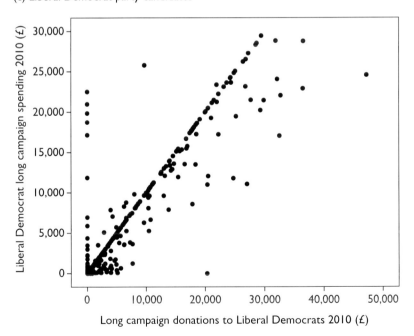

from the other two parties: the mean difference between the amounts spent and received was £3,146 and the median £1,197, with 10 per cent of them 'over-spending' (presumably from accumulated funds) by more than £10,000. A slightly larger number (131) 'under-spent', presumably keeping money in reserve for the later, short campaign, but in most cases only small amounts were involved – a mean of £2,771 and median of £993. On the short campaign, too (Figure 4.1[a]), about a quarter (148) of all Conservative candidates spent less than their donated income (mean £2,374; median, £731), and about the same number (139) 'over-spent' by about the same amounts (mean £2,898; median, £1,650). When the two campaigns are combined (Figure 4.3[a]), 235 candidates over-spent, but over half of them by less than £500 – although the maximum was over £31,000, and 22 of them 'over-spent' by more than £10,000. About the same number 'under-spent' (260), and again in most cases only a small amount of money was retained after the election was over: the median was just £355.

For the long campaign, Figure 4.2[b] shows a relatively small number of Labour candidates (81) spending more than their donated income; in most

Figure 4.3: The relationship between the total amount received in donations and the total amount spent on the 2010 campaign

(a) Conservative party candidates

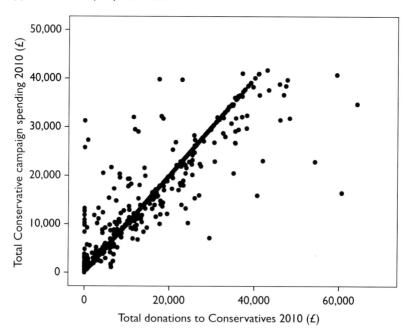

(b) Labour party candidates

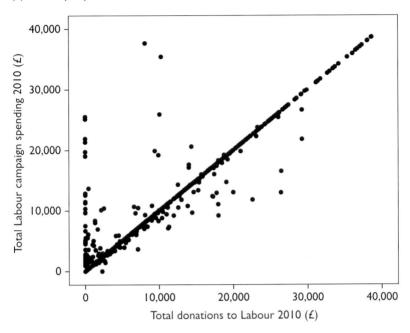

(c) Liberal Democrat party candidates

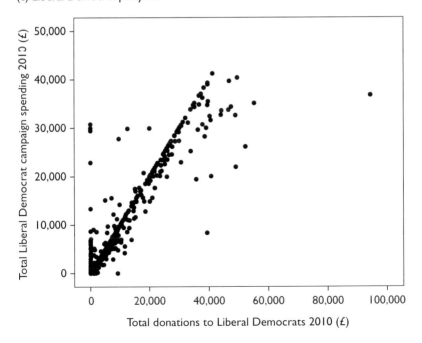

cases this 'over-spending' (presumably of money obtained through earlier donations) was less than £1,000. About the same number (84) 'under-spent' relative to the amount received in donations – presumably money was being retained for the short campaign. Indeed, this was probably the case: 121 Labour candidates spent more on their short campaigns than they received in donations then, a mean of £2,786 (although a median of only £1,572); in addition 99 spent less on that campaign than they received, although by less than £1,000 on average (mean £870; median, £252). Over both campaigns together, as Figure 4.3[b] shows, very few candidates spent substantially more than they received in donations (the mean for the 236 candidates was £2,315, although for half of them the 'over-spend' was less than £100). Fewer under-spent, and so had money 'left in the bank' after the election was over: 202 candidates in total spent less on the two campaigns than their donation income, but the mean surplus was only £742 and the median just £14.

The situation with Liberal Democrat candidates was very similar to that for their Labour counterparts. Figure 4.2[c] shows that a small number (66) 'over-spent' on their long campaign (mean £2,852; median £484), and a somewhat larger number (174) 'under-spent' (although not by much: a median of £624 and a mean of £2,071). An even larger number (236) 'under-spent' on their short campaigns – but by small amounts in most cases; the median was £295; fewer (141) 'over-spent', and again the sums were on average small (median £939; median, £2,059). Over the two campaigns together (Figure 4.3[c]) the great majority of candidates spent approximately what they obtained through donations: 173 spent more than they received, but for two-thirds of them that 'over-spending' came to less than £1,000. Many (321) spent less than they had received, but again in two-thirds of the cases the amount unspent was less than £1,000.

Is there any overall pattern to where a party either over- or under-spent on the campaigns relative to the value of the donations received? In electoral terms, one might expect over-spending to be most common in marginal constituencies where effort to win the seat is greatest, even if it means incurring debts that will have to be paid off later, whereas under-spending would be most concentrated in the safe seats – either those comfortably won by the party at the last election or those where there is no realistic expectation of victory and little incentive to spend money campaigning. There is relatively little evidence of this, however. Table 4.1 lists those constituencies where there was either under- or over-spending by their marginality; Table 4.2 repeats the analysis, but only for candidates who either under- or over-spent by more than £1,000.

Table 4.1: The distribution of constituencies according to whether candidates over- or under-spent on their 2010 General Election campaigns, by constituency margin

	OSL	OSS	OST	USL	USS	UST	ALL
Conservative							
Ultra-safe lost	43	70	94	45	42	73	225
Safe lost	15	16	33	23	26	45	101
Marginal lost	15	16	38	22	23	40	95
Marginal won	7	7	18	10	14	27	51
Safe won	19	17	24	17	21	37	76
Ultra-safe won	13	13	28	14	22	38	84
Labour							
Ultra-safe lost	20	49	67	25	28	41	173
Safe lost	12	13	26	10	8	18	64
Marginal lost	4	7	13	8	6	23	45
Marginal won	10	9	36	10	15	33	87
Safe won	12	10	27	12	16	38	91
Ultra-safe won	23	33	37	19	26	50	172
Liberal Democrat							
Ultra-safe lost	43	108	128	95	152	213	457
Safe lost	14	14	27	27	34	43	81
Marginal lost	5	10	10	15	15	20	31
Marginal won	3	4	6	15	5	17	28
Safe won	1	4	1	15	12	19	24
Ultra-safe won	0	1	1	7	9	6	10

OSL – over-spent on the long campaign; OSS – over-spent on the short campaign; OST – over-spent on both campaigns; USL – under-spent on the long campaign; USS – under-spent on the short campaign; UST – under-spent on both campaigns; ALL – total number of constituencies.

For Labour, there is some slight evidence supporting the argument regarding over-spending; in total, candidates spent more than their income from donations in 36 of the 87 seats that they were defending with majorities of less than 10 percentage points, but in many cases those over-spends were small: in only seven did they over-spend by more than £1,000, which compares with 34 seats where they over-spent by similar amounts despite having no realistic chances of victory there (that is, seats that they lost in 2005 by more than 20 points). Labour under-spending – especially of £1,000 or more – was, however, concentrated in their safest seats; moneys donated there were not spent on campaigns where victory was very likely, it seems. Turning to the Conservatives, again there is little evidence of 'excess' spending in the marginal seats that were so important to their overall

Table 4.2: The distribution of constituencies according to whether candidates over- or under-spent by more than £1,000 on their 2010 General Election campaigns, by constituency margin

	OSL	OSS	OST	USL	USS	UST	ALL
Conservative							
Ultra-safe lost	18	46	44	17	12	27	225
Safe lost	8	10	12	11	11	17	101
Marginal lost	9	8	9	10	9	15	95
Marginal won	7	5	7	6	9	12	51
Safe won	11	10	13	12	14	16	76
Ultra-safe won	7	8	9	8	15	17	84
Labour							
Ultra-safe lost	7	33	34	3	1	3	173
Safe lost	8	11	15	0	2	1	64
Marginal lost	2	4	3	1	0	1	45
Marginal won	5	5	7	3	2	5	87
Safe won	6	6	8	4	6	7	91
Ultra-safe won	13	23	23	9	7	14	172
Liberal Democrat							
Ultra-safe lost	11	45	45	26	27	46	457
Safe lost	9	12	11	14	15	20	81
Marginal lost	3	8	5	7	6	9	31
Marginal won	1	2	2	8	9	10	28
Safe won	1	3	0	12	9	13	24
Ultra-safe won	0	1	1	3	3	6	10

OSL – over-spent on the long campaign; OSS – over-spent on the short campaign; OST – over-spent on both campaigns; USL – under-spent on the long campaign; USS – under-spent on the short campaign; UST – under-spent on both campaigns; ALL – total number of constituencies.

strategy – indeed, candidates were more likely to under- than over-spend in such constituencies. Instead, again like Labour, many of the Conservative candidates who over-spent by more than £1,000 relative to the donations received were contesting seats that they had very little chance of winning (they lost there in 2005 by more than 20 percentage points). Liberal Democrat candidates, too, were just as likely to under- as over-spend by £1,000 in the party's marginal seats, although there was also much more under- rather than over-spending in the safe seats that they were defending.

Finally, Liberal Democrat candidates were very unlikely to over-spend in the seats that they won in 2005, especially those classified as either safe or ultra-safe, whereas they over-spent in around one-third of the marginal and safe seats where they lost then. They under-spent in 60 per cent or more of the constituencies that they won in 2005, however – and by more than £1,000 in those where their margin of victory was 10 percentage points or more. Under-spending was somewhat less likely in seats (especially those classified as marginal or safe) that were lost in 2005.

Individual donations to local parties

Entirely separate from the stipulations of the Representation of the People Act, which require candidates to report on their campaign expenditure and the donations received to cover that, are the requirements for separate reporting of all individual donations to a political party or any of its affiliated accounting units, under the PPERA 2000 (Part IV, Chapter III, Sections 62-69). As part of the goal to ensure both transparency with regard to the sources of donations to parties and that all of their moneys come from acceptable sources, parties must report all donations received in excess of a given amount, with that amount varying according to whether a donation was to the national party or to an accounting unit. For the latter, that sum during the period being analysed here was £1,000, although in some cases (and in the other parties more than the Conservatives) some smaller donations were reported and recorded, in part because of the requirement to report small donations from a single source if, when combined over the year, they exceeded the reporting threshold.[1] A register of all these donations, with details on the donor (classified by the Commission into eight types) as well as the recipient, is available on the Commission's website.

The overall trend in the value of all donations to each party over the period from 2001 to 2011 (that is, to their central party organisation as well as its accounting units) is shown in Figure 4.4 (see also Fisher, 2010). For Labour, there was an upward trend in the amount received until 2005, which paralleled and just exceeded that for the Conservatives; there was a similar, although shallower, trend for the Liberal Democrats, but their total income from donations was only about half of that received by their two opponents. Labour's income from donations fell substantially in 2006, however, but recovered thereafter, and in 2010 approximated the total received in the previous election year. After remaining relatively stable at its 2005 level until

---

[1] The minimum amount was increased by the Political Parties and Elections Act 2009, but its implementation in 2010 means that it had no substantial impact on the data deployed here.

Figure 4.4: Total donations to the three political parties (including their accounting units), 2001-11

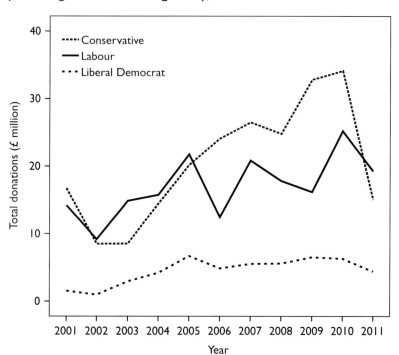

2007, on the other hand, the Conservative party's total income from donations then increased rapidly – with a slight dip in 2008 – and in 2010 was some 70 per cent more than its receipts in 2005. The Liberal Democrats also experienced an overall, steady rise after 2006, but in 2010 their receipts were only just under half those of Labour and 30 per cent of the Conservatives'. In the year after the 2010 contest, their income remained relatively stable, whereas Labour's fell by nearly one-quarter and the Conservatives' fell by 55 per cent, to some £4 million less than Labour's income. (Presumably the Liberal Democrats were able to attract donations having entered into the Coalition government.)

Most of those donations were not directed at constituency parties and other 'accounting units', however. If we look just at donations to accounting units that were either single- or multi-constituency parties, Figure 4.5 emphasises the clear advantage that local Conservative parties had in attracting donations, especially in general election years. In 2005 they attracted more than twice the money donated to their Labour opponents (£4.2 million against £1.9 million) – who in

**Figure 4.5: Total donations to the three political parties'
accounting units, 2001-11**

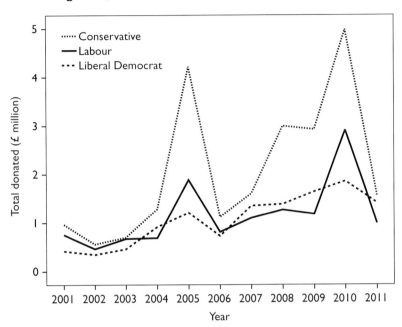

turn attracted about 50 per cent more than the Liberal Democrats.
Donations then fell in 2006 before beginning to increase: by 2010 each
raised substantially more than in 2005, but Conservative local parties
raised almost as much as the other two parties combined.

Table 4.3 shows the total number of donations, and the sums
involved, to accounting units that were either individual constituency
parties or groups of a small number of constituencies in a single local
organisation, thus omitting regional parties and a small number of
other organisations. These cover the four years leading up to the 2010
General Election, and thus refer to the local parties in place over
that period, whose overall finances were discussed in Chapter Three.
Where a donation was made to a multi-constituency accounting unit,
the money was allocated across those constituencies according to
their percentage share of the party's vote total at the 2005 General
Election. (Thus, with a two-constituency unit, where the party got
10,000 votes in one of the seats and 5,000 in the other, two-thirds of
the value of the donations were allocated to the first and one-third
to the second.) In each of the four years, the Conservatives were able
to attract substantially more money to their constituency parties than
either of their two opponents, although the total number of donations

Table 4.3: The number and total value of donations to local party accounting units, 2007-10

	Conservative		Labour		Liberal Democrat	
	N	**£**	**N**	**£**	**N**	**£**
2007	471	1,602,589	704	1,089,020	621	1,349,674
2008	710	2,999,898	836	1,266,584	590	1,383,989
2009	777	2,923,441	2,264	1,176,267	871	1,640,146
2010	1,131	4,982,876	2,273	2,911,285	666	1,856,553

to Labour parties was much larger. (In 2010, for example, the average donation to a Labour constituency party was £1,250, compared to £4,222 for the Conservatives and £2,950 for the Liberal Democrats.) The Conservatives substantially increased their number of donations in 2010, however, whereas Labour obtained almost exactly the same number and the Liberal Democrats over 200 less than in 2009.

Were these donations focused on the constituencies where they were most needed in terms of campaigning intensity – the marginal seats? Tables 4.4-4.6 explore this for each party in each of the four years, looking at both the number of constituencies that received one or more donations and the total value of money received. In these tables, given the volume of data available, we use the tenfold categorisation of constituencies employed in earlier chapters.

For Labour relatively small numbers of constituencies where the party lost by more than 10 percentage points in 2005 received donations, although the great majority of those where its margin of defeat was small did (Table 4.4). Most constituency parties in seats where Labour won in 2005 received at least one donation in each year, with the numbers increasing year-on-year as the next general election approached. Nevertheless, even in 2010 a not insubstantial number of the more marginal constituencies received no donations (10 of the 42 won by a margin of less than 5 points and five of the 45 won by 5-10 points), whereas 143 of the party's 172 safest seats (83 per cent) did receive donations. Some of the money was being given to places where it was less needed than others, therefore. Indeed, when we look at the total sums received, of the £6,792,139 donated over the four years, £2,298,903 (34 per cent) went to local parties where Labour's hold on the seat was safe (that is, it won there by more than 20 percentage points in 2005 so that the probability of the seat being lost in 2010 was small): this averaged £4,770 per constituency that received one or more donations. Against this, only about one-third of that total amount – £782,479 – was donated to the most marginal seats won by Labour

Table 4.4: The number of Labour constituency accounting units receiving donations, and their total value, 2007-10, according to constituency marginality

Constituencies with donations	2007	2008	2009	2010	ALL
Won 20%<	110	117	112	143	172
Won 15-20%	29	29	32	41	49
Won 10-15%	33	29	29	37	42
Won 5-10%	27	34	32	40	45
Won 0-5%	25	33	29	32	42
Lost 0-5%	17	18	24	25	31
Lost 5-10%	8	10	10	10	14
Lost 10-15%	8	4	5	7	18
Lost 15-20%	7	7	6	9	45
Lost 20%<	21	29	19	21	173

Total value of donations (£)	2007	2008	2009	2010
Won 20%<	383,407	392,061	469,350	1,053,545
Won 15-20%	151,950	117,805	151,957	348,219
Won 10-15%	116,691	177,103	148,734	433,052
Won 5-10%	129,113	126,441	114,825	351,189
Won 0-5%	86,710	220,325	130,882	344,562
Lost 0-5%	77,531	61,798	80,849	138,378
Lost 5-10%	23,953	64,550	22,830	67,537
Lost 10-15%	22,742	32,831	36,857	67,500
Lost 15-20%	10,976	18,334	10,662	42,542
Lost 20%<	55,909	53,299	55,571	86,978
TOTAL	1,058,982	1,264,457	1,222,517	3,246,183

in 2005 and where defeat was most likely in 2010 given the general shift in support towards its opponents, although because there were fewer constituencies in this category, this meant an average of £5,629 per constituency receiving any donations. If all of that income had been spent on campaigning in 2010, it was only about half-as-much again as the maximum allowed in the average constituency during the short campaign alone, and so would not have covered much of the total allowed for the long campaign as well. (A further £721,568 was donated to the 45 constituency parties – a constituency mean of £5,425 – won by 5-10 percentage points in 2005, many of which Labour was also in danger of losing given the Conservatives' lead in the opinion polls as the election approached.)

A very different pattern of donations is shown in Table 4.5 for the Conservatives, with much more money being raised in the marginal as against the safe seats – both those that the party was defending in 2010 and those where it was seeking to replace the incumbent. Donations in 2010 averaged £24,664 per constituency in receipt of one or more donations in the marginal seats with 2005 majorities of less than 5 percentage points that the Conservatives won then, £19,406 in the 45 where it lost by less than 5 points (donations were received in 39 in 2010), and £21,298 where the margin of defeat was between 5-10 points. By contrast, in 2010 only 55 of the 84 seats where the Conservative winning majority exceeded 20 points in 2005 received at least one donation in 2010 (and many fewer in each of the preceding

Table 4.5: The number of Conservative constituency accounting units receiving donations, and their total value, 2007-10, according to constituency marginality

Constituencies with donations	2007	2008	2009	2010	ALL
Won 20%<	35	41	39	55	84
Won 15-20%	20	21	19	33	50
Won 10-15%	8	7	9	16	26
Won 5-10%	6	9	10	14	16
Won 0-5%	13	23	21	29	35
Lost 0-5%	21	29	35	39	45
Lost 5-10%	19	32	33	37	50
Lost 10-15%	17	22	27	38	49
Lost 15-20%	9	19	23	32	52
Lost 20%<	14	22	30	49	225

Total value of donations (£)	2007	2008	2009	2010
Won 20%<	446,212	435,070	406,929	678,088
Won 15-20%	91,856	107,552	173,076	292,135
Won 10-15%	96,016	63,088	68,025	174,228
Won 5-10%	67,859	93,317	111,299	186,726
Won 0-5%	88,967	372,520	192,521	715,283
Lost 0-5%	182,139	457,579	530,641	756,821
Lost 5-10%	221,547	661,133	419,937	788,045
Lost 10-15%	202,478	443,822	377,804	513,137
Lost 15-20%	43,172	121,976	240,877	301,359
Lost 20%<	98,165	185,821	271,283	369,401
TOTAL	1,538,411	2,941,878	2,792,392	4,775,223

three years), and the average per constituency total received then was £12,328.

Finally, Table 4.6 shows that for the Liberal Democrats almost all of the constituency parties in seats that were won in 2005 received at least one donation in each of the four years (50 of the 62 in 2010), with the main exception being those where the margin of victory was more than 20 points (most of them were in Scotland, where in general the local units of all three parties are financially less healthy than in England). The amount of money donated to those parties in the last category was small – an average of just £7,404 per constituency over the four years, or £4,355 per constituency getting at least one donation. Much more was raised in the seats where its margin of victory was small – £720,651 – or £51,475 per constituency in those won by less than five points and £441,177 (£31,513 per constituency)

Table 4.6: The number of Liberal Democrat constituency accounting units receiving donations, and their total value, 2007-10, according to constituency marginality

Constituencies with donations	2007	2008	2009	2010	ALL
Won 20%<	5	3	5	4	10
Won 15-20%	12	11	12	12	12
Won 10-15%	10	9	9	10	12
Won 5-10%	10	13	12	11	14
Won 0-5%	12	13	13	13	14
Lost 0-5%	10	12	13	13	16
Lost 5-10%	9	11	11	12	15
Lost 10-15%	17	16	22	20	27
Lost 15-20%	27	25	34	33	55
Lost 20%<	102	100	126	141	456

Total value of donations (£)	2007	2008	2009	2010
Won 20%<	15,616	11,380	27,342	19,700
Won 15-20%	143,954	112,975	157,614	153,975
Won 10-15%	213,566	120,463	145,587	225,327
Won 5-10%	97,672	81,161	117,135	145,209
Won 0-5%	109,849	154,651	194,360	261,791
Lost 0-5%	92,815	71,156	124,586	126,515
Lost 5-10%	56,625	90,443	97,768	95,923
Lost 10-15%	171,818	77,121	136,191	190,908
Lost 15-20%	141,989	215,872	190,068	212,239
Lost 20%<	336,229	561,320	435,415	505,981
TOTAL	1,380,133	1,496,542	1,626,066	1,937,568

in those won by 5-10 points. Relatively large numbers of constituency parties where the Liberal Democrats lost in 2005 also received donations (in some because they were paired in multi-constituency accounting units with seats where the party won), including as many as one-quarter of those where defeat was by more than 20 percentage points (although the amounts received were relatively small: £3,088 per constituency among the 33 in that category that received donations in 2010, compared to £11,170 in the 13 in the most marginal winning group that obtained donations).

The donors

Who provides those donations? The Electoral Commission classifies donors into eight main types, and the number and value of donations in each category, for each party's local accounting units, over the period 2001-11 inclusive are shown in Table 4.7. Four major differences stand out.

First, Labour got a large proportion (43 per cent) of its money in donations from trades unions: these provided 53 per cent of all of its donations, averaging £1,452 each, compared to an average for all donations of £2,233. The unions provided much of the money but in smaller blocks than the other donors. In 1995, the party invited unions to sponsor constituency parties rather than individual MPs, hoping that this would see more donations focused on marginal constituencies.

Table 4.7: The main sources of donations to the three parties' constituency accounting units, 2001-11

	Labour		Conservative		Liberal Democrat	
	N	**£**	**N**	**£**	**N**	**£**
Company	435	1,031,808	1,466	6,552,266	405	1,143,349
Friendly Society	60	111,055	22	69,632	2	2,310
Individual	943	2,437,688	3,631	12,973,334	3,356	7,065,287
Limited Liability Partnership	32	69,174	18	49,144	1	1,008
Registered political party	510	743,843	–	–	–	–
Trade union	3,726	5,408,872	–	–	–	–
Trust	14	63,523	120	472,141	170	769,596
Unincorporated association	1,272	2,843,906	663	2,729,067	1,150	2,722,653
TOTAL	6,998	12,715,462	5,948	22,908,811	5,101	11,716,919

Most of the large unions donated to a large number of accounting units: over the decade, UNISON, for example, made 668 separate donations totalling £636,759 to over 130 different units. Neither of the other parties received any donations from trade unions to their local accounting units. Many of the union donations were to Labour's relatively safe seats, however, where in the past they had sponsored MPs; all but one of the Scottish constituency parties in receipt of National Union of Mineworkers (NUM) donations were former mining seats with very large Labour majorities, for example.

Table 4.8 looks in more detail at trade union donations to local Labour parties during the 2007-10 period on which most of the analyses here have concentrated. A total of 2,177 separate donations were made, to 799 different local accounting units,[2] with a total value of £2,963,100. Seventeen separate unions were involved, with five

Table 4.8: Donations to Labour constituency accounting units by trade unions, 2007-10

| | Number of | | |
Union	Donations	Constituencies	£
UNITE (includes Amicus and TGWU)	607	197	894,199
GMB	353	155	601,488
UNISON	463	129	497,834
USDAW	178	60	260,951
CWU	279	113	240,524
FBU	39	31	85,340
TSSA	37	13	57,600
UCATT	46	16	50,908
COMMUNITY	42	25	48,466
Musicians	11	11	43,000
ASLEF	53	16	42,950
CONNECT	6	2	38,500
NURMT	12	12	32,050
UNITY	9	9	28,300
PROSPECT	3	3	27,000
NUM	8	7	13,650
Durham Miners	1	1	350
TOTAL	2,177	799	2,963,110

[2] Most of the donations were to individual constituency parties but a few were to groups (in a single city, for example) which made it slightly difficult to produce an exact total of seats donated to. Some local parties got several donations from the same party; some got donations from more than one.

dominating the table in both the value of their donations and the number of recipient constituencies; the largest – Unite – was formed by the amalgamation of Amicus and the Transport and General Workers' Union (TGWU) in 2007. The smaller unions focused their money on a small number of constituencies: the Durham Miners' Union gave a small sum to one party only (Easington, where the local pit closed in 1993); Prospect (a union for managers, engineers and scientists) gave a single donation each to the very different constituency parties in Glasgow North West, Gloucester, and Ipswich, and Connect (a union for managers and professionals in the communications industry, which merged with Prospect in 2010) made two donations to Glasgow North West and four to Gloucester; the NUM made one donation each to six Scottish constituency parties and two to the Wansbeck seat in Northumberland. The larger unions, on the other hand, made donations (most of them relatively small) to a wide range of constituency parties. A total of 383 separate constituency Labour parties received at least one donation from one of the 17 unions; the largest was 20, to Livingston (a safe Labour seat in Scotland although the SNP performed well there in a 2005 by-election after the death of the sitting member, Robin Cook), although between them Derby North and South received 35 donations, 31 of them joint. The average number of donations per constituency was less than three, however.

Second, the Conservatives and Liberal Democrats relied to a much greater extent than Labour on donations from individuals – 57 per cent in the Conservative case (an average donation of £3,573) and 60 per cent for the Liberal Democrats (an average of £2,105). Labour's income from individuals was much less in total, but the average donation of £2,585 places their donors between the other two parties in the amounts given. The third difference is the Conservatives' much greater reliance on donations from companies (29 per cent of total income): its local parties not only obtained three times as many separate donations as either of its opponents from this source, but those donations were on average much larger – £4,470 compared to £2,372 from companies to Labour and £2,823 for the Liberal Democrats. Finally, only Labour accounting units reported donations from 'Registered political parties': all 510 of those were from the Co-operative Party, which made 561 separate donations to 153 different constituency parties (342 of the donations, totalling £554,737, went to 42 different constituencies whose MPs were sponsored by the Co-operative Party for at least part of the period 2001-11).

A third difference is that although all three parties raised substantial sums – nearly £3 million each – from unincorporated associations, in relative terms these provided twice as much of the total donated income for Labour and the Liberal Democrats as for the Conservatives. Many of these were organisations closely linked to the relevant political party, but not affiliated to them (illustrating the problems of regulating these aspects of party funding). Thus, for example, the Cannock Chase Liberal Democrat Council Group donated £7,118 to the party's Cannock Chase accounting unit over the 11-year period, and the Aberystwyth Liberal Association gave donations in kind (the use of premises) valued at £25,356 to the Ceredigion unit; the Norfolk Tote (in some cases called the Norfolk Tote and Bingo) made 173 separate donations totalling £103,607 to the South Norfolk Constituency Labour Party. Not all of these organisations were categorised as 'Unincorporated associations' by the Electoral Commission, however. Thus, for example, the Weymouth Labour Club, which gave 49 separate donations to the South Dorset constituency party, totalling £39,900, is classified as a Company; the Coggeshall Liberal Trust – classified as a Trust – gave £11,150 to the party's Braintree and Witham accounting unit; and the Bury Liberal Democrat Council Group – which donated £4,620 to the Bury accounting unit – was registered as a Friendly Society.

Table 4.9 gives data for the 10 largest unincorporated association donors to each party's local accounting units during 2007-10. With two exceptions, for both Labour and the Liberal Democrats these comprise the party's local government councillors in an area clubbing together to make donations to the local party, alongside the separate donations made by individual councillors (a particular feature of the Liberal Democrats). They make donations to a small number of local parties only – invariably those within the area served by their local council: the average Labour donation (£6,274) was more than twice that from a Liberal Democrat group (£3,051). Of the two exceptions, the SW East Labour Lotteries Group made five of its 12 donations to one constituency party – Ipswich – whereas the Broadstone and District Liberal Hall is the headquarters for the Mid Dorset and North Poole constituency party.

For the Conservatives, most of the large unincorporated association donors are groups associated with the party, but only one – that for Croydon – comprises members of the local council. Several are dining clubs: the United and Cecil Club coordinates dinners in a variety of locations and made donations to a wide range of constituency parties; others – such as the East Surrey Business Club and the Magna Carta Club – focus on their local party only (East Surrey and Surrey Heath,

Table 4.9: The largest ten unincorporated association donors to constituency accounting units, by party, 2007-10

Unincorporated association	Number of		£
	Donations	Constituencies	
Conservative			
United & Cecil Club	83	38	260,300
Midlands Industrial Council	10	4	186,244
Carlton Club	15	10	97,035
Leamington Fund	1	1	64,500
The Oak Ball	3	3	58,725
Croydon Councillors	6	1	52,546
East Surrey Business Club	11	1	44,000
Magna Carta Club	3	1	37,500
Business Fore	5	2	34,000
National Conservative Draw	11	7	34,000
Perth Conservative Club	1	1	34,000
TOTAL	149	69	902,850
Labour			
Newham Labour Group	7	1	134,805
Lambeth Labour Group	7	3	123,812
Croydon Labour Group	14	3	98,726
St Helens Labour Group	22	2	94,504
Haringey Labour Group	8	2	85,506
Islington Labour Group	19	2	57,075
Tower Hamlets Labour Group	5	2	36,500
Leeds Labour Group	15	6	35,700
SW East Labour Lotteries	12	5	34,285
Hackney Labour Group	8	2	33,147
TOTAL	117	28	734,060
Liberal Democrat			
Oldham LD Council Group	15	2	108,512
Richmond upon Thames LD Council Group	17	1	80,240
Newcastle upon Tyne LD Council Group	14	3	73,500
Broadstone & District Liberal Hall Committee	29	1	64,999
Kirklees LD Council Group	34	4	64,332
Cambridgeshire County LD Council Group	18	4	56,200
Basingstoke LD Council Group	23	2	39,637
Gateshead LD Council Group	14	1	36,412
Lewisham LD Council Group	14	1	29,415
City of York LD Council Group	12	2	26,583
TOTAL	190	21	579,830

respectively).[3] As with the other two parties, therefore, unincorporated associations are a means by which members and supporters of the Conservative party raise money themselves and direct it to local constituency parties; the only difference is that in the Labour and Liberal Democrat parties the predominant source is their local government-elected representatives.

A considerable proportion of the money donated to accounting units was thus being redistributed from one part of a political party's organisational structure to another, although not from the central party organisations. This was also the case with some of the donations from individuals. Among the 943 Liberal Democrat individual donations over the full decade, for example, 41 were from MPs (totalling £308,852), another 232 (£491,027) were from individuals who self-identified as local government councillors, and a further 22 (£76,636) were from either peers or members of other elected bodies. In their annual accounts for 2010, for example, the local parties for Oldham East and Saddleworth and for Oxford West and Abingdon respectively reported incomes of £39,512 and £39,470 from the local Liberal Democrat council group. Similarly in the Labour party, 126 of the individual donations (£509,840, one-fifth of the total) were received from MPs: no self-identified councillors gave money to the party's accounting units, however. Individual elected members donating to local parties was also not characteristic of the Conservative party: only 48 of the 3,631 donations from individuals were from MPs, for example, totalling £244,207; again, there were none from self-identified councillors.

Finally, Table 4.10 shows that all three parties obtained substantial sums from company donors, but in total the Conservatives received twice as much as the other two combined; the average Conservative donation at £10,520 was much larger than that to its two opponents – Labour, £4,544, Liberal Democrat, £3,107. These sums are small overall relative to the amounts donated to the central party organisations in recent decades – mainly to the Conservatives and to a lesser extent Labour – which have been the focus of much attention from those who claim that such donations are a means by which business people gain political access. Websites such as searchthemoney.com scour all of the material published by the Electoral Commission and in the Register

---

[3] The National Conservative Draws Society was highlighted as a 'private members' society' by a trade union website (http://union-news.co.uk/2012/03/revealed-tory-union-members-donate-1m-to-keep-cameron-in-downing-st). Most of its donations go to the party headquarters, but seven constituency accounting units received money during 2007-10.

Table 4.10: The largest 10 company donors to constituency accounting units, by party, 2007-10

Company	Main activity	Number of		£
		Donations	Constituencies	
Conservative				
JCB Research	Construction equipment	26	13	285,000
Crescent Properties	Construction	23	1	273,029
Caledonia	Investment trust	25	12	168,000
Stalbury Trustees	Conservative lobbyist	35	25	148,006
Albert Building	Office buildings	26	1	98,149
AB Produce	Agricultural servicing	20	2	72,579
Chester & County	Property	12	1	63,000
Norbrook Labs	Veterinary pharmaceuticals	3	1	43,000
Canary Wharf	Property management	4	2	43,800
Growth Financial	Investment	4	1	35,000
TOTAL		178	59	1,229,563
Labour				
Barnes and Richmond Labour Club		10	1	56,720
Kingswood Labour Club		1	1	40,000
River Front Properties	Property development	7	1	25,602
Urban Visions	Property development	10	1	21,934
BM Creative	Entertainment agent	4	3	20,000
GLC	Hedge fund	2	2	20,000

(continued)

Table 4.10: The largest 10 company donors to constituency accounting units, by party, 2007-10 (continued)

Company	Main activity	Number of		£
		Donations	Constituencies	
Labour (continued)				
Ruobal Properties	Property development	10	1	18,197
Castle Point Gas & Heating	Plumbing	4	1	17,500
Opal Property	Property development	4	1	10,901
Bestways	Wholesaler	1	1	10,000
TOTAL		53	13	240,854
Liberal Democrat				
Joseph Rowntree Reform Trust	Charity	42	10	232,771
Hereford Liberal Club		23	1	79,605
Dawley Estates	Property development	20	2	64,781
Reading Liberal Club		61	2	60,314
Betterworld	Book retailer	19	14	52,500
Merthyr Tydfil Car Auctions	Automobiles	6	3	47,400
Hampden Buildings	Estate management	12	1	33,000
Scarborough Liberal Clubhouse		7	1	31,850
Magdalen Hall Co	Political activities	14	1	21,873
IPA Consulting	Management consultancy	3	1	19,000
TOTAL		207	36	643,094

of Members' Interests to identify the main donors and recipients. Its website lists the amounts received by all Conservative MPs, including donations to their local party and those received from individuals as well as companies and other organisations.

Whereas companies and their owners give money to a national party because they support (and in most cases hope to benefit from) its policies, most of those contributing to a local party are probably seeking support from an MP on local issues. This is illustrated by the nature of the top 10 company donors to each of the three main parties in Table 4.10, which lists not only the donors but, where it has been possible to identify them by web searches, their main business. Many are in either property development or construction and are locally focused companies donating to local parties. Among Conservative donors, for example, all 23 donations by Crescent Properties went to the Hampstead & Highgate party, and on the Labour list all 10 from Urban Visions went to the Rochdale constituency party, whose co-founder was Simon Danczuk, MP for Rochdale since 2010. Similarly Ruobal Properties focused all of its donations on party organisations in Hertfordshire, and Hampden Buildings, an Aylesbury estate management company, gave all of its 12 donations to the Aylesbury Liberal Democrats. Companies in other types of business similarly focused their donations on a small number of constituencies in areas where they operated; the wholesaler Bestways made a donation to the Bolton South East Labour party, for example; Merthyr Tydfil Car Auctions gave money to three South Wales Liberal Democrat constituency parties; and AB Produce made several donations each to Conservative accounting units in Lancashire West and Leicestershire North West (the company's main base is in South Derbyshire).

Overall, therefore, company donors to constituency parties involve local businesses providing money for local campaigns, perhaps as a general expression of support for the party's policies, but perhaps too in the hope that their support might be reciprocated by assistance with their local projects. But there are some exceptions: Labour's two largest company donors were local Labour Clubs that had been incorporated; and Magdalen Hall Company (which made 14 donations to the Colchester Liberal Democrats) is classified by one website (192.com) as 'Activities of political organisations'; its building (its main asset, a former church hall) is leased to Colchester Liberal Democrats to house both the constituency party's own activities and the local Liberal Democrat MP's constituency office, and 34 per cent of its share capital is owned by them – they have the right to nominate two directors.

Conclusions

The sources of funds used by candidates to finance their general election campaigns are far from transparent. In most cases, their returns to the Electoral Commission of the amounts spent on both their long and short campaigns in 2010 exactly equalled the amount spent; no information is given as to the source(s) drawn on, but the clear implication is that the money was received as a single sum, either directly from the local party or indirectly through a fighting fund or similar organisational structure (such as the collective units – Gloucestershire Conservatives, for example, and the North Wiltshire Group, discussed in Chapter Three). In some cases, it may be possible to reconstruct the sources of income from local party accounts, but because most of these have a turnover that does not require them to make annual returns to the Electoral Commission, as shown in Chapter Three, this is only possible for a minority of candidates. In the majority of cases – and the great majority of Labour and Liberal Democrat candidates – the sources of their campaigning funds are unknown.

A partial corrective to this situation is the requirement for all individual donations to local parties to be reported to the Electoral Commission. These data, although informative, provide a far from complete picture, however. The amounts received through donations to local parties in 2010 reported in Table 4.3 cover only around half of the total expended on the long and short campaigns reported in Table 2.1: 54 per cent in the case of the Conservatives, 49 per cent for Labour, and 39 per cent for the Liberal Democrats. (Some donations received in previous years may have been retained for use on the 2010 campaign, but there is little evidence of local parties accumulating reserves for that purpose, although the transfer of money to fighting funds undoubtedly was designed for that purpose.) Furthermore, although those data provide some enlightenment on income sources, in a substantial number of cases – although varying across the three political parties – many of the reported donations are from bodies associated with the parties themselves but legally independent of them, in that they are not registered as accounting units and so are not subject to the transparency requirements legislated for since 2000.

FIVE

Party funding futures

The research reported in the preceding chapters has shown that money matters in constituency campaigns at British general elections. Candidates who spend relatively large amounts in the last few months and weeks before election day in general run more intensive campaigns than those who spend relatively little: they contact more voters, display more posters, distribute more leaflets, and have more canvassers working for them on the streets and doorsteps. Not surprisingly, in general more is spent in marginal constituencies either defending narrow majorities or seeking victories where the margin of defeat last time was small. But even within that group of seats there is considerable variation in campaign intensity: some candidates and their local parties are better able to raise money for their campaigns than others in comparable circumstances.

Analysis of local parties' annual accounts suggests that this variation in campaign intensity reflects the relative health of local parties. Few local Labour parties have an annual income or expenditure exceeding the £25,000 threshold for reporting their financial situation to the Electoral Commission, for example, and although on that measure the Liberal Democrats have more healthy local parties than Labour, compared to the Conservatives their local foundations for conducting intensive local campaigns are also relatively weak across the country. Those local parties with weak finances tend to have fewer members and are unable to attract much money through donations and other fundraising devices (on which see Friedman, 2013). The result is that their candidates' campaigns tend to lack intensity. This was exemplified by Unlock Democracy's 2006 survey of 286 local parties, the report of which included a section entitled 'National wealth, local squalor' (Graham, 2006). At the 2005 General Election, outside the marginal constituencies there was little evidence of direct contact between local parties and electors: 'at least 67 per cent of the population received no personal contact from any of the three main parties'; and in safe Labour seats this figure was estimated as 82 per cent. (On contact patterns at the 2010 General Election, see Johnston et al, 2012a, 2012b.)[1]

[1] A survey by the Electoral Reform Society of the distribution of leaflets at local government elections in 2013 came to a similar conclusion (www.electoral-reform.org.uk/blog/where-are-my-leaflets).

In some respects the lack of local resources has become increasingly irrelevant, as the parties centralise aspects of the local campaigns. Thus Unlock Democracy's report noted that in 2005 the Conservatives, rather than mobilise resources to contact voters on their doorsteps, spent £4.5 million on direct mail targeted at just 800,000 potential voters in marginal seats (the total electorate then was over 44 million). Their average local expenditure per voter on the short campaign in the constituencies then was 7 pence, but on those 800,000 targeted voters it spent 80 times that amount: 'Rather than working on the principle of convincing as many voters as possible of your argument through time consuming personal contact, it targets people [by direct mail] who on the basis of statistical data are likely to support the party'. The report claimed that such 'targeting itself is a major contributing factor to increasing voter alienation and disengagement', US and British research having shown that people are more likely to be convinced to turn out by face-to-face contact, and it questioned whether 'the minimum level of campaigning in lesser target seats is providing a sufficient level of communication to the electorate to sustain good, informative, participatory democracy'. Local parties need both people and money but 'the more political parties centralise their campaign operations, the more local activism dwindles, meaning that parties have to centralise and target resources even more' – a vicious downward spiral.

Fisher and Denver (2008, 2009) have charted this shift between the 1992 and 2005 elections: the average number of members in the local parties surveyed fell from 1,542 to 892 for the Conservatives, from 444 to 349 for Labour and 166 to 137 for the Liberal Democrats (although for both the Conservatives and Liberal Democrats the averages were higher in 2005 than they were in 2001, when a further Labour landslide was widely expected: the figures for 2001 were 646 and 130 respectively). Given the fall in membership and the implications this had for the ability to mount labour-intensive local campaigns (Fisher, 2000), the parties had to develop new means of contacting voters including telephones, direct mail and the internet. Fisher and Denver calculated indices of traditional (that is, labour-intensive) and modern (greater use of technology) campaigning, and showed that substantial decline in the former over the four elections was compensated by comparable growth in the latter, especially in the parties' target seats. Parties, they concluded, were modernising their local campaigning procedures 'partly through the availability of technology and partly through necessity (due to membership decline)' (Fisher and Denver, 2009, p 208) – but their assessment of the impact of the two suggested that voters were more likely to respond positively to the traditional forms of campaigning:

> Computers, call centres, direct mail and the like may help and may represent the best that parties can do in the circumstances, but they are simply not an adequate replacement for doorstep canvassing, leafleting, putting up posters, number taking at polling stations and knocking-up on the day. (p 209)

The trend continued in 2010, with even greater emphasis on modern campaigning methods (Fisher et al, 2011); nevertheless, analyses once again showed that, irrespective of the amount spent on the local campaign, the more campaign workers a candidate had in the constituency (which included both party members brought in from other seats where the outcome was more certain as well as non-member volunteer helpers), the greater the percentage of the electorate canvassed face-to-face and the number of campaign workers active on polling day itself, the better the outcome (Hain, 2012; Fisher et al, 2013a).

The parties are increasingly managing local constituency campaigns from their central offices, therefore, although at the 2010 General Election only two of them were able to provide funding to local parties to enhance that activity. Both the Conservatives and, to a lesser extent, the Liberal Democrats invested large sums in the years preceding the 2010 General Election on target seat campaigns, aimed at laying the foundations – through high visibility profiles for their candidates – for the final push in defending seats where there was a possibility of defeat, and seeking victories where their opponents' hold was relatively weak. Although those campaigns had a crucial local component, however, they too, and especially the Conservatives', were only part of a wider strategy, much of which involved the central part of the organisation, through telephone polling and direct mailings. In the last few months before polling day, those two parties distributed little money towards their candidates' expenses, however, and funding of local campaigns had to rely on donations and other contributions that the local organisations and their candidates could raise. But, as Kavanagh and Cowley (2010, Chapter 11) detail, the central organisations continued their locally focused but nationally and regionally driven campaigning in what one Liberal Democrat campaigner called the 'direct mail election ... [with] more paper delivered to more houses than any campaign in British history' (p 232). Labour, for example, distributed 8.3 million items through the mail between 2008 and early 2010, across 138 seats, and followed this up later in 2010 with 2.6 million further letters to those identified as its 'core supporters' in the targeted seats and 4.8 million 'swing voters' – the latter in particular focused on those who had previously voted Liberal Democrat, warning them that to do so again could result in a Conservative victory. Three-quarters of Labour's expenditure nationally went on those direct mailings, and a donation of £200,000 on the final weekend before election day allowed it to send out a further 400,000 items, which arrived on election-eve. Although it lacked the financial resources to fund its local parties' campaigns, Labour also ran an activist- and volunteer-staffed national telephone call centre which contacted 4-7,000 voters daily during the final campaign weeks (and 10,000 in the last week); its database was built up over the preceding years, and relevant information sold to constituency campaign organisations for a small price (Kavanagh and Cowley, 2010). Nevertheless, the party – like its opponents – believed that such materials complemented local activity only, and that 'where we work, we win'; its own surveys indicated that the more voters contacted in a constituency the better the Labour candidate's relative performance. Thus the Conservatives had a financial edge, but their opponents could counter this – at least in the last few hectic weeks – by intensive campaigning on the streets and doorsteps undertaken by volunteers (Fisher et al, 2011, 2013a).

Money alone cannot buy electoral success, therefore: it is a necessary, but far from sufficient, component of a campaign. The last two decades have seen considerable concern expressed, including by the political parties themselves, about the amount of money spent on election campaigns, with several inquiries (some conducted within and others outwith the state apparatus) into its extent and nature, with suggestions for reform. The next section reviews some of those recent considerations of the issue, as a framework for a final discussion bringing the results of the research reported here into the ongoing debates about party funding and its possible reform. (A full chronology of the various initiatives on the reform of party funding is provided by Hitchins and Gay, 2009, updated in Kelly, 2013.)

The reform of party funding, 1997-

In November 2011, the Committee on Standards in Public Life (CSPL, 2011) published its report, *Political party finance: ending the big donor culture*. This was the latest in a series of reports seeking to reform party funding produced in the last two decades, none of which has had the full impact its authors hoped for. Changes have been made – notably through the PPERA 2000, the Political Parties and Elections Act 2009, and, in a minor but important way, the Election Administration Act 2006. The major reason why these Acts have only partially achieved the reform sought is because there has been a lack of consensus among the main political parties on the way forward. All have claimed a desire to achieve a full package of reforms and made manifesto commitments to that end, but they have been unable to agree on what that package should contain. Although a party with a majority in the House of Commons could pass legislation to achieve its own goals (even though it may face considerable opposition in the House of Lords), this has not been attempted with regard to the issues that most separate the parties. It is generally accepted that such a major constitutional change should have all-party agreement, and that has been elusive.

This chapter does not provide a full history of those various reform attempts of the last two decades. Two reports from the House of Commons Library – *The funding of political parties* (Gay et al, 2007) and *In brief – party funding* (Kelly, 2012) – outline the major developments; a number of books on this subject have been published recently (see, for example, Ewing, 2007; Rowbottom, 2010; Ewing et al, 2011); and Koß (2011) has placed the issue in a theoretical and comparative international context.

The Committee on Standards in Public Life was established in 1994 following a number of financial 'scandals' involving MPs; its terms of reference were extended in 1997 by the then Prime Minister to enable it to investigate and produce its 1998 report, *The funding of political parties in the United Kingdom* (CSPL, 1998). It noted three main aspects of the contemporary situation relevant to its inquiry (p 1):

- '... the parties' belief that elections can only be won by the expenditure (mainly on advertising) of vast sums of money [that] has given rise to something of an arms race ... [which] in turn has put enormous pressure on party fundraisers to devise innovative ways of attracting donations';
- The perception, stemming from this situation, that the growing number of large donations 'gives credibility to accusations that money buys access to politicians'; from which
- 'It is a small step from the thought that money buys access (encouraged by some party fundraisers) to the widespread public perception that money can buy influence.'

The Committee reported that it found no evidence that influence had been bought (though see the anecdotal – albeit very partial – evidence to the contrary in Friedman, 2013), but that nevertheless the perception is that it is 'extremely damaging' (see the essays in Ewing and Issacharoff, 2006). To counter that situation, it made a range of proposals aimed very largely at ensuring transparency through clear rules regarding from whom donations could be accepted, the public disclosure of all donations above a certain threshold, the auditing and publication of party accounts, and the establishment of an independent Electoral Commission to oversee and enforce this new regime. No limits were suggested for the size of donations, but it was recommended that, to slow the 'arms race', there should be a limit (suggested as £20 million) on the amount that a political party could spend nationally on a general election campaign; that limit should be additional to the regulated amounts that candidates could spend on their campaigns, as discussed in Chapter Two earlier. The Committee's detailed arguments (p 123) suggested that integration of those amounts into the national totals would not only be administratively cumbersome but also potentially inequitable; for example, candidates may have no control over national spending, but if their party had over-spent on their candidacies they could face punishment for something of which they personally were not guilty. A further consequence could be that the parties nationally would direct virtually all of their resources into a relatively small number of target seats, which was democratically undesirable.

This report led to the publication of a White Paper and draft Bill, which became the PPERA 2000. An early evaluation by the Committee – *The first seven reports: a review of progress* (CSPL, 2001) – indicated that the great majority of its recommendations had been implemented. The report thus established the foundations for an evolving system of regulation based on three of the Committee's seven principles of public life, adumbrated when it was established – integrity, accountability and openness. Its key guiding principle regarding party funding was transparency. Its general argument was that rather than impose a regulatory regime that could be cumbersome to administer, a regime requiring returns, which would be published, on from whom money was obtained and how it was spent, would be the best way of both ensuring that parties acted ethically and holding them to account. Some regulations were suggested and implemented – on from whom donations could and could not be accepted, for example, and on total expenditure by a party in the year before a general election, with the consequent necessity for political parties to be registered, and the Electoral Commission was established as an independent regulatory body, but the overall intent was that openness would ensure accountability without a burdensome set of regulatory procedures.

In 2004, following an internal review, with external consultation, of the operation of the 2000 Act, the Electoral Commission published *The funding of political parties: report and recommendations*, as part of its statutory requirement to keep that and other matters under review. Its recommendations were set within a clear statement of the important roles that political parties play by:

- crystallising political, economic and social interests within society and offering voters alternative policies reflecting those interests;
- integrating individuals and groups within the political system;
- organising campaigns to mobilise voter support for policies and thus 'make possible the conduct of effective government' (p 7);
- recruiting political players as candidates for public office; and
- making public policy.

To undertake those functions, parties must be adequately funded, and their funding sources should be transparent. Evaluation of the current situation suggested an imbalance between the national and local components of the main political parties. The Commission believed that 'the electorate is better served by campaigns that engage directly with voters' (p 3) rather than the more remote activities channelled through the national media as well as impersonal contacts such as direct mailings; its research indicated consistently that 'voters respond better to local communications and campaigning than national level political advertising' (p 59).

To achieve a change in the national–local balance the Commission recommended that national spending limits on general election campaigns should be reduced by about one-quarter from the then current levels (around £19 million); there should also be 'a significant increase in candidate spending limits to encourage more activity at the local level' (p 4) and greater transparency in the reporting of local income and expenditure. The recommendation that 'candidates' spending limits be raised to enable more activity at the local level' was not accompanied by specific figures, although the Commission suggested that they should be approximately doubled and apply to a four-month period ending on polling day (p 61; the regulated period for expenditure on elections to both devolved bodies and the European Parliament was four months, although this did not also apply to candidates' spending; those bodies had fixed terms so that it was much more straightforward to have a defined period ending on election day).

These recommendations did appear somewhat paradoxical, given the observation that 'as the statements of accounts data show, the pressure to raise significant sums of money to fund election campaigns has tended to place considerable strain on party finances, calling into question the financial viability of some. In the context of a closely fought campaign, the pressure to spend up to the current expenditure limits will be greater, placing further pressures on limited party resources' (pp 57-8; this comment appears to be mainly directed at spending on campaigns nationally but, as the data discussed in Chapter Two earlier clearly indicate, the pressures observed at the national level are even greater in many local parties). There is an implicit assumption that by increasing spending limits, parties would be able to raise more money to fund their campaigns ('a higher limit would provide the opportunity for candidates to run more effective campaigns to ensure that their messages reach more voters'; p 61) – but (as the analyses reported here suggest) such facility may be much greater in some parties (notably the Conservatives) than others.

The Commission also recommended that the cost of any local campaigning activity, within whatever period is set for spending subject to an expenditure limit, should apply 'regardless of when the person is declared to be a candidate' (p 63). This would cover expenditure clearly aimed at promoting an individual's cause with a local electorate but not covered by the current regulations because of what was known as the 'triggering' issue. There had long been uncertainty as to the period for which the 'short campaign' regulations in the Representation of the People Act applied. This was clarified in the 2000 Act as being 'after the date when he becomes a candidate', defined as the date on which Parliament was dissolved or, if later, the date on which either the person was nominated or the candidacy was self-declared. As such, it did not cover expenditure before Parliament was dissolved, an issue of increasing concern to the Labour party given the experience of the large donations made by Lord Ashcroft and others to local Conservative target seats before the 2005 General Election campaign. (Electoral Commission data show that Lord Ashcroft's company, Bearwood Corporate Services Ltd, made 135 separate donations to local accounting units in 2004-05, totalling £914,067.37; during the same period, two others with whom he worked on that target seat strategy – the Midlands Industrial Council and Lord Leonard Steinberg – made 44 grants totalling £413,189.95 and 15 totalling £115,480.53 respectively.)

These issues were taken up by the House of Commons Constitutional Affairs Committee in 2006, which published a report, *Party funding*.

It too saw 'merit in the focus of campaigning being shifted from the national to the local level' (p 28), and recommended a 'modest' increase in local spending limits. It also noted that, because of the increased number of elections now being held, particularly in the parts of the UK with devolved institutions, and the growth of what has become known as 'continuous campaigning', it agreed with witnesses who told the Committee that, in effect, there is now no 'fallow period ... when parties are not using their money for electioneering' (p 30). Instead of extending the regulated period somewhat, as the Electoral Commission had recommended, therefore, the Committee argued for a package of measures that would 'enable the expenditure of all parties, both at local and national level, to be capped over a five-year accounting period', with each election having its own expenditure caps within that overall figure (p 32; implicitly, such regulations would exclude local government elections and apply only to elections for the House of Commons, devolved bodies and the European Parliament).

In its response to that report (Constitutional Affairs Committee, 2007), the Labour government noted that declining party membership has stimulated changes in campaigning strategies, leading 'to a reduction in the number of local activists ... [that] subsequently reduced the direct contact that parties have with members of the public' (p 2). It expressed its concerns thus (p 5):

> Campaigning is a core activity for political parties which provides information and encourages participation and engagement. It is the means by which political choices are presented to the voters. However, we are concerned about the negative public perception of impersonal and expensive campaigns and their potential impact on participation and engagement should campaign costs continue to escalate.

It therefore agreed with the Committee's recommendations for a tighter cap on national spending and a modest increase in local spending limits that would be regulated for a longer period of time (p 6), although recognising that separating out national from candidate-centred local spending would be difficult. There was an implicit assumption that raising the limits would encourage more fundraising activity and spending, which the evidence of the last decade discussed in the preceding chapters discredits. In 2010 only a few local parties – especially those in some target seats – were able to raise and spend anything like the maximum allowed on their candidates' campaigns; raising the maximum is therefore as likely to allow a relatively small number of (especially Conservative) local parties to spend even more on their candidates' campaigns, and make the unevenness portrayed in our earlier chapters more pronounced. This could change, if the Conservatives find it more difficult to raise money and one of the other parties is able to increase its donations substantially, but it is extremely doubtful that all three parties could become well-funded simultaneously.

Following a further scandal – the so-called 'cash for honours' issue – in March 2006 the Prime Minister asked a former senior civil servant, Sir Hayden Phillips, to review the funding of political parties, with particular reference to:

- the case for state funding and whether it should be enhanced by a cap on the size of donations; and
- the transparency of parties' funding.

Sir Hayden published *An interim assessment* in October 2006 which included a full review of the various issues, surveyed the main choices available and set out questions for further discussion. The options discussed were:

- Minimum change to the status quo, which comprised two main elements:
  - limits on candidate spending on both of what is now termed the 'short campaign' and the national campaign (the latter were set in the PPERA 2000, as £30,000 multiplied by the number of seats that the party contests, so that for a party contesting all 632 seats in Great Britain in 2010 the limit was just under £19 million[2]); and
  - the various reporting requirements for donations and annual accounts also introduced in that Act.
- Increased transparency and greater control on expenditure.
- A cap on donations in addition to greater transparency and expenditure control.
- To compensate for the probable loss of income, greater levels of public funding for parties, which could be based on:
  - a general subsidy to each party based on its popularity (probably measured by its number of votes at the previous election);

---

[2] The deposit for candidates – returned if they obtain over 5 per cent of the votes cast – is £500, so the total initial cost of fielding candidates in all 632 seats would be £316,000.

- a targeted subsidy to support particular activities (such as policy development); and
- a voter-led incentive scheme, in which parties could receive public funding through, for example, tax relief on donations going either to the party or to the donors, matching funding, a voucher scheme by which electors make a donation to a party when they vote, and a grant per party member.

Sir Hayden submitted his final report, *Strengthening democracy: fair and sustainable funding of political parties*, six months later (Phillips, 2007). His main conclusions were that:

- the status quo with no cap on donations is unsustainable, and a cap should be introduced, with extended regulation;
- expenditure on general election campaigns should be reduced;
- 'The price of a fairer, more stable system of party political financing may be some increase in public funding, that should in turn be linked to measures designed to encourage greater democratic engagement';
- better and clearer information for the general public on sources of party income; and
- an expanded role for the Electoral Commission was needed to implement a new regime.

Much of what he recommended was common ground between the political parties, but two issues remained in contention: the design of a limit on donations and controls on party spending. Regarding the latter, he recommended that they apply for the full period between elections, and comprise two parts: a total to cover running costs for the full five years (perhaps £150 million), and a 'general election premium' (of perhaps £20 million). Those figures would exclude all accounting units spending less than £40,000 per annum (and therefore include the amounts spent by some of the larger ones, as discussed in Chapter Three, but create a potential loophole that some local parties could exploit) as well as candidates' campaign expenses.

Sir Hayden further recommended that a final settlement should be reached by consensus, should 'respect the interests of smaller parties and of parties which have yet to be created', and 'Nothing should be agreed until everything is agreed'. In his letter to the Prime Minister, he said that there is 'an overriding public interest in acting now to reform party funding', which 'will require tough decisions on all sides', and he recommended that the government 'invite the three largest parties to come together to make a determined effort to solve the remaining areas of dispute'; he agreed to chair such discussions.

Six months later, *The Guardian* (31 October 2007) reported that those talks had failed and Sir Hayden had 'given up hope of achieving agreement'. It claimed that the sticking points were: the Conservatives' demand that all donations be capped at £50,000, 'including any money raised by individual trade unions', which Labour rejected; and Labour's demand for new regulations on expenditure by candidates between general elections, which the Conservatives resisted. In *The Guardian's* view the talks collapsed because 'each party [was] anxious that the other might manage to entrench financial advantages in law'. Sir Hayden confirmed this in a retrospective paper (Phillips, 2012), which focused on the five formal meetings of representatives from the three largest parties that he chaired in 2007, as well as many bilateral sessions he held with individual parties. All of the discussions were based on four principles: that nothing should be agreed until all was agreed; that a fair system need not initially be uniform in its application but should aim for a common outcome over time; that a new settlement should be reached by consensus; and that any solution should be constructed to serve the long-term interests of Parliament as a whole, not short-term party advantage. After the early discussions, when he perceived 'a chance to escape from that trap of short-termism and myopia', he circulated a draft agreement, which proposed a cap of £50,000 on all donations, which would apply to trade unions, but their members' affiliation fees would not be aggregated into a single union donation. On tighter spending controls, he repeated his limit for running costs over the five-year cycle as £150 million as well as a £20 million general election premium, with how those sums should be disaggregated by year and between parts of the party organisations left to them to determine individually. Finally, on public funding he proposed a matching scheme comprising a £10 state allocation for every £10 raised in donations as well as a pence-per-vote allocation based on the results of the last general election.

No agreement was reached, however, because the two largest parties had different priorities. For the Conservatives, large donations were the main problem because they believed that the general public distrusted big donors – whether individual, corporate or trade union (and the role of affiliation fees in the latter; the Conservatives wanted individual union members to agree to any part of their fee being part of such a donation; on the issue of trade union contributions, see Ewing, 1982, 2011). For Labour, the main issue was the spending arms race – for a relatively brief period in the 1990s, given the unpopularity of the Conservatives and New Labour's assiduous courting of business support, Labour attracted substantial donations from wealthy individuals but these soon declined, and it was clear that they were unlikely to become a permanent source of substantial income. In addition, both were wary about the likely public response to proposals for state funding. The main reasons for the failure to agree were political, and with the high hurdle of consensus on all issues this meant that if any party had a problem with any part of the package, the exercise would fail. Sir Hayden wondered whether the parties really wanted the talks to succeed:

> It turned out that it had been better to travel hopefully than to arrive as when we were in sight of our destination the passengers started to argue about where they wanted to go. As we were on a democratic trip, the crew could not insist that we stuck to the itinerary we had proposed to them and which they initially responded to positively. (p 322)

The Guardian's 31 October 2007 leader concluded that 'The fact that all main parties found fault with Sir Hayden's sensible proposals surely counts in their favour. They should form the basis of any new law'. Instead, the Labour government decided to proceed with legislation reflecting its own position, and in June 2008 the Home Secretary published a White Paper, *Party finance and expenditure in the United Kingdom: the government's proposals* (Ministry of Justice, 2008), based on parts of Sir Hayden's list. This was followed by publication of a Political Parties and Elections Bill 2008, which addressed the issue of preventing candidates from spending unlimited amounts on their local campaigns prior to the dissolution of Parliament. In previous legislation, expenditure was only regulated in the period after an individual became a candidate for a constituency, officially after Parliament was dissolved and an election called (although most candidates were 'adopted' by their local parties well before that date). This was replaced in the Bill by the statement that:

> A reference ... to a candidate at an election, in relation to election expenses, includes (where the context allows it) a reference to a person who becomes a candidate at the election after the expenses have been incurred.

This means that, according to the House of Commons Research Paper (Gay and White, 2008), any individual's expenditure is subject to regulation whenever it is incurred if it was 'intended to promote their election' (that is, over the full five years of the election cycle). The maximum amount that could be spent was not specified, since this was covered by previous legislation, and could be amended, by Order in Council, at any time.

This proposal was subject to considerable debate in Parliament, and the Electoral Commission raised substantial concerns regarding its implementation and regulation: how, for example, does one determine whether spending three or more years before an expected election counts towards promotion of a candidate's cause? The government recognised this, and when the Bill returned to the House of Commons from the Committee stage (where discussion of the issue had been curtailed), it introduced amendments that created the limits on 'long campaign' spending in the final months before Parliament was dissolved, as long as that did not occur earlier than 55 months after the previous election (these are detailed above, in Chapter Two). Such a measure covering a longer period had initially been proposed as part of an Electoral Administration Bill in 2005 but was withdrawn in the face of considerable and widespread opposition. Once again, such a proposal lacked support from opposition parties (especially the Conservatives), and in its place the government proposed regulation of spending on specified matters in the last months of a Parliament before dissolution, even if the expenditure was incurred before that period but the materials were used after the 'trigger' date (which, for the first application of the regulations, would be set at 1 January 2010). Alternative trigger dates were suggested in Parliamentary debates during 2008-09 to lengthen the period (to either 10, 18 or even 36 months before the last day on which an election could be held, for example), but the opposition parties indicated that they were content with the government's proposals; these were added to the Bill without a division and implemented at the next year's general election. The items of expenditure covered by the regulations, as set out in the Electoral Administration Act 2006, were:

- advertising of any nature, whatever medium used;
- unsolicited material addressed to electors, whether by name or to their address;
- transport of any persons to any place, by whatever means;
- public meetings of any kind;
- the services of an election agent; and
- accommodation and administrative costs.

These headings were used in the published reports of spending on the long and short campaigns at the 2010 General Election (see Table 2.2 earlier).

The Committee on Standards in Public Life returned to the issue in 2010, following the 2009 'MPs' expenses scandal'; it recognised that although there had been substantial changes in the regulation regime following its 1998 report, nevertheless there were still issues that needed to be addressed because of continued 'high levels of public suspicion', a 'situation that is unsustainable, damaging to confidence in democracy' and thereby presenting a 'serious need for reform' (CSPL, 2011, p 8). It made four main recommendations: the first two dealt with donations, that there should be a total limit of £10,000 in donations from an individual or organisation to a party within a calendar year, and that this requirement should include trade unions; one was concerned with campaign spending – the existing limits should be cut by 15 per cent; and the final one proposed public funding to parties, at a rate of around £3 per vote obtained in a Westminster election and £1.50 per vote in elections to devolved bodies and the European Parliament.

The case for a cap on donations continued earlier arguments. That for a reduction in campaign spending was introduced because 'it would be unacceptable, in current circumstances, to ask taxpayers to provide a higher subsidy without simultaneously obliging the parties to cut their spending' (p 10). The detailed recommendations regarding the latter were (p 14):

> 16 The parties should open discussions with a view to replacing the different limits on campaign spending for different elections with a single limit covering all elections in a single Westminster Parliamentary cycle;
> 17. The long and short campaigns should, for simplicity, be combined into a single regulated period for candidate spending in line with the four month period for elections to the devolved legislatures and the European Parliament;
> 18. Existing definitions of regulated campaign expenditure should be looked at again in the light of the standardisation of party accounts, to guard against significant under-reporting.

With regard to spending on the national campaigns in the 365 days preceding a general election, the Committee noted that the spending limits set in the 2000 Act had not been changed since; although this meant that there had been a real terms decline in the total that could be spent of some 30 per cent, it had received virtually no evidence that those limits were burdensome in 2010. Instead, it reported that 'We received evidence to suggest that political parties could and should reduce their campaign spending, particularly on billboard advertising and direct mailing, both of which are unpopular with many voters' (p 56), with one Liberal Democrat MP telling the Committee that much campaign expenditure is 'actually rather wasteful and badly applied'. The Committee further noted that both Labour and the Liberal Democrats had reduced their spending on such items in 2010 because of financial constraints, which demonstrated that 'the use of volunteers and the internet made it possible to run reasonably effective campaigns at less cost' (p 59). Regarding spending by candidates, the report said very little, noting that few spent close to the allowed maxima in 2010 (although Conservative candidates spent on average at least half as much again as their Labour and Liberal Democrat opponents); it therefore concluded that there was 'no compelling case' for increasing the limits (p 57).

In its detailed arguments, the Committee noted that although the introduction of regulated expenditure in the four-month 'long campaign' period increased transparency, this was of little 'useful purpose' (p 81) because so few candidates spent much during that period in 2010; the Electoral Commission, responsible for collating the returns, had argued that they introduced 'additional confusion and complexity'. (In 2010, 130 out of 631 Conservative candidates reported spending £15,000 or more during the long campaign period, of which 74 spent more than £20,000; the comparable figures for Labour candidates were 48 and 24 respectively, and for Liberal Democrats 63 and 35.) With the introduction of fixed-term parliaments, it would be easier to have a single regulated period. The Committee reported that it received conflicting advice regarding the impact of candidate spending, but noted the paradoxical situation that the regulations could be circumvented by national campaigning targeted on particular seats but with no reference to the candidate. It accepted that parties would concentrate their efforts on targeted marginal seats and did not think it 'appropriate to introduce new rules to prevent this'. Nor did it think there should be any regulation outside the statutory period; some witnesses had expressed concern about the target seats campaign masterminded by Lord Ashcroft for the Conservatives prior to 2010, but the Committee did not 'see anything improper about the parties behaving in this way provided the rules about donations and the actions of third parties are followed' (p 82). Indeed, it concluded that 'some of the resentment was caused by the source of the funds, the donor's alleged residence and the nature of the campaigning rather than the targeting of the seats'.

Labour and parts of the media frequently raised concerns about Lord Ashcroft's tax status, given the large donations from his company, Bearwood Corporate Services Ltd, to the Conservative party. Between 2007-10 it made 17 separate donations: only three were in cash (totalling £575,000), with the non-cash majority totalling £3,240,266. In addition, Lord Ashcroft's wife (Ms Susan Anstey) made six donations to the party between 6 May 2008 and 30 June 2009, totalling £393,120, which included donations of £250,000 in December 2008 and £124,520 in June 2009. The 2000 legislation outlawed all donations from outside the UK and a Labour MP asked the Electoral Commission to investigate whether the law had been broken in this case, The investigation took 14 months. The Commission reported that party officials refused to be interviewed and there was a problem because of 'Lord Ashcroft's inability to provide key documents, which he said had been destroyed' (*The Guardian*, 4 March 2010), and found that 'it had enough evidence to clear his £5.1m in donations as "legal, permissible and correctly reported"'.[3]

In response to Labour's attacks on the Conservatives' reliance on large donations from wealthy individuals, their opponents stressed the importance of Labour's many donations received from trade unions. A document published in 2010 immediately prior to the general election focused on one of the country's biggest unions, Unite, whose campaigning for Labour was being run by Charlie Whelan, formerly a special political adviser to Gordon Brown when he was Chancellor of the Exchequer (hence the pamphlet's subtitle, 'Charlie Whelan's new militant tendency'; Conservative party, 2010). It quoted a former Labour General Secretary, Peter Watt (who in 2010 published his exposé of his period of office under the title *Inside out: my story of betrayal and cowardice at the heart of New Labour*) as saying that, 'It is absolutely fair to describe the Labour party as the political wing of Unite'. The Electoral Commission's data show that between 2005 and 2010 Unite made 559 separate donations to Labour, totalling £14,792,314 – many to the central party but many also to local accounting units. The Conservatives' assessment of this expenditure 'since Q3 2005' (probably ending with the fourth quarter of 2009)

---

[3] See www.electoralcommission.org.uk/__data/assets/pdf_file/0009/87219/ Case-summary-Bearwood-Corporate-Services.pdf

claimed that 90 accounting units with incumbent Labour MPs had received £303,918.25 from Unite (this included £33,052.38 to 13 constituency parties represented by members of the cabinet), and 58 with non-incumbent candidates had received a further £156,643.56. In addition to that expenditure, Unite staff assisted Labour's 2010 campaigns; the union sent out direct mail and set up a telephone bank that targeted its members living in 90 constituencies where the margin of Labour's victory in 2005 was smaller than the number of local Unite members. (The Conservative party also pointed out that, in addition to its trade union income, Labour received £12,942,808 from Lord David Sainsbury between 2001-10, including some £6.5 million from 2007 on; he was Minister for Science and Innovation from 1998 to 2006.)

To date there has been no action on the Committee on Standards in Public Life's recommendations, and although the parties individually have committed themselves to further reform, the Coalition government formed in 2010 has not published any proposals. However, in 2013 two backbench MPs as well as a Liberal Democrat peer published a draft Bill (Tyrie et al, 2013) for a phased process of reform based on both the Committee and Sir Hayden Phillips' recommendations. It would end the public subsidy to candidates involved in the distribution of one free item of mailing to each elector, replacing them by a single booklet incorporating material from all candidates wishing to avail themselves of the opportunity – which, they estimated, would save £47 million over a six-year period, with that money being used to provide the recommended public subsidy to parties. It introduces, among other items, a cap on donations and loans to parties, their MPs and members (which would include candidates) and party associations ('where the membership of the association consists wholly or mainly of members of the party', thereby covering the current 'accounting units'); it sets out a framework for dealing with the collection of affiliation fees from trade unions and other organisations; introduces a system for regulation of 'third party expenditure' (see below); and reduces the overall spending cap for parties *and* their candidates at each general election, with limits on how much can be spent in any single constituency. Contemporaneously, the Electoral Commission (2013) published its recommendations for changing the current regulatory framework within the UK party and election finance laws (without proposing substantive alterations to those regulations), which included combining the 'long' and 'short' campaign periods, while noting that this 'would allow significantly higher levels of spending close to polling

day and could disadvantage candidates with relatively limited funds'
(p 96).[4]

Refocusing campaigns

A major message that emerges from much of the discussion about party
funding since the mid-1990s is that there should be more emphasis on
local, candidate-centred, campaigns at general elections and a reduction
in the very substantial expenditure on the national campaigns which
many, especially in parties whose financial resources in 2010 precluded
major spending then, believed to be unproductive. The arguments for
more local campaigning presented this as relatively inexpensive because
it would involve volunteers undertaking the canvassing, with money
just needed for leaflets and other supporting materials as well as the
costs of maintaining a staffed office. This revived concentration on local
activism would, it was hoped, reinvigorate local democracy, although
there was a widespread realisation that party memberships were much
smaller than in the early- and mid-20th century and unlikely to grow
again to those levels. Nevertheless, in some parties there was a desire
to constrain this hoped-for revival of local campaigning, because of
a fear that parties and candidates with access to substantial financial
resources could gain an electoral advantage.

The evidence discussed earlier in this book sustains that argument.
A large body of research over recent decades has invariably shown that
the amount spent by candidates on their general election campaigns is
significantly related to their shares of the votes cast – more money spent
means more votes (especially if the candidate is not of the governing
party), and less for their opponents. The money does not buy the votes,
but it contributes significantly towards the campaigning effort. Most
is spent on either advertising material (mainly leaflets and posters)
or staff, without whom it would be harder to organise and conduct
long-term campaigns. Without posters and, especially, leaflets, it is hard
to bring the candidate to the attention of a constituency's 70,000 or
more electors, and canvassers encountering potential supporters on the
street or doorstep want to leave something tangible to remind them

---

[4] Neither document includes recommendations that data on spending on local campaigns be collected and published by a central body – the Electoral Commission –
thereby ensuring transparency and full accountability. For example, the data quoted
in the Introduction to this book on spending at the 2013 Eastleigh by-election could
only be obtained from the local returning officer (at a fee), and that material is destroyed after one year.

of that contact and the promise they may have made to support the candidate. Thus higher levels of spending on materials and staff imply more intensive campaigns; even if it is the case, as some of the evidence presented to committees of inquiry discussed above suggests, that voters respond more readily to face-to-face interactions with candidates and party workers than more impersonal contacts. Nevertheless, money is needed to oil those campaigning activities and those who have more of it available tend to perform better.

Spending is not the only valid indicator of a campaign's intensity of course: some local parties may be able to mobilise more campaign workers than others, including both party members from other constituencies who have been convinced their efforts are more valuable there than in their own seats where the outcome is more certain, as well as non-party members, willing to work for the party but not to join it. The 2010 survey of constituency agents discussed in Chapter Two, for example, found that of 277 Conservative local parties, 79 had volunteers sent into their constituency from elsewhere, and 195 recruited non-party members to aid their campaigning; the comparable figures were 89 and 275 respectively for the 379 Labour agents surveyed, and 41 and 290 of the 350 Liberal Democrats (Fisher et al, 2013a).

Where were these tactics deployed? Looking first at the Conservatives, we focus on the marginal seats that they lost in 2010 and where victory was necessary if they were to form the next government. Of the constituencies for which we have data, spending was on average slightly higher on the short campaign in those where volunteers from other constituency parties were involved than in those where they were not (90 and 86 per cent of the maximum permitted respectively), and many more leaflets were produced locally (mean values of 144,727 and 95,750); the constituency parties that received volunteers also had more members on average (363) than those that did not (303). Almost all of the local parties involved recruited non-member campaigners; the small number that did not on average produced only 31,667 leaflets each compared to 142,788 for those that did recruit non-members. Clearly in general the more active local parties running the more intensive campaigns were also more likely to have volunteers directed to help them by the national and regional campaign coordinators and also to recruit non-members to participate in their activities, particularly leaflet delivery (Fisher et al, 2013a).

For Labour, we looked at the constituencies that they won by only narrow margins in 2005 and where their defensive strategy was focused in 2010. As with the Conservatives, the local parties that received volunteer workers sent in from other seats on average spent more on the short campaign (79 per cent) than those that did not (71 per cent), and produced many more leaflets locally (84,935 as against 35,772). Again, almost all recruited non-members; the small number that did not produced many fewer leaflets (17,500 on average) than those that did (72,963). Finally, for the Liberal Democrats we looked at all of their marginal constituencies, both those won in 2005 and those lost: around half had volunteers from other local parties and they on average spent 89 per cent of the maximum on their short campaigns as against 81 per cent by those with no such outside assistance. For all three parties, therefore, those whose local parties recruited non-members to participate in their campaigns tended to be those that were running the more intensive local campaigns in any case: to those that have (or are better prepared) shall be given.

In general, therefore, the more campaign workers involved the more that the party's candidate spent on the short campaign, as the graphs in Figure 5.1 show for each. These cover all local parties for which we have both short campaigning expenditure returns and reports of the number of workers from the agents' survey discussed in Chapter Two.

Figure 5.1: The relationship between the amount spent by each party on its candidates' short campaigns and the number of workers who participated in that campaign

(a) Conservative party

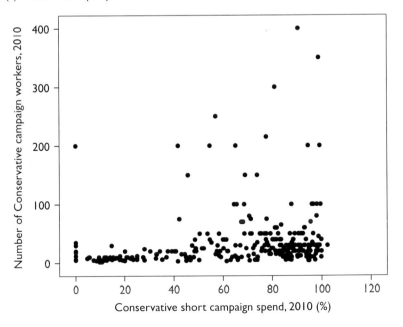

(b) Labour party

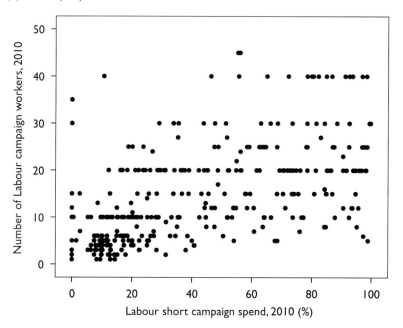

(c) Liberal Democrat party

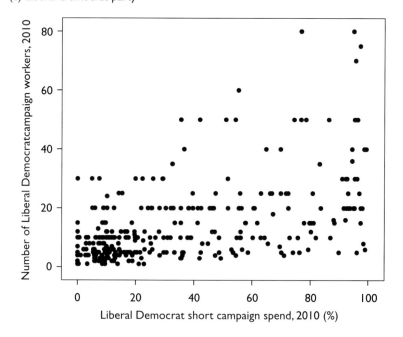

For each party there is a reasonably close relationship between the two indices of campaign effort, but in a relatively small number of constituencies in each case there were many more workers than usual for that amount of expenditure. The general relationships are rather hidden by the small number of outliers in those graphs – constituencies where there were many more campaign workers than average given the amount spent. There were few where there were many fewer workers than average for a given expenditure level. In Figure 5.1[b], therefore, we exclude the eight constituencies where Labour deployed 100 or more campaign workers in order to depict the general relationship more clearly. Labour mobilised few campaign workers in those constituencies where it spent very little – or vice versa – but there was only a small number where it spent a considerable amount but had just a small number of people out canvassing. (The considerable number of seats where the agent reported either 10, 20 or 40 workers suggests that rounding was frequently employed in the responses rather than exact numbers; it may have been that many agents did not know the exact numbers.) And the 'extra' workers helped: evidence shows that where a local party was able to mobilise more campaign workers than was the average for one spending that amount on the short campaign, the better its candidate's performance (Fisher et al, 2013a,b). Writing in *The Guardian* on 24 April 2000, Peter Preston claimed that party activists made no difference – he referred to 'the essentially peripheral role of their card-carrying foot soldiers'; several letters to the paper published two days later argued exactly the opposite, citing academic research, and the analyses reported here confirm their position.

Although some concern was expressed about levels of local spending in the debates and proposals regarding funding reforms summarised above, especially because of Labour's concern over the Ashcroft-inspired target seat campaigns, in general it has received less attention than either national spending levels or the many issues relating to donations. This may be because the amounts local parties spend are individually relatively small in comparison with the national expenditure but, as the totals discussed in Chapter Two suggest, in aggregate they are far from insignificant. For example, reported expenditure at the 2010 General Election by the national parties, according to the Electoral Commission, was: Conservatives, £16,682,874; Labour, £8,009,483; and Liberal Democrats, £4,787,593.[5] On the long and the short local campaigns combined (which cover only four months compared to the

[5] See https://pefonline.electoralcommission.org.uk/Search/CampaignExpenditure Search.aspx

full 12 months preceding the election for the national parties), their respective expenditure was £9,143,388, £5,959,672 and £4,712,340 (see Table 2.1). Thus Conservative candidate spending was 55 per cent of the cost of the party's national campaign (or approximately one-third of the party's total expenditure on the election); Labour's candidates spent 74 per cent of the national amount (that is, 43 per cent of its expenditure was in the constituencies); and Liberal Democrat candidates' campaigns in total came to 98 per cent of the central party's spending (some of which, as Chapter Four shows, went in donations to the local parties). Candidate spending is not a small component of the total expenditure on general election campaigns, therefore, and these figures do not include the amounts raised and spent before 2010, as well as, for the Conservatives and, especially, the Liberal Democrats, the substantial grants made to local parties in target seats to lay the foundations for the final months and weeks of the campaign.

Local donations

Although much of the debate about party funding focused on capping the size of individual donations (or the total amount any one donor could give in a single period, usually a year) most of this – at least implicitly – concentrated on donations to the national party organisations. Donations to local parties received little attention because although, as just indicated, the total amount spent is large, it has been spread across more than 600 constituencies where, in general election years at least, the maximum amount that can be spent in each during the last few months before polling day is little more than £40,000. Raising such relatively small amounts through large donations (compared to the situation for the national party organisations) is unlikely to pose the dangers that are seen to threaten politics where 'big money' is involved. Where very large donations are made there is the fear that (potentially, if not realised) this could be buying influence, particularly over government policy. This argument has considerable credence when applied to parties nationally, but it is unlikely that individuals or organisations with large sums that they were prepared to give to political parties would consider that donating them to a single candidate would be personally beneficial, although the party accounts discussed in Chapter Three show that local parties (and their MPs) are able to arrange for supporters (such as members of the Conservatives' Patrons' Clubs and local businesses; see Chapter Four) to meet with ministers and other leading figures for relatively small sums.

Very large donations to local parties are unlikely, therefore, and Table 5.1 confirms this with data on all of those received by local party accounting units (both single- and multiple-constituency) between 2001, when regulation began, and the end of July 2012. For each of the three parties the average donation, whether measured by the mean or the median, was relatively small; the median was very similar for both Labour and the Liberal Democrats (£1,500 and £1,550 respectively), but nearly £1,000 bigger for the Conservatives, who attracted larger sums on average from their backers (although each of the other two were more likely to report smaller ones – in some cases because the donors gave several donations during the year that totalled more than the specified figure above which reporting was required). Many individual donations were small; for Labour, the smallest tenth of donations (that is, in the lowest decile; Table 5.1) were below £400, whereas for the Conservatives and Liberal Democrats they were below £1,125 and £1,000 respectively.

Nor were there many large donations: for the Conservatives only 10 per cent (the upper decile) exceeded £7,250, whereas the comparable figure for the other two parties was £3,318 for Labour and £4,200 for the Liberal Democrats. Each got only a small number of very large donations. Labour constituency parties got only 11 exceeding £25,000, for example; four of the largest were from individuals (Lord David Sainsbury gave £50,000 to Tower Hamlets Labour party in 2009 and the other three, from individuals with no identifiable public profile, were given to individual parties). The remaining seven were, in effect, 'transfers' within the party, such as the three donations in 2009–10 (totalling £86,300) from Newham Labour Group to Newham Campaign Forum. For the Liberal Democrats only

Table 5.1: Individual donations to local parties, 2007-10

	Conservative	Labour	Liberal Democrat
Minimum	205	50	60
Lower decile	1,125	376	1,000
Lower quartile	1,500	750	1,200
Median	2,497	1,500	1,550
Upper quartile	5,000	2,000	2,314
Upper decile	7,250	3,318	4,200
Maximum	200,000	54,000	248,590
Mean	3,891	1,826	2,310
Standard deviation	6,547	2,261	4,905
Number of donations	6155	7290	5,389

nine donations exceeded £25,000; six came from individuals (in March 2005, Tim Farron, the party's – successful – candidate gave £30,000 to his Westmorland and Lonsdale constituency party: he won by just 267 votes), and the remaining three were from other organisations within the party classified as trusts (for example, Summerseat Liberal Club gave £248,590 to the Bury local accounting unit). Finally, the Conservatives received 42 separate donations exceeding £25,000. Eleven were from companies, but this included two that were, in effect, intra-party transfers; there were also five from trusts and unincorporated associations. The remaining 26 were from individuals: Richmond Park constituency party received three totalling £192,311.55 in 2007-10 from its candidate, Zac Goldsmith; the Conservative candidate for Meon Valley, George Hollingbery, gave his local party £52,499.15 in two donations in 2009-10; and David Mowat, the party's candidate in Warrington South, gave £40,000 in 2010.

Local parties and funding reform

Most of the recent proposals for reforming party funding comprise a package that caps the size of donations, reduces party expenditure overall and recommends an increase in public funding for party activities; there is already some of the latter, such as the 'Short money' provided to assist opposition parties with policy development, but the additional money would be a contribution to both recurrent costs of party management and organisation as well as those of electoral campaigning.[6] In addition, there is the anticipation that one consequence of such a package being implemented would be an increase in the volume of local – relatively inexpensive – campaigning activity undertaken as now by members and other volunteers. The electorate is believed to be more responsive to such personal campaigns than the impersonal direct mailings and telephone calls that increasingly characterise modern attempts to canvass their support; if the parties are unable to raise large sums to fund these centralised activities, they might direct more of their attention to the local scale, and perhaps

---

[6] The Committee on Standards in Public Life estimated (Chapter 11) that if its full package of reforms were adopted, that is, the impact of a donations cap and some compensatory public funding, and there were no other changes, between 2001 and 2010 the net impact on the Conservatives and Labour respectively would have been a loss of income of £5 million and £5.8 million (that is, about £0.5 million per an-num), whereas the Liberal Democrats would have had a net increase of £3.8 million.

encourage donors to make contributions there. What might the pattern look like under different scenarios?

The status quo

Since the substantial changes introduced in the PPERA 2000, there has been little alteration to the funding regime, apart from the extra restrictions – which focused on the local parties – in the Political Parties and Elections Act 2009. More importantly, there is little evidence that any further significant changes are likely since all-party agreement on a package has failed to materialise. Unless there is a major shift in opinion, or one party is prepared to promote substantial change without support of the others (very unlikely in the context of the 2010-15 Coalition government), therefore, the current regime will probably continue at least until after the 2015 General Election, and quite possibly for some years thereafter.[7]

It is difficult to argue other than that, in financial terms, the Conservatives will retain a substantial advantage under that regime at the local level, which reflects their larger number of local accounting units that are financially relatively healthy as well as their greater ability to raise money through donations, fundraising activities and appeals than is the case with either of their opponents – although, as Chapter Three showed, apart from those that owned property, very few local Conservative parties had substantial assets on which they could draw. Furthermore, the relative financial health of the Conservative party centrally compared to its two opponents means that it is much better placed to undertake the types of activities engaged in between 2007-10, masterminded by Lord Ashcroft, that built up candidates' public profiles in a substantial number of marginal seats and laid the foundations for their success against opposition candidates with fewer available resources. Indeed, by late 2012 the party had identified 80 target seats for its 2015 campaigns – 40 won in 2010 by fairly small majorities that must be won again and a further 40 where the incumbent must be defeated to ensure an overall majority government for the next quinquennium. Local parties were instructed that candidates must be adopted by the end of 2012 so that campaigning on their behalf

---

[7] There are indications, however, that Labour may make commitments in its 2015 General Election manifesto to introduce reforms without all-party consensus: see http://www.telegraph.co.uk/news/politics/labour/10290412/Labour-threatening-a-5000-cap-on-party-donations.html and http://www.theguardian.com/politics/2013/sep/06/senior-lib-dems-labour-party-funding

could begin in 2013 and by December 2012 several had already been adopted;[8] in the following month Labour announced the 106 target seats on which it would focus its local campaigns.[9]

Within a year of the 2010 result, Lord Ashcroft had undertaken extensive polling to identify which types of voters could be attracted to the Conservative 'brand' and ensure a winning coalition in 2015. His report, *Project Blueprint: winning a Conservative majority in 2015* (Ashcroft, 2011: it was updated in September 2011 and July 2012 with *Phase 2* and *Phase 3* documents based on later polls, and then in October 2012 with a second, poll-based, report: *Blue collar Tories? In pursuit of the strivers*), made no mention of a target seat strategy, but it is clear that having identified who the party needs to target, he and his associates are also clear where. Labour started targeting marginal seats in 2012; immediately after the Chancellor of the Exchequer's Autumn Statement in December it used online media to target voters in 60 constituencies where the Conservative majority in 2010 was less than the number of families receiving in-work tax credits. The Conservatives responded with their own online advertisements in the same 60 seats, contrasting 'hard-working families' with 'people who don't work', and asking who was more deserving of support, with the party chair emphasising the speed of their response, which was followed up by detailed leaflets distributed in the same constituencies.[10]

Whether either of the other two parties will be able to emulate the programme being stimulated by Lord Ashcroft's strategy must be in doubt, given their financial situations. Of course, party fortunes can change, even in the short term, and the Conservatives may find that unpopularity with the electorate sees a reduction in the amount of money that they can allocate to the task. Indeed, for the first three-quarters of 2012, Labour closely matched the Conservatives' fundraising efforts according to the Electoral Commission's reports. The Conservatives attracted 514 separate donations, totalling £10,485,172, whereas Labour received 469, to a total value of £9,428,770; the Liberal Democrats attracted 324 donations during the same period, to a value of £1,873,971. Further, there is the potential of major donors

---

[8] See http://conservativehome.blogs.com/parliament/4040-seats/

[9] See http://news.sky.com/story/1035423/labour-expects-60-seat-majority-in-2015

[10] See http://conservativehome.blogs.com/thetorydiary/2012/12/cchq-launches-at-tack-ad-in-marginal-constituencies-hardworking-families-vs-people-who-dont-work. html; http://politicalscrapbook.net/2012/12/tory-hardworking-family-used-to-pro-mote-christian-home-schooling/

deserting the Conservatives and instead offering support to their right-wing UKIP opponents.[11]

In 2015, the election once again will almost certainly be substantially focused on the marginal constituencies, and by 2012 the Conservatives were laying the foundations for a target seat campaign. If their opponents are to counter it, they, and especially Labour, will need to respond to a greater degree in the years preceding the election, as well as in the long and short campaigns of the final months, than they did in the past. Although in relative terms the 2012 data suggest that Labour nationally is attracting as much in donations as the Conservatives, nevertheless there is little evidence that Labour's local parties are improving their relative situation from that shown in the analyses in Chapter Three. If that remains the case, then it is very unlikely that, without substantial transfers from central funds, they will be able to match Conservative spending in the long and short campaigns leading up to the 2015 campaign across all constituencies, let alone in the preceding years.

If there is no uprating in the amounts that can be spent on the two regulated campaigns, then around £40,000 will again be the maximum that can be spent on each candidate's campaign. In some marginal constituencies their opponents may match the Conservatives' spending on both the long and short campaigns. For example, in 2011 Lord Ashcroft conducted polls in 41 marginal constituencies that the Conservatives won in 2010 from either Labour or the Liberal Democrats. In the 33 where Labour came second, the Conservatives outspent Labour in 18 in 2010 on the long campaign and in 27 on the short; in the eight where the Liberal Democrats came second the Conservatives spent most on both the long and the short campaign in only three. If Labour and the Liberal Democrats can maintain strong parties in such constituencies, therefore, they may be able to compete on relatively equal financial terms with the Conservatives in 2015, which suggests that their central parties should focus in the years preceding the next election in sustaining those local parties. In 2010,

[11] Stuart Wheeler, who gave the Conservatives £5 million in a single donation in 2001, was expelled from the party after giving £100,000 to UKIP in 2009, and subsequently became a UKIP treasurer: see www.bbc.co.uk/news/uk-politics-12152655; www.kentnews.co.uk/news/former_tory_donor_stuart_wheeler_predicts_great_things_for_ukip_in_kent_1_1660939. He subsequently donated £473,237.25 to UKIP, as well as £140,000 to his Trust Party that he established in 2010. He contested Bexhill and Battle at that year's general election, winning 5 per cent of the votes; the party's other candidate won 1 per cent in Perth and North Perthshire: http://unlockdemocracy.org.uk/blog/entry/donor-of-the-week-stuart-wheeler

Labour had local parties that returned their annual accounts to the Electoral Commission (that is, had an income in excess of £25,000) in 14 of the 33 of those seats that it lost to the Conservatives, as did all eight of the Liberal Democrats in those where they were defeated by Conservative candidates. So the two parties had reasonable foundations on which to base an attack on the Conservatives' incumbency; against that, in 2010 their Conservative opponents had such financially healthy local parties in 32 of the 41 seats where such a strong challenge might be anticipated.

In December 2012, details were released naming 20 of the 40 seats which the Conservatives didn't win in 2010 that were included in its target seats campaign aimed at victory at the next general election; of those 20, 13 were won by Labour in 2010 and the other seven by the Liberal Democrats. Of those 20 seats, the Conservatives had a single-constituency local party with a 2010 income exceeding £25,000 in 13, and 10 of them had received target grants in 2009. On average the Conservatives spent £15,367 there on the 2010 long campaign and £10,002 on the short campaign. They therefore had a solid foundation on which to launch the start of their 2015 campaigns in many of those seats. Against that, in the 13 Labour-held seats where the Conservatives were launching their challenge, only five had a single-constituency Labour local party with an income of £25,000 or more in 2010; on average, Labour spent £9,155 on the long campaign in those 13 (the Conservative mean spend was £12,097) and £9,359 on the short campaign (Conservative, £9,420). Finally, in the seven seats being defended by the Liberal Democrats, that party had a single-constituency local party with an income exceeding £25,000 in six (the seventh was part of a two-constituency London borough local party). In 2010 the Liberal Democrats spent on average £15,925 on the long campaign, compared to the Conservatives' £21,442, and £10,290 on the short campaign (Conservative, £11,081).

Finance is only one component of a successful local campaign, of course. Money spent locally on leaflets and posters is likely to have a limited impact if it is not accompanied by intensive campaigning on the doorsteps and in the streets, which requires a substantial local organisation as well as volunteer activists. Very few of the agents employed by candidates to run their local campaigns are full-time professionals; many are volunteers. As part of their 2015 target seats campaign, the Conservatives are placing paid organisers in each of the 80 chosen constituencies. The Liberal Democrat and – again especially – Labour parties may find this very difficult to match. In 2012 they showed that they were able to both direct volunteers to and recruit non-member canvassers in marginal constituencies, to work alongside local members. This may be extended, but it may be taking place in the context of continuing declines in local party membership. The pool on which to draw to organise locally and deliver intensive campaigns may be weak in many places, and could be a further call on scarce central funds.

In the immediate post-war decades, it became the conventional wisdom among political commentators and academics that local campaigning was at best obsolescent. It occupied the energies of local activists but to little effect, because the 'real' campaigns were now being fought through the national media – increasingly television. It is likely that this was always an over-interpretation, and certainly the revival of the Liberal party from 1970 on was built to a very large extent on intensive local campaigns, albeit in a relatively small number of constituencies. (An excellent example of this is given in Paddy Ashdown's 2009 autobiographical discussion of how the party built its local base in Yeovil; see also Ashdown and Bruce, 1985.) From then on, too, analyses of the impact of spending and other campaigning activities have all demonstrated the importance of local canvassing in mobilising support, especially in the marginal seats where general elections have been won and lost. The parties centrally have recognised this, and there has been increased integration of the national and local campaigns. No longer are candidates in those key seats left to their own, and their agents' and activists', devices in how and to what intensity they organise their campaign. Increasingly, a party's central office becomes involved. Before the 2001 General Election, for example, Labour, which had a substantial majority in the House of Commons, encouraged its MPs defending relatively marginal seats to spend more time in their constituencies – 'key seat status' would be awarded and extra assistance provided for their 2001 campaigns if they contacted at least 26,000 households (a minimum of 100 per week), raised at least £10,000 locally and retained at least 90 per cent of the party's existing members there. Backbenchers representing marginal seats certainly spent less time voting in the Commons and more, it was assumed, campaigning in their constituencies; and in those seats both turnout and the Labour party's share of the votes cast fell by less than the national average (Johnston et al, 2002).

The success of Lord Ashcroft's target seats campaigns in 2005 and 2010 (Johnston and Pattie, 2007; Cutts et al., 2012), the impact of the Liberal Democrats' 'continuous campaigns' (as illustrated by Cutts', 2006, detailed studies of one constituency), and other initiatives all point to a greater importance of local campaigning in the future, a trend that the political class seems to accept because it identifies benefits to be gained from more personal interaction between parties, candidates and voters and less from the arms race of central spending on massive national advertising campaigns that characterised recent general elections, although in 2010 neither Labour nor the Liberal Democrats had the resources to undertake much of this, in any case. If the 2010 party leaders' televised debates are repeated in 2015, these may become the dominant element of the 'national' campaigns, especially if there are parallel debates between, say, each party's main financial spokesperson. There may then be a significant rebalancing, with the parties paying much more attention to their local campaigns. But with declining memberships this may pose a considerable problem – local parties are relatively weak in a majority of constituencies and, unless more members and supporters can be recruited and money raised, more intensive, longer-term local campaigns will have to be increasingly coordinated from the centre. The seeds of such a change have already been sown, as a greater proportion of leaflets are printed centrally, direct mailings go out from one location rather than a large number, and volunteers are directed to the constituencies where their work 'on the ground' is most needed (which depends, of course, on party members and others being convinced that campaigning elsewhere than in their home area is to the party's greater benefit). These centralising tendencies are likely to be increased as scarce resources (both financial and human) are carefully managed.

All of these changes will probably accentuate a growing trend in British electoral politics – the focus on a small proportion of constituencies that are marginal and the relative neglect of the majority of constituencies where the outcome is fairly certain. Elections are determined in parts of the country only; increasingly, voters there will become the focus of more and more attention from the parties whereas their contemporaries elsewhere, to a greater extent than at recent elections, are largely ignored. The latter group may have some contact with one or more of the local candidates, and even receive a leaflet, but, unlike the residents of marginal constituencies, their support will not be intensively canvassed. (At the 2005 General Election, the notional results suggest that only 95 of the 632 seats in Great Britain would have been won with majorities of less than 5 per cent of the votes cast if that election had been fought in the new constituencies in place for the 2010 contest, and a further 75 by margins of 5-10 per cent; 76 of the 170 seats held by margins of less than 10 points changed hands in 2010, compared to only 34 of the remaining 462.)

Of course, this depends on certain assumptions, one of which is that the proportion of marginal constituencies – those that can be won or lost by a shift in the partisan leanings of the voters by no more than 10 percentage points – will remain the same. After the 2010 General Election some commentators argued that the post-war era of two-party dominance, with one of them likely to get a working majority in the House of Commons with little more than 40-42 per cent of the votes, had come to an end. Small single-party parliamentary majorities or coalitions were now the most likely outcome (Curtice, 2009, 2010). Indeed, some heralded a three-party system (four-party in Scotland and Wales), but election results do not bear this out in terms of local contests (Johnston and Pattie, 2011b). In most constituencies at recent elections only two parties have been in contention, and England is characterised not by a three-party system in its constituencies, for example, but rather by three two-party systems; in most seats two of the three parties dominate and the other occupies a relatively poor third place. (In seats where Labour and the Conservatives occupied the first two places in 2010, for example, they averaged 37.8 and 37.3 per cent of the vote total respectively, whereas the Liberal Democrats averaged only 17.1 per cent; where the Conservatives and Liberal Democrats occupied the first two places, their respective vote shares averaged 48.8 and 32.0, while Labour's was 12.7.) Campaigning then focuses on three types of two-party marginals. This may change, although it is unlikely to do so very quickly, and of course a party may suddenly redirect some of its campaigning to unexpected places (as the Liberal Democrats did at Redcar in 2010 where Labour's majority of 31 percentage points was unexpectedly overturned).

One further unknown is the role of new technology. The rise of the 'internet election' has been promised throughout the last decade, but with little apparent impact – certainly in contrast to the last two US presidential elections. But the use of social media in various forms of political organisation has increased markedly, and it may be that this affects the next general election much more than previously. Of the more than 13,000 respondents to the 2010 BES post-election survey, only 71 reported that they had been texted by Labour during the campaign, with 89 reporting that they had been contacted via Twitter and 411 by email (although see Graham et al., 2013); the comparable figures for contact by the Conservatives were 120, 102 and 905, and for the Liberal Democrats 231, 129 and 422. This contrasted with 870, 1249 and 727 who had been visited at home by people canvassing for the three parties respectively, and 5,088, 5,629 and 5,052 who had received leaflets. As the parties build up their databases of email and Twitter addresses, they will almost certainly make greater use of these in the future which, while far from cost-free, allow for relatively easy, bespoke and targeted messages, whose impact it is as yet hard to predict.

With a reform package

The preceding arguments have suggested that if the stalemate regarding party funding reform continues, in an era of constrained financial resources and falling memberships the political parties are likely to further concentrate their campaigning activities for the 2015 General Election in a relatively small number of marginal constituencies, where the local campaigns are likely to be more centrally coordinated, if not directed, than previously. This might appear to be in line with some reformers' desire to redirect party–elector interaction towards face-to-face modes, and thereby revive democracy. The majority of the electorate would probably be largely ignored in such an exercise, however, and even where there is contact it is likely to involve intensive canvassing for support focused almost entirely on each party's identified supporters, to ensure that they don't waver and/or fail to turn out on election day. Those committed to its opponents – and in particular the places where they are concentrated (Johnston et al, 2012a) – will be very largely ignored.

Would it be very different if the proposed funding reforms were in place, involving a limit on large donations, a cap on the amount spent throughout the election cycle and not just on a period immediately preceding a general election, as well as an element of public funding to compensate in part for the loss of the large donations? One consequence of the first and third items in this package would undoubtedly be a reduction in the overall financial resources available to the parties, since it is very unlikely that the public funding allocations would fully replace lost income from large donors, and that the parties themselves could raise substantial additional income from small donors as well as other fundraising activities. For the former to occur, there would have to be a substantial change in attitudes to political donations, and given the greater attractiveness of one of the parties to relatively wealthy individuals, this would almost certainly not result in an equal increase in such income across all three.

The same factor would undoubtedly also operate with regard to fundraising, especially at the local level. Recent experience shows that the Conservative party is better able to raise substantial sums through local events than the others, undoubtedly because its members and supporters are in general better off; in addition, such events involve much time-consuming work by either or both paid staff and volunteers, and their numbers are declining. The stimulus to join a party is much less now than it was in previous decades, when there was a clear ideological divide between the Conservatives and Labour, and a large percentage of the electorate identified strongly with one of those parties. With the rise of valence politics fewer voters are now committed permanently to any party (Crewe and Särlvik, 1983; Clarke et al, 2009); they are more likely to change their allegiance according to their evaluation of the relative success/potential of one or more of the parties in managing the national economy and delivering personal benefits, and if there is less incentive to join a party, there is also less stimulus to donate money to it, unless you perceive clear potential personal benefits if it forms the next government and disadvantages if it does not.

With donation caps and some replacement public funding, therefore, the situation is unlikely to be very different from that sketched out above for a status quo regime – increasing centralisation of campaigns focused on target seats – although if each local party received a grant of £5 for each vote that it received at the preceding election, then after the 2010 General Election 618 local Conservative parties, 619 local Labour parties and 620 local Liberal Democrat parties would receive enough to cover the full costs of the next short campaign and 564, 522 and 526 respectively would receive sufficient to cover both the long and the short maxima then – that is, enough for a 'fully funded' campaign in all of the seats where they had any chance of victory.[12] But what if the new regime also involved limits on spending for a longer period than that currently covered so that it incorporated any spending by both the central parties and their local accounting units, which included promoting the individual candidates' cause? If those limits did not place a cap on spending in individual constituencies for the full period, then again there would continue to be a focus on the target seats, with parties directing as much as possible there. Furthermore, as the Electoral Commission (2013) noted in its proposals for a revised regulatory framework, the result of removing a specific cap on candidates' spending during the 'short campaign' (by incorporating it within a longer period) could result in parties focusing very intensive, expensive campaigning (as at Eastleigh in 2013) during the last few weeks and days before the election in the most marginal seats, thereby removing the attempt at ensuring a relatively level inter-party expenditure playing field that has been in place since 1883.

---

[12] Calculation of the exact sum would be slightly difficult after a review of constituencies by the Boundary Commissions, but far from insuperable.

There would be problems with regulating such expenditure, however, as was argued by the Electoral Commission and others during the debates over the 2006 and 2009 Acts. What spending counts as promoting the individual candidate rather than her/his party, even if a person's candidature has been declared? It would be very difficult to separate out the various components of the expenditure, especially in the first years of a five-year electoral cycle, and requires a single, centralised set of accounts for each party incorporating all of its local units (irrespective of their income and expenditure levels).

Another issue would also be raised were there such a cap on spending, whether by the party as a whole wherever it is spent, and on what or by individual candidates. The regulations as they currently are phrased for the long and the short campaigns refer to spending to promote individual candidates. But what about spending by people or groups outwith the party – for example, by organisations wanting to promote a party and its candidates for their particular interests? Such 'third party' spending became of concern when the European Court of Human Rights declared that the UK's maximum allowed expenditure of just £5 by a third party breached the European Convention on Human Rights (Ewing, 2011). The PPERA 2000 introduced new restrictions on what it termed 'controlled expenditure' by third parties. It regulated any spending on the 'production and publication of election material which is made available to the public at large or any section of the public (in whatever form and by whatever means)' which is intended either to 'promote or procure electoral success' for one or more registered parties or candidates that 'advocate (or do not advocate) particular policies' or, more generally, to 'enhance the standing [of any candidate or registered party] … with the electorate in connection with future relevant elections (whether imminent or otherwise) and any such material is election material even though it can reasonably be regarded as intended to achieve any other purpose as well' (with a note indicating that 'candidates includes future candidates, whether identifiable or not'). Those 'third parties' that wish to spend more than £10,000 in England or £5,000 in one or more of the other three countries during the regulated period must be registered with, and provide accounts to, the Electoral Commission, and donations to those 'third parties' must also be reported. The limits set for a third party's expenditure at a general election, for the 365-day period immediately preceding polling day, were: in England, £793,500; Scotland, £108,000; Wales, £60,000; and Northern Ireland £27,000 (which is equivalent to an average expenditure of £1,500 per constituency). There are, however, additional controls on third party expenditure that either promotes or disparages a particular candidate; for this, the limit was set at £500 for a general election.

These regulations have had little impact to date. In late 2012 the Electoral Commission's Register of Third Parties contained just 21 entries; some were single-issue organisations (such as the Paddington Development Trust and the League Against Cruel Sports), and others have a broader remit (such as Common People, 'a radical, green, left-leaning group'); yet others represent specific groups within society, such as the Board of Deputies of British Jews and five trade unions – including Unite, which campaigned heavily in marginal seats for Labour at the 2010 General Election; and two individuals. The Commission's register of spending by third parties has 28 entries, although five of them refer to the same organisation. (The Young Britons' Foundation is self-described as a 'non-partisan, not-for-profit educational, research and training organisation that promotes conservatism in schools, colleges and universities' to combat 'left-wing bias in the education system and the mainstream media'; it spent £134,859.91 on advertisements in May 2010.) The total spent during 2010 was £2,970,205.35, with the largest amount (£671,167) by the trade union Unite.

The potential for using third parties in campaigning, and thereby avoiding the regulations that apply to political parties, is quite considerable, especially if the internet is used as the main medium for making contact (Ewing and Rowbottom, 2011; Rowbottom, 2011; Pinto-Duschinsky, 2011), as is the case in the USA where Political Action Committees (PACs) and SuperPACs now make major contributions because they can spend unlimited amounts independently of a party or candidate. A party's supporters (individuals, companies etc) could set up multiple third parties to promote its policies, with each spending up to the substantial maximum annually – the regulations currently only preclude the same person being responsible for more than one third party.[13] The limits on spending to support an individual candidate are much tighter, but again several

---

[13] As part of its response to growing concerns about the role of lobbyists in Parliament and MPs being paid by them, the Conservative party leader announced in June 2013 that as part of its crackdown on such activities, the government proposed to introduce an 'anti-sleaze' Bill that, among other things, would preclude 'third-party organisations affiliated to parties and any organisation contributing £100,000 or more' from spending more than a relatively small amount on political advertising in the year preceding a general election, a move that would have a particularly large impact on those (pro-Labour) trade unions that run their own campaigns as well as donating to the party's. See www.guardian.co.uk/politics/2013/jun/03/cameron-moves-union-funding-labour

linked groups could be established, with each spending up to the maximum allowed. Furthermore, although the limit for spending to promote (or disparage) a candidate by any one registered third party is only £500, the costs of some campaigns – such as emails to all of a member's organisation living in a specific constituency – may not be large.

If limits were to be placed either on total spending by a party and its accounting units for the full electoral cycle or for a longer period of spending than is currently the case on a candidate's campaign, then it is likely that the 'third party option' will be more widely used, as realised in the proposals tabled by Tyrie et al (2013). Its regulation could be difficult, however, particularly if messages are sent from addresses and/ or using internet service providers outside the UK (see Ewing and Rowbottom, 2011).

In July 2013 the coalition government introduced a Transparency of Lobbying, Non-Party Campaigning and Trade Union Administration Bill. Although its main aims were to constrain the activities of political lobbyists, through registration, and the political activities of trades unions, its provisions with regard to non-party campaigning had a much wider impact. After lengthy debates in both Houses of Parliament and much lobbying activity, the Bill received Royal Assent in late January 2014 and its clauses related to non-party campaigning will thus have an impact on the 2015 general election. (For full discussions of the Bill's contents and the debates see James et al., 2013, and Gay et al., 2014.) All non-party organisations campaigning for particular policies have to register with the Electoral Commission if they spend more than £20,000 in England or £10,000 in one of Northern Ireland, Scotland or Wales, with that threshold applying to the period from 19 September 2014 in the case of the 2015 General Election. The 'controlled expenditure' by such non-parties covered by the legislation is similar to that applying to political parties, and the total that any one organisation can spend is limited to two per cent of the maximum allowed for the political parties in each of England, Northern Ireland, Scotland and Wales. Where expenditure exceeds a specified threshold the permission of the party concerned must be obtained and if the expenditure is focused on particular constituencies, the maximum expenditure allowed is £9,750 per constituency, and £5,850 in the period after the dissolution of Parliament. When a non-party organisation campaigns for or against an individual candidate, there is a maximum expenditure of £700. All of this regulated expenditure must be reported to, and monitored by, the Electoral Commission. Many of those likely to be impacted by these new regulations foresaw problems in their implementation – not least because staff costs have to be included in the controlled expenditure totals: there is to be a review within 18 months of the 2015 election.

Conclusions

Much concern has been expressed in recent years about the decline of party membership in Great Britain (Whiteley and Seyd, 2002), which is also a characteristic of many other mature democracies. McGuiness (2012), for example, has shown that by 2008 membership of both the Conservative and the Labour parties was lower (at below 500,000 in the former case and 200,000 in the latter) than at any time since 1948; at its peak the Conservative party had six times as many members as now (around 1950), and Labour had five times. The Liberal Democrat membership (including its forerunner parties) has similarly declined from a peak in 1960 to only about one-fifth of its size then. This very substantial decline has been particularly severe in areas where each party is not especially strong electorally, which means an absence of substantial human resources with which to mount campaigns at elections at all levels.

Declining membership also means problems in sustaining income, not only through (increasing) individual subscriptions, but also in mounting activities to raise funds to spend on election campaigns. Yet at the same time, many aspects of those campaigns are becoming more expensive, putting even greater pressure on the main parties, all three of which have indicated a wish to constrain the amounts that can be spent. At the local level, those amounts have been controlled for over a century, and the limits have not been increased with inflation. Nevertheless, many local parties have been unable to raise as much money as the law allows them to spend on their candidates' campaigns, even in marginal constituencies where the outcome can have a significant influence on the overall result. Many candidates – especially from the Labour and Liberal Democrat parties – have in consequence been disadvantaged by this lack of resources, especially where they have been unable to counter the relative absence of finance by recruiting more volunteer helpers. Concern has thus been expressed at the advantage that some candidates (especially Conservative at recent elections) have enjoyed because of their greater financial resources (and the grants that the central party organisation has provided for canvassing in pre-election years).

The parties are very aware that intensive local campaigns bring electoral benefits, especially those that involve much party/candidate–

voter personal interaction. They have thus restructured their activities by increasingly focusing, through central direction and some funding, their canvassing and campaigning on the minority of seats that are identified as marginal. Debates have continued regarding how those activities should be regulated and the amounts of money spent on them constrained but, as with other aspects of those debates on funding, all-party agreement on the way forward has not been forthcoming. Even were such agreement to be achieved, however, it is likely that the current trends of centralisation and target-seat concentration will continue, with new ways found to circumvent limits to what can be spent, where, and when.

In conclusion

The February 2013 Eastleigh by-election, discussed in the Introduction, illustrates the foundations for the Liberal Democrats' successes at both by-elections and general elections since the 1970s. Those have been built on combinations of a strong local activist cohort, a substantial local government base (the party held all of Eastleigh's local government seats at the time of the by-election, and their candidate was one of its local councillors there; see Terry, 2013), and continuous campaigning based on local issues and claimed policy delivery,[1] funded by local money-raising efforts aided by grants from the party's central office and the Association of Liberal Democrat Councillors.[2] The party's problem, however, is that it has only been able to build such foundations in a minority of the country's parliamentary constituencies, and it lacks the funding to extend that base very substantially. Most of its local parties, as illustrated here, are small, with few members and insubstantial incomes and, of course, at a general election it cannot focus all of its campaigning efforts, and mobilise large numbers of party activists and volunteers, on one seat, as was the case at Eastleigh and other by-election successes in recent decades.

That situation is not peculiar to the Liberal Democrats. Labour, as again we have demonstrated here, and as the party's officials and campaign managers have admitted, is in an even weaker position overall, with very few large and active constituency parties having substantial sources of local income that can be used to sustain an organisation (with staffing and infrastructure) and to fund intensive campaigns. Few of those local parties had incomes of £25,000 or more in the years leading up to the 2010 General Election, and the party centrally was unable to contribute to their campaigning costs, when a

---

[1] A poll conducted by Lord Ashcroft in 213 marginal constituencies in March 2013 showed that 27 and 20 per cent of respondents had received leaflets or other materials from the Liberal Democrats in seats that the party held and which were targeted by either the Conservatives or Labour respectively, whereas only 4 and 1 per cent had received anything from the Conservatives and 4 and 6 per cent from Labour. The full details are available at http://lordashcroftpolls.com/2013/03/marginal-territory-the-seats-that-will-decide-the-next-election/#more-2052

[2] The party's president, Tim Farron, was quoted as responding to the question 'How do you get to be a Liberal Democrat MP?' as saying '... by becoming a nutter and working your socks off and doing the traditional Liberal Democrat grassroots building up a seat from nothing'. See www.politicshome.com/uk/article/73767/tim_farron_surviving_the_storms.html

number of their Conservative opponents were able to spend as much as £40,000 during the three months before polling day, virtually all of that money being raised locally with no subsidies from Central Office. Some constituency Labour parties were able to mobilise substantial numbers of canvassers and campaigners (including volunteers) despite their financial frailties, but these were largely last-minute responses to local situations and could not be replicated across the country.

The data presented in this book have shown that, in terms of both membership and money, the Conservatives had by far the strongest network of local parties in the period preceding the 2010 General Election, and were able to enhance that foundation in a considerable number of target seats through grants from a relatively healthy central organisation.[3] And yet, as Eastleigh revealed, even where there is apparently a relatively healthy local party organisation (the local Conservative party had 174 reported local members there in 2009 and a 2010 income of £48,217), there may be little campaigning activity other than at election time; the Liberal Democrats have shown (and as illustrated by Cutts, 2006, and Cutts and Shrayne, 2006) that maintaining contact with their supporters across the full electoral cycle – itself requiring a phalanx of committed party workers and not-insubstantial funds – pays dividends at the ballot box every five years.

As local party organisations wither in many parts of the country – with few members and little money – so more of the work preparing for general elections has been undertaken at the parties' London and regional headquarters, usually involving paid staff rather than volunteer helpers and with some of the work 'outsourced'. Given the greater attention paid at elections over the last three decades to the importance of local campaigning, however, especially in targeted marginal constituencies, this is a somewhat paradoxical situation: party officials, operating at some distance from the grassroots, have had to take greater responsibility for delivering effective constituency campaigns, including the mobilisation and management of local workers. This is costly (extensive telephone polling operations, for example), but the parties are also finding it increasingly difficult to raise money for their central office operations and are having to depend on a small number of donors willing to provide the needed financial resources, which

---

[3] There are, however, fears that this will not be repeated for 2015 given the reported decision of the mastermind (and substantial funder) of that programme, Lord Ashcroft, not to continue his donations. See www.thesundaytimes.co.uk/sto/news/article1220456.ece

raises substantial questions regarding those donors' impact – real or potential – on the parties' policies and actions.

For at least two decades this financial situation has been the source of considerable concern, within the political parties as well as with several think-tanks and commentators more generally. Several inquiries have been held and recommendations delivered, but the changes – notably the establishment of the Electoral Commission which oversees regulations designed to achieve greater transparency with regard to the parties' income and expenditure and limits to both sources and the amounts that can be spent on campaigns – have not been far-reaching, and there is little likelihood of more extensive reforms occurring in the near future because of the absence of all-party agreement on their nature.

Among the major goals of several of the sets of recommendations for change have been ending the central parties' dependence on large donors, and stimulating a revival of local democracy through more active party branches. The analyses reported here have provided little evidence of substantial foundations on which such a shift could be built. In many parts of the country local party organisations are moribund, with few members and little money; even at general elections in winnable seats some local parties are unable to raise the relatively small sum (about £12,000) that can be spent on campaigning in the last few weeks before polling day and, as a consequence, a majority of voters never even get a leaflet telling them who a party's candidate is. Canvassers (both party members and volunteers) are mobilised in some areas – in relatively large numbers in a few, although not comparable to those involved at key by-elections such as Eastleigh – with important effects on the outcome, but there is no evidence of any widespread revival. There are occasional surges, as after the formation of the SDP in 1981 and Tony Blair's election as Labour leader in 1994, but these are never sustained. Membership of a political party is no longer something that most citizens even consider, let alone giving money to and working for.

Parties matter, nationally, regionally and locally, for the successful operation of mass representative democracy, and money matters too: if those parties are to flourish and exercise power, whether in local, regional or national government, they need money to sustain their activities, including their campaigns to win representation. In contemporary Britain most local parties are not flourishing, and there is little evidence to suggest that they will again, whatever strategies might be devised to promote their health. Money may be a key component of effective local campaigning. But it cannot, of itself, cure the deeper malaise afflicting political parties' grassroots organisations in the UK.

References

Ashcroft, M.A. (2010) *Minority verdict: the Conservative party, the voters and the 2010 Election*, London: Biteback Publishing.

Ashcroft, M.A. (2011) *Project Blueprint: winning a Conservative majority in 2015* (http://lordashcroftpolls.com/wp-content/uploads/2011/12/project-blueprint.pdf).

Ashcroft. M.A. (2012) *Blue collar Tories? In pursuit of the strivers* (http://lordashcroftpolls.com/wp-content/uploads/2012/10/BLUE-COLLAR-TORIES.pdf).

Ashdown, P. (2009) *A fortunate life: the autobiography of Paddy Ashdown*, London: Aurum.

Ashdown, P. and Bruce, M. (1985) *Growth from the grassroots*, London: Liberal Party.

Bale, T. (2010) *The Conservative party from Thatcher to Cameron*, Oxford: Polity Press.

Bogdanor, V. (1983) *Multi-party politics and the constitution*, Cambridge: Cambridge University Press.

Bogdanor, V. (1986) 'Letter to the Editor', *Environment and Planning A*, vol 18, p 1537.

Bowers, P., Gay, O. and Pyper, D. (2013) *Transparency of Lobbying, Non-Party Campaigning and Trade Union Administration Bill*. Research Paper 12/51. London: House of Commons Library.

Butler, D.E. and Kavanagh, D. (1992) *The British general election of 1992*, Basingstoke: Macmillan.

Butler, D.E. and Stokes, D.E. (1969) *Political change in Britain: forces shaping electoral choice*, London: Macmillan.

Butler, D.E. and Stokes, D.E. (1974) *Political change in Britain: the evolution of electoral choice*, London: Macmillan.

Clarke, H.D., Sanders, D., Stewart, M.D. and Whiteley, P. (2009) *Performance politics and the British voter*, Cambridge: Cambridge University Press.

Conservative Party (2008) 'Cash Gordon: Charlie Whelan's new militant tendency' (http://issuu.com/conservatives/docs/cashgordon).

Constitutional Affairs Committee (2006) *Party funding*, HC 163-I, London: The Stationery Office.

Constitutional Affairs Committee (2007) *Government response: party funding*, Cm 7123, London: The Stationery Office.

Cowley, P. and Kavanagh, D. (2010) *The British General Election of 2010*, Basingstoke: Palgrave Macmillan.

Crewe, I. and King, A. (1995) *SDP: the birth, life and death of the Social Democratic Party*, Oxford: Oxford University Press.

CSPL (Committee on Standards in Public Life) (1998) *The funding of political parties in the United Kingdom*, Cm 4057-I, London: The Stationery Office.

CSPL (2001) *The first seven reports: a review of progress*, London: CSPL.

CSPL (2011) *Political party finance: ending the big donor culture*, Cm 8208, London: The Stationery Office.

Curtice, J. (2009) 'Neither representative nor accountable: first-past-the-post in Britain', in B. Grofman, A. Blais and S. Bowler (eds) *Duverger's law of plurality voting*, New York: Springer, pp 27-46.

Curtice, J. (2010) 'So what went wrong with the electoral system? The 2010 election result and the debate about electoral reform', *Parliamentary Affairs*, vol 63, pp 623-38.

Curtice, J. and Steed, M. (1982) 'Electoral choice and the production of government: the changing operation of the electoral system in the United Kingdom since 1955', *British Journal of Political Science*, vol 12, pp 249-98.

Curtice, J. and Steed, M. (1986) 'Proportionality and exaggeration in the British electoral system', *Electoral Studies*, vol 5, pp 209-28.

Cutts, D.J. (2006) 'Continuous campaigning and electoral outcomes: the Liberal Democrats in Bath', *Political Geography*, vol 25, pp 72-88.

Cutts, D.J. (2013) 'Local elections as a "stepping stone": does winning council seats boost the Liberal Democrats' performance in general elections?, *Political Studies* (doi 10.1111/J12029/1467-9248)

Cutts, D.J. and Shryane, N. (2006) 'Did local activism really matter? Liberal Democrat campaigning and the 2001 British general election', *British Journal of Politics and Industrial Relations*, vol 8, pp 427-44.

Cutts, D.J., Johnston, R.J., Pattie, C.J. and Fisher, J. (2012) 'Laying the foundations for electoral success: Conservative pre-campaign canvassing before the 2010 British general election', *Journal of Elections, Public Opinion and Parties*, vol 22, pp 359-75.

Denver, D.T. and Hands, G. (1997) *Modern constituency electioneering: local campaigning in the 1992 general election*, London: Frank Cass.

Denver, D.T. and Hands, G. (2002) 'Post-Fordism in the constituencies? The continuing development of constituency campaigning in Britain', in D.M. Farrell and R. Schmitt-Beck (eds) *Do political campaigns matter? Campaign effects in elections and referendums*, London: Routledge, pp 108-26.

Electoral Commission (2004) *The funding of political parties: report and recommendations*, London: Electoral Commission.

Electoral Commission (2013) *A regulatory review of the UK's party and election finance laws. Recommendations for change*, London: Electoral Commission (www.electoralcommission.org.uk/__data/assets/pdf_file/0003/155874/PEF-Regulatory-Review-2013.pdf).

Detterbeck, K. (2005) 'Cartel parties in Western Europe?', *Party Politics*, vol 11, pp 173-91.

Evans, G., Heath, A. and Payne, C. (1999) 'Class: Labour as a catch-all party?', in G. Evans and P. Norris (eds) *Critical elections: British parties and voters in long-term perspective*, London: Sage Publications, pp 87-101.

Ewing, K.D. (1982) *Trade unions, the Labour party, and the law: a study of the Trade Union Act, 1913*, Edinburgh: Edinburgh University Press.

Ewing, K.D. (2007) *The cost of democracy: party funding in modern British politics*, London: Hart Publishing.

Ewing, K.D. (2011) 'The trade union question in British political funding', in K.D. Ewing, J. Rowbottom and J.-C. Tham (eds) *The funding of political parties: where now?*, London: Routledge, pp 54-73.

Ewing, K.D. and Issacharoff, S. (eds) (2006) *Party funding and campaign financing in international perspective*, Oxford: Hart Publishing.

Ewing, K.D. and Rowbottom, J. (2011) 'The role of spending controls: new electoral actors and new campaign techniques', in K.D. Ewing, J. Rowbottom and J.-C. Tham (eds) *The funding of political parties: where now?*, London: Routledge, pp 77-91.

Ewing, K.D., Rowbottom, J. and Tham, J.-C. (eds) (2011) *The funding of political parties: where now?*, London: Routledge.

Fisher, J. (2000) 'Small kingdoms and crumbling organizations: examining the variation in constituency party membership and resources', *British Elections and Parties Review*, vol 10, pp 133-50.

Fisher, J. (2010) 'Party finance: normal service resumed?', *Parliamentary Affairs*, vol 63, pp 778-801.

Fisher, J. (2012) 'Local regulation and political activity at the local level in Britain', in K.D. Ewing, J. Rowbottom and J.C. Tham (eds) *The funding of political parties: where now?*, London: Routledge, pp 110-24.

Fisher, J. and Denver, D.T. (2008) 'From foot-slogging to call centres and direct mail: a framework for analysing the development of district-level campaigning', *European Journal of Political Research*, vol 47, pp 794-826.

Fisher, J. and Denver, D.T. (2009) 'Evaluating the electoral effects of traditional and modern modes of constituency campaigning in Britain, 1992-2005', *Parliamentary Affairs*, vol 62, pp 196-210.

Fisher, J., Cutts, D. and Fieldhouse, E. (2011) 'The electoral effectiveness of constituency campaigning in the 2010 General Election: the triumph of Labour', *Electoral Studies*, vol 30, pp 816-28.

Fisher, J., Fieldhouse, E. and Cutts, D. (2013a) 'Members are not the only fruit: volunteer activity in British political parties at the 2010 General Election', *British Journal of Politics and International Relations*, vol 15, pp 75-95.

Fisher, J., Johnston, R.J., Cutts, D., Pattie, C.J. and Fieldhouse, E. (2013b) 'You get what you (don't) pay for: the impact of volunteer labour and candidate spending at the 2010 British General Election', *Parliamentary Affairs* (doi: 10.1093/pa/gst006)

Friedman, B. (2013) *Democracy Ltd. How money and donations corrupted British politics*. London: Oneworld Publications.

Gay, O., Bowers, P. and Pyper, D. (2014) *Transparency of Lobbying, Non-Party Campaigning and Trade Union Administration Bill: Lords Amendments*. Standard Note SN/PC/6796, London: House of Commons Library.

Gay, O. and White, I. (2008) *The Political Parties and Elections Bill*, Research Paper 08/74, London: House of Commons Library.

Gay, O., White, I. and Kelly, R. (2007) *The funding of political parties*, Research Paper 07/34, London: House of Commons Library.

Gould, P. (1998) *Unfinished revolution: how the modernisers saved the Labour party*, London: Little, Brown & Co.

Graham, J. (2006) *Local politics: a case for treatment? A survey of local constituency parties across Great Britain*, London: Unlock Democracy.

Graham, T., Broersma, M., Hazelhoff, K. and van 't Haar, G. (2013) 'Between broadcasting political messages and interacting with voters', *Information, Communication & Society*, vol 16, pp 692-716.

Hain, P. (2012) *Outside in*, London: Biteback Books.

Hitchins, A. and Gay, O. (2009) *Party finance – a chronology*, Standard Note SN/PC/04527, London: House of Commons.

House of Commons Library (2012) *Membership of UK political parties*, Standard Note SN/SG/5125, 3 December, London: House of Commons.

House of Commons Political and Constitutional Reform Committee (2013) *The Government's lobbying bill*. Seventh Report of Session 2013-2014. London: The Stationery Office, HC 601

James, M., Newson, N. and Tudor, S. (2013) *Transparency of Lobbying, Non-Party Campaigning and Trade Union Administration Bill (HL Bill of 2013-14) – Lords Library Note*. LLN 2013/028, London: House of Lords Library.

Johnson, R.W. (1972) 'The nationalisation of English rural politics: Norfolk South West 1945-1970', *Parliamentary Affairs*, vol 26, pp 8-55.

Johnston, R.J. (1977) 'The electoral geography of an election campaign: Scotland in October 1974', *Scottish Geographical Magazine*, vol 93, pp 98-108.

Johnston, R.J. (1985) *The geography of English politics: the 1983 General Election*, London: Croom Helm.

Johnston, R.J. (1986) 'A space for place (or a place for space) in British psephology: a review of recent writings with especial reference to the general election of 1983', *Environment and Planning A*, vol 18, pp 599-618.

Johnston, R.J. (1987) *Money and votes: constituency campaign spending and election results*, London: Croom Helm.

Johnston, R.J. (2012) 'Seats, votes, and the spatial organisation of elections revisited', in G. Gudgin and P.J. Taylor, *Seats, votes, and the spatial organisation of elections*, Colchester: ECPR Press, pp ix–xxxix.

Johnston, R.J., Cowley, P.J., Pattie, C.J. and Stuart, M. (2002) 'Voting in the House or wooing the voters at home: Labour MPs and the 2001 general election campaign', *Journal of Legislative Studies*, vol 8, pp 9-22.

Johnston, R.J., Cutts, D.J., Pattie, C.J. and Fisher, J. (2012a) 'Spending, contacting and voting: the 2010 British general election in the constituencies', *Environment and Planning A*, vol 44, pp 1165-84.

Johnston, R.J., Cutts, D.J., Pattie, C.J. and Fisher, J. (2012b) 'We've got them on the list: canvassing and voting in a British general election campaign', *Election Studies*, vol 31, pp 317-29.

Johnston, R.J. and Pattie, C.J. (1997) 'Where's the difference? Decomposing the impact of local election campaigns in Great Britain', *Electoral Studies*, vol 16, pp 165-74.

Johnston, R.J. and Pattie, C.J. (2006) *Putting voters in their place: geography and elections in Great Britain*, Oxford: Oxford University Press.

Johnston, R.J. and Pattie, C.J. (2007) 'Funding local political parties in England and Wales: donations and constituency campaigns', *British Journal of Politics and International Relations*, vol 9, pp 365-95.

Johnston, R.J. and Pattie, C.J. (2008a) 'The financial health of political parties in English constituencies, 2004-05', *Journal of Legislative Studies*, vol 14, pp 500-16.

Johnston, R.J. and Pattie, C.J. (2008b) 'How much does a vote cost? Incumbency and the impact of campaign spending at English general elections', *Journal of Elections, Public Opinion and Parties*, vol 18, pp 129-52.

Johnston, R.J. and Pattie, C.J. (2010) 'The local campaigns and the outcome', in N. Allen and J. Bartle (eds) *Britain at the polls 2010*, London: Sage Publications, pp 203-39.

Johnston, R.J. and Pattie, C.J. (2011a) 'Local parties, local money and local campaigns: regulation issues', in K.D. Ewing, J. Rowbottom and J.-C. Tham (eds) *The funding of political parties: where now?*, London: Routledge, pp 92-109.

Johnston, R.J. and Pattie, C.J. (2011b) 'The British general election of 2010: a three-party contest or three two-party contests?', *The Geographical Journal*, vol 177, pp 17-26.

Johnston, R.J., Pattie, C.J. and Allsopp, J.G. (1988) *A nation dividing? The electoral map of Great Britain 1979-1987*, London: Longman.

Johnston, R.J., Pattie, C.J. and MacAllister, I.D. (1999) 'The funding of constituency party general election campaigns in Great Britain', *Environment and Planning C: Government and Policy*, vol 17, pp 391-410.

Johnston, R.J., Pattie, C.J., Fisher, J., Cutts, D.J. and Fieldhouse, E. (2013) 'The long and the short of it: local campaigning at the 2010 British general election', *Political Studies*, vol 61(S1), pp 114-137.

Katz, R.S. and Mair, P. (1995) 'Changing models of party organization and party democracy: the emergence of the cartel party', *Party Politics*, vol 1, pp 5-28.

Katz, R.S. and Mair, P. (2009) 'The cartel party thesis: a restatement', *Perspectives on Politics*, vol 7, pp 753-66.

Kavanagh, D. (1970) *Constituency electioneering in Britain*, London: Longmans.

Kavanagh, D. (1995) *Election campaigning: the new marketing of politics*, Oxford: Blackwells.

Kavanagh, D. and Cowley, P. (2010) *The British general election of 2010*, Basingstoke: Palgrave Macmillan.

Kelly, R. (2012) *In brief – party funding*, Standard Note SN/PC/6123, London: House of Commons Library.

Kelly, R. (2013) *Party funding: background and developments since November 2011*, Standard Note SN/PC/6123, London: House of Commons Library.

Kirchheimer, O. (1966) 'The transformation of West European party systems', in J. LaPalombara and M. Weiner (eds) *Political parties and political development*, Princeton, NJ: Princeton University Press, pp 177-200.

Koß, M. (2011) *The politics of party funding: state funding to political parties and party competition in Western Europe*, Oxford: Oxford University Press.

Lawrence, J. (2009) *Electing our masters: the hustings in British politics from Hogarth to Blair*, Oxford: Oxford University Press.

McAllister, I. (2002) 'Calculating or capricious? The new politics of late deciding voters', in D.M. Farrell and R. Schmitt-Beck (eds) *Do political campaigns matter? Campaign effects in elections and referendums*, London: Routledge, pp 22-40.

McGuiness, F. (2012) *Membership of UK political parties*, Standard Note SN/SG/5125, London: House of Commons Library.

Mair, P. (1998) *Party system change: approaches and interpretations*, Oxford: Oxford University Press.

May, J.D. (1972) 'Opinion structure of political parties: the special law of curvilinear disparity', *Political Studies*, vol 21, pp 135-51.

Ministry of Justice (2008) *Party finance and expenditure in the United Kingdom: the government's proposals*, Cm 7329, London: The Stationery Office.

Norris, P. (1995) 'May's law of curvilinear disparity revisited: leaders, officers, members and voters in British political parties', *Party Politics*, vol 1, pp 29-47.

Norris, P. (1997) 'Political communications', in P. Dunleavy, A. Gamble, I. Holliday and G. Peele (eds) *Developments in British politics*, Volume V, Basingstoke: Macmillan, pp 75-88.

Norris, P. (2000) *A virtuous circle: political communications in postindustrial societies*, Cambridge: Cambridge University Press.

Panebianco, A. (1988) *Political parties: organization and power*, Cambridge: Cambridge University Press.

Pattie, C.J. and Johnston, R.J. (1996) 'Paying their way: local associations, the constituency quota scheme and Conservative party finance', *Political Studies*, vol 44, pp 921-35.

Pattie, C.J. and Johnston, R.J. (2009a) 'The Conservatives' grassroots "revival"', *The Political Quarterly*, vol 80, pp 193-203.

Pattie, C.J. and Johnston, R.J. (2009b) 'Still talking, but is anybody listening? The changing face of constituency campaigning in Britain, 1997-2005', *Party Politics*, vol 15, pp 411-34.

Pattie, C.J. and Johnston, R.J. (2012) 'The electoral impact of the UK 2009 MPs' expenses scandal', *Political Studies*, vol 60, pp 730-50.

Phillips, Sir Hayden (2006) *The review of the funding of political parties: an interim assessment*, London (www.official-documents.gov.uk/document/other/0117037184/0117037184.pdf).

Phillips, Sir Hayden (2007) *Strengthening democracy: fair and sustainable funding of political parties*, London: The Stationery Office.

Phillips, Sir Hayden (2012) 'The funding of political parties', *The Political Quarterly*, vol 83, pp 318-24.

Pinto-Duschinsky, M. (1981) *British political finance, 1830-1980*, Washington, DC: American Enterprise Institute.

Pinto-Duschinsky. M. (2008) *Paying for the party: myths and realities in British political finance*, London: The Policy Exchange.

Pinto-Duschinsky, M. (2011) *The finance of the three largest British political parties, 2005-2010*, Research paper prepared for the Committee on Standards in Public Life Review of Public Funding (www.public-standards.org.uk/Library/13th_Report___Political_party_finance_FINAL_PDF_VERSION_18_11_11.pdf).

Pulzer, P.J. (1967) *Political representation and elections in Britain*, London: George Allen & Unwin.

Rallings, C. and Thrasher, M. (1995) *Media guide to the new parliamentary constituencies*, Plymouth: Local Government Chronicle Elections Centre.

Rallings, C. and Thrasher, M. (2007) *Media guide to the new parliamentary constituencies*, Plymouth: Local Government Chronicle Elections Centre.

Rawlings, H.F. (1988) *Law and the electoral process*, London: Sweet & Maxwell.

Rowbottom, J. (2011) *Written evidence to the Committee on Standards in Public Life Review of Public Funding* (www.public-standards.org.uk/Library/All_written_evidence_political_party_finance_21_11_11.pdf).

Särlvik, B. and Crewe, I. (1983) *Decade of dealignment*, Cambridge: Cambridge University Press.

Schmitt-Beck, R. and Farrell, D.M. (2002a) 'Studying political campaigns and their effects', in D.M. Farrell and R. Schmitt-Beck (eds) *Do political campaigns matter? Campaign effects in elections and referendums*, London: Routledge, pp 1-21.

Schmitt-Beck, R. and Farrell, D.M. (2002b) 'Do political campaigns matter? Yes, but it depends', in D.M. Farrell and R. Schmitt-Beck (eds) *Do political campaigns matter? Campaign effects in elections and referendums*, London: Routledge, pp 187-93.

Seyd, P. (1998) 'In praise of party', *Parliamentary Affairs*, vol 51, pp 198-208.

Steed, M. (1966) 'The results analysed', in D. Butler and A. King, *The British general election of 1966*, London: Macmillan, pp 386-415.

Terry, C. (2013) *From councillors to MPs: looking beyond the 2013 local elections*, London: The Electoral Reform Society (www.electoral-reform.org.uk/blog/from-councillors-to-mps).

Triesman, D. (2000) 'The causes of corruption: a cross-national study', *Journal of Public Economics*, vol 76, pp 399-547.

Tyrie, A., Whitehead, A. and Tyler, L. (2013) 'Funding democracy: breaking the deadlock' (www.fundingukdemocracy.org).

vanHeerde-Hudson, J. (2011) 'Playing by the rules: the 2009 MPs' expenses scandal', in D. Wring, R. Mortimore and S. Atkinson (eds) *Political communication in Britain: the leader debates, the campaign and the media in the 2010 General Election*, Basingstoke: Palgrave Macmillan, pp 241-60.

vanHeerde-Hudson, J. and Fisher, J. (2013) 'Parties heed (with caution): Public knowledge of and attitudes towards party finance in Britain', *Party Politics*, vol 19, pp 41-60.

Vivyan, N., Wagner, M. and Tarlov, J. (2012) 'Representative misconduct, voter perceptions and accountability: evidence from the 2009 House of Commons expenses scandal', *Electoral Studies*, vol 31, pp 750-63.

Watt, P. (2010) *Inside out: my story of betrayal and cowardice at the heart of New Labour*, London: Biteback Books.

Whiteley, P. and Seyd, P. (1994) 'Local party campaigning and electoral mobilization in Britain', *Journal of Politics*, vol 56, pp 242-52.

Whiteley, P. and Seyd, P. (2002) *High-intensity participation: the dynamics of party activism in Britain*, Ann Arbor, MI: University of Michigan Press.

Index

Note: The following abbreviations have been used – *f* = figure; *n* = note; *t* = table